The Japanese and Peru

THE JAPANESE AND PERU 1873-1973

C. Harvey Gardiner

UNIVERSITY OF NEW MEXICO PRESS
Albuquerque

©The University of New Mexico Press, 1975
All rights reserved. Manufactured in the United States of America
Library of Congress Catalog Card Number LC 75-17371
International Standard Book Number ISBN 8263-0391-9
First Edition

TO
Frank E. Vandiver
and
Nelson Gardiner
men admired

Introduction

In recent generations the Japanese and Peruvians, like the rest of the world, have developed widening perspectives. If one considers the relations between these two Pacific nations, an important segment of a new perspective on Latin America emerges. Long ago discovery, conquest, and settlement dictated European perspectives on Latin America. Later a strongly developed "mother-hen" complex by the United States inspired another, an Anglo-American, perspective on the area. Still later certain components of national pride, among them *indianismo,* fostered special focuses on the region by Latin Americans themselves. One much desired perspective, that from Africa, proves difficult of achievement in terms of the availability of accepted historical ingredients. A second neglected region, the transpacific world, differs considerably from Africa, however, in that its ties with Latin America, overwhelmingly a matter of record in the nineteenth and twentieth centuries, can readily be documented.

But, within the whole of Latin America, what makes the Japanese-Peruvian record especially significant? Of all Latin America, Peru first prompted the attention of modern Japan, via international incidents born of the coolie traffic. Peru became the first Latin American state with which Japan established diplomatic relations, which have recently entered their second century. Of all Spanish America, Peru received the largest number of Japanese immigrants and the Andean state also led Latin America in attracting Japanese scholars to the study of her native culture. No other Latin American land has indulged such massive anti-Japanese rioting and journalistic outbursts, and similarly none can match the severity with which Peruvian authorities handled Japanese-Peruvians during World War Two. More recently still, in terms of trade, Peru has consistently been a leading Latin American supplier to Japan and likewise an important recipient of Japanese investment capital.

Trade that once revolved around fans, toys, and other trivia now includes sophisticated machinery and the raw materials of technically advanced industry. Trade that was nonexistent as recently as 1947 now flows at an annual rate in excess of a quarter of a billion dollars. Now joint-venture Japanese-Peruvian enterprises are heralding a future of unknown dimensions and significance. Attesting to this, the number of Peruvian chief executives and cabinet officials who have journeyed to Japan on business exceeds that of any other Latin American country. An account of Japanese relations with Peru, however, is part of a larger theme, that of the Japanese and Latin America, almost all of which awaits frontier-minded historians.

Japanese and Peruvian relations have constituted a maze of interlocking diplomatic, economic, and social considerations, a dispassionate study of which nonetheless must place primary emphasis on the Japanese factor, for a number of reasons. In the first place, it has been a matter of the Japanese going to Peru, not Peruvians going to Japan. This has meant that the Japanese faced the strange setting, the different language, the alien culture—all challenges that registered differently on succeeding generations. Accordingly, as a study in migration and acculturation, the Japanese and their descendants deserve and receive the heavier emphasis.

In the economic sphere—and Japanese-Peruvian relations have increasingly revolved around trade and investment—Japan has been dominant. Need for raw materials caused Japanese surveys and missions to scour Peru; Japan's desire for wider markets for her manufactured goods led to the bringing of "floating fairs," exhibits, and trade centers to Peru. Similarly Japan has invested heavily in Peru and has sent many technicians there without equivalent Peruvian activity in Japan. Both the relative stability of Japanese currency and the accuracy of their statistics encourage the use of their records.

Certain features of the present study invite comment. Most of the century-long account features a thematic organization rather than a strictly chronological presentation. To fortify such general themes as migration, occupations, friction, trade, education, investment, and cultural activities, details featuring human aspects of the relationship have joined the generalities regarding policies and practices. Although metropolitan Lima-Callao does constitute the primary focus for the Japanese and their descendants, this study also turns to other relevant areas of the country.

Acknowledgments are extended to many institutions and individuals. In Japan generous assistance was received from Director General Minoru Izawa and his staff at La Sociedad Latino-Americana (Raten Amerika Kyōkai); from Naomasa Oshimoto, Chief of the Research Section of the Japan Emigration Service (Kaigai Ijū Jigyōdan); from Masao Yoshida and Hiroshi Mitani at the National Diet Library; from Tōru Tamai and Kokichi Morimoto of the Federation of Economic Organizations (Keidanren); from the library of Mitsui Bussan Kabushiki Kaisha (Mitsui Products Company); from Sen Nishiyama of the United States embassy staff; from Kyōaki Murata of *The Japan Times;* and from librarians at the Universities of Tokyo, Rikkyō and Seikei. Additional assistance came from the Japanese Foreign Office (Gaimushō) and from Ambassador José Carlos Mariátegui, head of the Peruvian mission in Tokyo.

In Peru Ambassador Tetsuo Ban and his staff in the Japanese embassy have provided printed works and other materials. Additional materials have come from the *Peruvian Times*.

In the United States staff members of the following institutions have extended generous assistance: the University of Illinois at Urbana, the Library of Congress, Columbia University, the Latin American Collection of the University of Texas at Austin, Stanford University, Washington University, St. Louis Public Library, the Columbus Memorial Library of the Pan American Union, and the Department of Justice, Washington, D.C. The Japanese Consulate General in Chicago and the Japan Trade Centers in Chicago and Houston have generously cooperated.

At Southern Illinois University, Dr. John Clifford aided this study through the acquisition of microfilm copies of numerous manuscript materials, including the Japanese Foreign Office files of the period 1868-1945 regarding Latin America. Charles Holliday assisted with interlibrary loans and Charles T. Goodsell provided publications. During the period 1968-71 the Office of Research and Projects of Southern Illinois University extended support to this project. Gratitude for the research opportunity that accompanied a Fulbright lectureship in Tokyo is also directed to those, in Washington and Carbondale, who made it possible.

C.H.G.

Contents

	Introduction	vii
	Tables	xii
1.	Of Coolies and Diplomats	1
2.	The Japanese Immigrants, 1899-1941	22
3.	Early Diplomatic and Commercial Relations	42
4.	Cultural Collision	61
5.	The Turbulent Decade, 1941-51	81
6.	Diplomatic, Social, and Cultural Affairs, 1945-68	94
7.	Trade, Investment, and Technical Assistance, 1945-68	111
8.	In a Revolutionary Era, 1968-73	127
9.	Retrospect and Prospect	156
	A Select Chronology of Japanese-Peruvian Relations	159
	Notes	165
	Bibliography	181
	Index	193

Tables

1.	Emigration of Japanese to Peru, 1906-1909	30
2.	Distribution of Japanese in Peru, 1910	32
3.	Emigrants and Emigration Companies, 1898-1923	33
4.	Emigration of Japanese to Peru, 1910-21	34
5.	Emigration of Japanese to Peru, 1924-30	36
6.	Economic Survey of the Japanese in Peru, 1927	37
7.	Movement of Japanese in and out of Peru, 1931-37	38
8.	The Japanese in Peru, by Department and Sex, 1940	40
9.	Economic Activity, 1940	40
10.	Marital Status, 1940	41
11.	Age Groups and Sex, 1940	41
12.	Japanese Trade with Peru, 1896-1910	56
13.	Japanese Trade with Peru, 1911-18	58
14.	Japanese Trade with Peru, 1919-30	58
15.	Japanese Trade with Peru, 1931-41	59
16.	Barber Shops in Lima, 1904-24	64
17.	The Japanese and Peru, 1925	68
18.	Language of Instruction, Hours Weekly	77
19.	Emigration of Japanese to Peru, 1951-70	100
20.	Japanese Trade with Peru in Relation to Japanese Trade with All of Latin America, 1947-68	114
21.	Japanese Exports to Peru and Selected Other American Trading Partners, 1947-68	116
22.	Japanese Imports from Peru and Selected Other American Trading Partners, 1947-68	117
23.	Japanese Exports to Peru, 1961-68—Values and Major Categories	117
24.	Japanese Imports from Peru, 1961-68—Values and Major Categories	118
25.	Overseas Japanese Remittances to Japan, 1967	132
26.	Western Hemisphere Japanese Communities, 1970	133
27.	Japanese Trade with Peru in Relation to Japanese Trade with All of Latin America, 1969-73	139
28.	Japanese Exports to Peru and Selected Other American Trading Partners, 1969-73	140

29. Japanese Imports from Peru and Selected Other American Trading Partners, 1969-73	140
30. Japanese Exports to Peru, 1969-72—Values and Major Categories	140
31. Japanese Imports from Peru, 1969-72—Values and Major Categories	140
32. Levels Attained in Japanese Trade with Leading Latin American Trading Partners, 1951-73	141
33. Vehicle Production, 1971-73	149
34. Japanese Purchases of Peruvian Fish Meal, 1965-72	150
35. U.S. Foreign Aid to Peru, 1948-72	153
36. U.S. Direct Investment in Peru, 1955-71	154

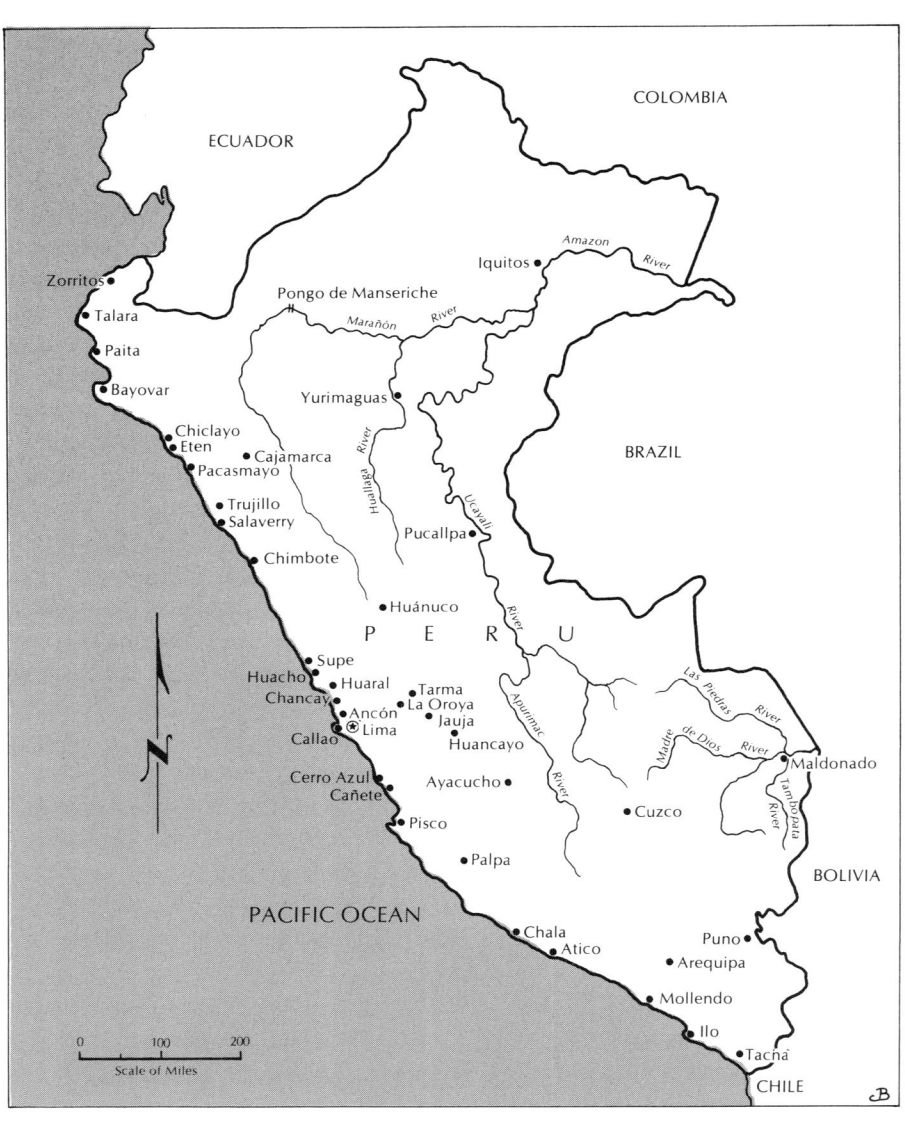

1

Of Coolies and Diplomats

In the wake of Commodore Perry's visit, the emergence of Japan into the modern world did not immediately include Latin America. When the first Japanese mission went abroad in 1860 to exchange treaty ratifications with the United States, its contact with Latin America was brief and unimportant. The Japanese concluded their Pacific voyage at Panama. A hurried railroad trip, during which the novelty of the train drew more attention than did Panama or the Panamanians, brought the travelers to Aspinwall on the Caribbean coast. There they promptly took ship for the United States. On the return trip, which completed their circumnavigation of the earth, their brief glimpse of Brazil proved no more significant than had the passage across Panama. Nor was the visit to Bahia, Brazil, in 1870, by two Japanese sailors aboard a British ship at all meaningful.[1] In the meantime unscheduled maritime drama had forced an opening in Japanese-Peruvian relations.

In 1868 the 198-ton bark *Cayaltí*[2] precipitated a marine mixup of seemingly unlimited dimensions. An American-built vessel, reportedly either of Peruvian or Chilean ownership, flying the flag of the United States, and commanded by a Portuguese skipper who had a Peruvian crew and a cargo of Chinese coolies, the *Cayaltí* executed a voyage that introduced modern Japan to independent Peru amid charges of mutiny, piracy, and murder.

In mid-January the *Cayaltí* weighed anchor at Callao for a routine coasting voyage to Peruvian ports rather than the epochal transpacific adventure that ensued. The most important cargo below the closed hatch consisted of forty-nine Chinese men earmarked, as coolies, or contract laborers, had been since 1849, for Peruvian cotton and sugar plantations.

As the *Cayaltí* approached Pacasmayo, the Chinese burst onto the deck. Ah Cow, one of the leaders, attacked the boatswain with an axe. As a crowd of Orientals rushed toward him, the knife-wielding Peruvian dived overboard. Other members of the crew, overpowered, were temporarily removed to the forecastle. Four others, seeking refuge in the rigging, witnessed the coolie victory in such despair that they also jumped into the sea. Only two members of the ship's complement escaped death—the Chinese cook and Captain Manuel de Nicolini; the later quickly pledged to return the unhappy Chinese to their native land. All remaining members of the crew, as well as seven Chinese, lost their lives during the ten-minute struggle which shifted control and changed the course of the vessel.

The voyage scheduled to end in a few days continued for months. Provisions dwindled and the *Cayaltí* suffered typhoons and calms while working an uncertain course across the northern Pacific. Although the *Cayaltí* never encountered another ship, she did touch land. On one occasion supplies were picked up at an unidentified island "where it was warm." Months later all aboard were cold and hungry when another island was visited and remembered because the natives wore skins and had sledges drawn by dogs. There the captain and cook, who had gone ashore for provisions, refused to return to the vessel. Some time later, after being trapped for days in an ice pack, the *Cayaltí* made yet another landfall. Though unidentified, it surely was in the Kurile Islands, for there the Chinese, on payment of sixteen dollars, picked up the Japanese pilot who took the ship into Hakodate, one of the few ports in Japan at which American consuls then functioned.[3]

On August 19, American Consul E.E. Rice went out to the *Cayaltí* and boarded her. A hurried check disclosed she had flown the flag of the United States, a fact which intensified his interest. Some success attended his search for the ship's papers but consternation marked his return on deck as he discovered a member of the trading firm of Thompson and Bewick hoisting their house flag in place of the American ensign. A flaring of tempers and a flurry of words embittered Rice and he speedily turned the ship over to Japanese authorities who agreed that the forty-two Chinese aboard the *Cayaltí* be taken ashore for examination and safekeeping. The role of the Japanese, relative to both ship and passengers, mounted, as did the air of mystery.[4]

For Minister Van Valkenburgh, informed by Consul Rice, the *Cayaltí* reinforced the concern he entertained regarding northern Japan where decisive engagements were then shaping up in the civil war between supporters of the emperor and of the shogun. The months that witnessed initial contacts which made Japan aware of Peru also settled the conflict that ushered Japan into the modern world under imperial rule.[5]

In this same period Peru was flirting with so much chaos at home and experiencing so much friction in her European relations that she failed to face the transpacific world with widening outlook, either in policy or practice. During the 1860s, tensions born of alleged abuse of Basque immigrants provoked demands from Spain for apology and indemnity, and led to islands seized, treaties negotiated and disavowed, and ports blockaded and bombarded. There was turmoil related to the 1867 liberal constitution and the specter of economic ruin for a nation overly dependent upon mismanaged guano revenues. In addition, the administrative discontinuity featuring military figures in Lima and disavowed diplomats abroad guaranteed that the case of the *Cayaltí* would continue to involve Americans rather than Peruvians.[6]

Van Valkenburgh, a general turned diplomat, instructed Rice not to take delivery of the ship and to avoid taking any action in the matter without specific instructions. Turning to the U.S. Asiatic squadron, the diplomat asked Rear Admiral J.C. Rowan to dispatch one of his units to Hakodate.[7]

While Van Valkenburgh was inviting the U.S. Navy onto the scene, Consul Rice was amassing information and reaching conclusions. Sixty days after the arrival of the *Cayaltí,* he wrote, "It is now nearly a certainty that the coolie bark is American built . . . and will undoubtedly be handed over to me by the Japanese Government." "My present opinion," he added, "is that the bark should be sold here for the benefit of whom it may concern, and the Coolies be sent to the Coal mines for a term of years as Pirates."[8]

Commander Earl English took the U.S.S. *Iroquois* into Hakodate and promptly instituted a thorough survey of the *Cayaltí*. He pronounced the hull sound and seaworthy, the windlass broken, and all the boats missing except a single small one. The fore topmast was twisted and cracked and broken yardarms had been crudely spliced. Some booms and yards had disappeared. Rice's words,

"How the Chinamen ever got in here is, indeed, a mystery" seemed to echo in the surveyors' report.[9]

Other complications also developed. J.H. McColley, the American consul at Callao, had certified the crew list. Clear, too, was the fact that the ship, reputedly Chilean-owned, had flown the American flag for more than three years, the better to escape capture by Spanish naval units during the lengthy hostilities in which Chile and Peru joined against Spain.[10]

Both before and during the survey of the vessel, eight of the forty-two surviving Chinese presented testimony. Each man made a lengthy statement of his experience aboard the ship. Differing in details, those accounts nonetheless afforded the basis for winnowing the general experience all had known.[11]

Meanwhile the outcome of the survey led Consul Rice to act while others—Commander English, Admiral Rowan, Minister Van Valkenburgh and Secretary of State Seward—engaged in a round-robin of correspondence. He informed the Japanese authorities at Hakodate that the bark was American property. Despite Van Valkenburgh's admonition that he not take delivery of the ship, Rice wrote the Japanese, "Accordingly I have taken possession of said bark 'Cayalti' and until the Chinamen and Bark can be disposed of in a proper manner have to request your assistance as provided by Treaty."[12] Apparently he based his appeal on article nine of the Treaty of Amity and Commerce negotiated in mid-1858 by Consul General Townsend Harris, wherein it read, "When requested by the American consul, the Japanese authorities will cause the arrest of all deserters and fugitives from justice, receive in jail all persons held as prisoners by the consul, and give to the consul such assistance as may be required to enable him . . . to maintain order among the shipping."[13]

Concern about the ship also renewed Rice's friction with certain Britons. While charges of looting were pending against the Chinese, the *Cayaltí* remained at anchor, its passengers comfortably housed in a one-time army barracks.[14]

The complicated circumstances suggested a number of possible courses of action. When Felipe de la Torre Bueno, the Peruvian consul at Macao—the Portuguese colony from which most Chinese contract labor usually embarked for Peru—claimed the vessel, Van Valkenburgh refused to take action until it was clear he had a right to do so. Rear Admiral Rowan, sharing Rice's assessment, declared, "these coolies are guilty of Piracy" and urged that they be tried in courts of Japan, China, or the United States.[15] In addition, Rice and the Japanese authorities in Hakodate, with the Chinese detained, money impounded, and ship expenses mounting and unpaid, gave Minister Van Valkenburgh reasons enough for soliciting instructions from Washington.

Secretary of State William H. Seward, advocating noninvolvement in the case, insisted, "It appears doubtful whether any of our citizens are interested in the vessel, and this Government can certainly take no part in reducing the coolies to the servitude from which they have escaped." Later, when apprized of Rowan's stress on piracy, Seward vigorously rebutted that, citing "their object in capturing the vessel was not robbery and plunder."[16] The desire of the Chinese to return to their native land, Seward pointed out, paralleled the *Amistad* case which some years earlier had led to a favorable decision by the United States Supreme Court.[17]

Although American authorities desired to leave the case entirely to the Japanese, the *Cayaltí* affair refused to go away. In mid-1869 Consul McColley added from Callao another confusing dimension to the case. He certified and forwarded a declaration by Juan Cudina, an American resident in Callao, that he, as sole owner of the *Cayaltí,* authorized her sale.[18] In due course the Department of State, insisting there was insufficient evidence that the vessel was American, fortified its previous hands-off position by declaring that even if the vessel and her owner were American, both had violated the Act of February 19, 1862, which prohibited the coolie trade.[19]

While the *Cayaltí* gradually deteriorated at Hakodate, more sudden changes beset the interested American officials. Seward relinquished the reins of the Department of State to Hamilton Fish, General Van Valkenburgh surrendered the legation to the Nevada politician C.E. DeLong, and Consul A.C. Dunn replaced E.E. Rice at Hakodate. To substantiate his charge that Rice's disgraceful conduct of the business of the consulate included fraudulent transactions, Dunn referred to the *Cayaltí*. Only one item of correspondence concerning the case remained in the files. To all else, in December 1870, he added, "The said Bark lies in the Harbor."[20]

A diplomatic headache for American officials, a source of friction between Americans and Englishmen, and an expense and embarrassment to the Japanese authorities, the *Cayaltí* incident proved something less than a prod and inspiration to Peruvians. However, it clearly demonstrated the need for better communications between Peru and Japan. Accordingly no surprise attended the request, on March 15, 1870, by the Minister of Foreign Affairs of Peru, that the United States government permit its ministers in Japan and China to represent Peru in its dealings with those governments.

As the 1870s dawned, this wider ranging international outlook of Peru derived from a number of circumstances. President José Balta, inaugurated in mid-1868 and destined to serve a full four-year term, brought some measure of continuity to political administration. Secondly, this was a time of extravagant optimisn concerning Peruvian economic prospects. These high hopes were based on the guano, nitrates, and copper which sought foreign markets, and the banking, utility, and other commercial enterprises whose ultimate success would also result in increased foreign trade. To all else, and specifically related to the Far East, the continuing Peruvian need for Chinese laborers faced changes abroad. For more than two decades—since 1849—the importation of thousands of Chinese coolies had partially met Peruvian labor needs. In due course, however, Chinese law prohibited the overseas recruitment of such workers. For a time cooperative Britons moved the coolies through Hong Kong but British authorities plugged that channel of supply and Peru became totally dependent upon Portuguese Macao. By 1870 the gnawing fear that the Portuguese would yield to combined Anglo-Chinese pressures led President Balta to consider a direct diplomatic approach to China. The proximity of China and Japan, plus the fact that less than vigorous relations were anticipated with either, led Peru, like various other governments, to couple the two Asian states in initial diplomatic endeavors. However, Balta's efforts to send Foreign Minister José Antonio García y García to China in 1870 and 1871 were rebuffed by García, causing Peruvian-Far Eastern relations to be conducted, if at all, by diplomats of friendly powers.[21]

The United States, having helped to open Japan to the world in the 1850s, readily acceded to the Peruvian request which initiated Japanese-Latin American diplomatic relations. Secretary of State Fish wrote recently installed Minister C.E. DeLong, "In view of the friendly relations existing between the United States and Peru, I will consequently thank you to attend to any matter which may be entrusted to your charge by the Government of that Republic so far as this can be done compatibly with other instructions from this Department."²² The *Cayaltí* issue had demonstrated to Peru the need for representation in Japan, and a second shipload of Chinese would soon occupy Minister DeLong as custodian of Peruvian interests in that country. This, in turn, would hasten Peru into direct diplomatic relations with Japan.

The calm of summer broke suddenly when the Japanese Foreign Office informed DeLong that the *Cayaltí,* which was still anchored at Hakodate and incurring needless expenses, would be sold by the governor of Hakodate if not claimed within 120 days. DeLong hastened to claim the vessel in the name of Peru and then, in mid-November, wrote to Lima, requesting instructions. DeLong briefly stated the two-year-old history of the *Cayaltí* in Japanese waters, concluding with the admonition that if the ship were not quickly sold at auction she probably would not yield the sum needed to cover the expenses which already exceeded two thousand dollars. Five days earlier DeLong had written the Peruvian Foreign Office that he would be happy to negotiate a treaty between Japan and Peru on the same terms as had other nations. The precise motivation for this offer is unclear: was it an expression of his willingness to serve Peru, a desire to shed the responsibility for Peruvian affairs, or the wish of a political extrovert to thrust himself into the limelight? However, at the close of 1870, in the season that found Consul Dunn denouncing Rice's handling of the *Cayaltí* case and DeLong awaiting instructions from Lima, inaction set in on all fronts—Peruvian, Japanese, and American.²³

This calm of 1871 and early 1872 quickly dissipated due to the complications attending a second Peruvian coolie ship, the *María Luz* in Japanese waters.²⁴ At first the American legation in Yokohama side-stepped involvement. When Captain Ricardo Herrera appealed for aid, Chargé d'affaires C.O. Shepard, acting in the absence of Minister DeLong, replied, "Although always ready and anxious to render aid and assistance to vessels bearing the Peruvian flag and engaged in legitimate business, I *cannot,* under the circumstances, extend my protection." Shepard rebuffed the appeal because the skipper of the *María Luz* had admitted that his ship was carrying several hundred Chinese to Peru.²⁵

Three days earlier, on July 7, the 109-foot bark *María Luz,* out of Macao with approximately 230 Chinese, had been driven by stormy weather to seek shelter in Yokohama harbor. Her stay there included not only the refusal of the American diplomat to assist the ship's captain but also an episode which, involving the ranking British diplomat, made the *María Luz* an international issue.

Under cover of darkness one of the Chinese escaped from the Peruvian ship, swam to the *Iron Duke,* and sought refuge aboard that British vessel. The exhausted fugitive, transferred by the British consul to the Japanese authorities, was speedily returned to the *María Luz.* However, this episode, followed by similar ones, fanned the suspicions of British Chargé d'affaires Robert G. Watson. He urged the Japanese Foreign Office to conduct an inquiry.

Watson, in describing the fugitive's case, expressed his suspicions that the so-called Chinese passengers were being ill treated and insisted that the barbarity characteristic of the coolie traffic between Macao and Peru led him to conclude "that Japan should not permit its hospitality to be abused to the possible injury of natives of China." Watson not only insisted upon an inquiry, he also suggested procedures—interrogation of the ship's officers, testimony from the alleged passengers, and the study of relevant contracts and regulations. Lest Japanese reluctance engender inaction, he reminded Foreign Minister Soyeshima "that as the ship is under the flag of a country having no treaty relations with Japan no other power can control your right to take proceedings . . . ."[26] Because of Watson's prodding communication, British humanitarianism overcame official American reluctance, Japanese indifference, and Peruvian ignorance; the *María Luz* case blossomed into an international incident which occupied many minds for almost a half decade and inspired wider and more significant aspects of Peruvian-Japanese relations.

Within forty-eight hours of Watson's appeal to the Japanese Foreign Office, the Kanagawa prefectural authorities requested the presence of Captain Herrera and the Chinese fugitive whom the police had returned to his ship. Next the Kanagawa officials had Municipal Director E.S. Benson of Yokohama visit the *María Luz.* Benson intimated that the Chinese could not risk telling the truth while aboard ship.[27]

Captain Herrera, anxious to get back the ship's papers which he had deposited with the prefectural officials, complained that his expenses came to $250 daily. Emphasizing his desire to depart, he informed the governor of Kanagawa, "if my papers are not returned to me and the expenses of my detention here guaranteed, the care of the ship, the Chinese, etc. will be yours because I will abandon the vessel, the passengers, etc. and I will return to my country."[28] Obviously Herrera hoped his threat to dump unwanted individuals and expense-inducing property into the lap of the Japanese authorities would lead them to halt the inquiry and release his ship. That same day another authorized survey of the *María Luz* took place.[29] Quickening the interest of the Japanese, the report filed by the two investigators delayed the departure of the Peruvian ship and challenged her anxious captain's bluff.

By this time Minister DeLong, having returned to his post, was reversing Chargé Shepard's refusal to assist Peruvian interests. Shepard and DeLong interpreted Fish's instructions differently. Shepard allowed American opposition to the coolie traffic to override all else, eliminating totally any cooperation in the *María Luz* case. On the other hand, DeLong apparently felt that cooperation was to be extended until specific instructions to the contrary came from Washington. Shepard, in turn, could insist that a Peruvian citizen, not the Peruvian government, had referred the present case to the American legation. DeLong, meanwhile, sensed that imperfect transpacific communications required early handling of a case which only belatedly could come to the attention of authorities in Lima. To all else, DeLong's reversal of the American position quite possibly stemmed, in part, from a real and growing personality conflict between himself and Shepard.

First DeLong urged the Japanese to give Herrera a prompt and fair public trial. Next he more fully assumed the role of diplomatic representative for Peru by addressing to the Peruvian Foreign Minister a dispatch supplemented by eight enclosures. As he sought Peruvian approval of his action, the American minister also hoped to establish communications with Lima. During 1870-72 his unanswered dispatches inclined DeLong "to the belief that they were never received."[30]

To facilitate the proceedings by the prefecture of Kanagawa and to relieve the Chinese of physical and psychological restraints, all of them, as well as Captain Herrera, went ashore. The testimony of a number of Chinese contributed to a judgment sustaining the charge that Herrera had subjected his alleged passengers to cruel treatment. The Kanagawa prefecture pronounced Herrera guilty, but recommended leniency. In consideration of the delays and inconveniences suffered, the court recommended that the Peruvian captain be pardoned and allowed to depart with his vessel. Herrera insisted that the Chinese also be returned to the *María Luz*. While the issue was taking form, another attack on the proceedings of the prefecture arose.

Since this was a time when all foreign powers jealously guarded their extraterritorial rights and viewed Japanese judicial proceedings with jaundiced eyes, the foreign consuls closely followed this inquiry. Leading the opposition to the action by the Kanagawa authorities was Acting Consul General E. Zappe of Germany. On five counts, the most important of which denied the competency of the Japanese authorities, the German repudiated the finding and recommendation of the prefectural authorities. His cogent arguments immediately drew the attention of fellow consuls. Three, the Danish, Portuguese, and Italian representatives, endorsed the findings of Zappe. In support of the activities and decisions of the Japanese, British Consul Robertson stood alone. Between the extremes of repudiation and acceptance were two consuls, the Dutch and the American.[31]

Captain Herrera's request, directed to the prefectural government, that "the Chinese passengers who have been taken from . . . the bark *María Luz* . . . be sent back again," evoked an immediate response. The authorities informed him that "each of those Chinese declines to return on board of the ship, and can only be compelled to do so by this kenchō [prefectural authorities], after a judgment to that effect regularly obtained in an action brought before me." At once this suggestion that Herrera institute legal action led the Peruvian skipper to lay the prefecture's letter before DeLong, saying, "I now humbly beg to crave your excellency's assistance in this matter."[32]

DeLong promptly wrote the Foreign Office, reminding the Japanese that he abhorred the coolie trade, that Herrera was powerless to approach the Foreign Office, and that the American minister had assumed obligations in reference to Peruvian interests. Desirous of precise information on points about which he wished to communicate with the Peruvian Foreign Office, DeLong put four queries to the Japanese minister.

"I am not to be understood," Minister Soyeshima replied, "as admitting that this government is under any obligations to receive any communication from you in behalf of the government of Peru." While jolting DeLong's position as an official representative of Peruvian interests, the Japanese did treat DeLong's queries "as his [Herrera's] representative and for his information, but not for the information of the Peruvian government." Devastating to the American minister's effort to speed the return of the Chinese to the *María Luz* was Soyeshima's assertion, "I know of no law, custom, or precedent which requires this government, or any other government to force any person to return to a ship against his will unless he be a fugitive, criminal, or a deserting seaman."[33] Sensing that litigation was the only avenue open to him, Captain Herrera began the action by which he hoped to force the Chinese back aboard his ship.

Aware that the *María Luz* deserved Peruvian attention, DeLong again wrote the Foreign Office from which he, as yet, had received no communication. Along with the prefecture's judgment went copies of recent correspondence concerning both the proceedings and the Chinese. He added copies of the testimony, ship's papers, and all other items offered in evidence during the trial, hoping for "your excellency's approval of my action."[34]

The fate of hundreds rested on a few test cases. Herrera's counsel, Frederick V. Dickens, filed petitions regarding two of the Chinese, Chiong and Sia Jam, petitions that were intended to force all the Chinese back aboard the *María Luz*. Attorney John N. Davidson, defense counsel, answered those petitions with his objections. Simultaneously the expenses resulting from the stay ashore of the Chinese produced additional friction. When Dickens learned that either more money must be paid to cover the twenty dollars per diem expense of the Chinese or they would be allowed to go at large, vigorous protest accompanied the payment which kept the Chinese under Japanese detention.[35]

In the meantime, the Japanese Foreign Office had circumscribed DeLong's role as the representative of Peru. It drew upon a precedent of 1867, when the United States had been protecting the interests of several nations' citizens in war-ravaged Mexico, and it had learned that while official mediation would not be acceptable the introduction of good offices privately would be admitted. The Japanese Foreign Office indicated its adherence to the approach employed by Mexico. While clarifying one issue, Soyeshima muddied other diplomatic waters when he added, "It may even happen that they [Peruvians] will be regarded more favorably than other foreigners who betray distrust by insisting upon being under the jurisdiction of their respective consuls."[36] This bald assertion that a citizen of a country not enjoying extraterritorial rights in Japan might receive better treatment than one whose government did enjoy such rights enraged DeLong, even as earlier portions of the communication had mollified him.

On September 27 Taku Oye, who had presided over the hearings, handed down decisions in the two cases. In both instances he announced, "The judgment of the Court is for the defendant."[37] Turned over to a Chinese government commission for repatriation, the Chinese ceased to be pawns in this extended international confusion.

Minister DeLong quickly summarized matters for both Washington and Lima. His dispatch to Fish, accompanied by thirteen enclosures, prompted the diplomat to say, "This completes the history of the matter up to this date." To the Peruvian Foreign Office went a sequence of negative reporting—the court decision against Captain Herrera, a reiteration of the opposition of the United States to the coolie traffic, and the limited role accorded him as the representative of Peru by the Japanese authorities, a combination that surely affected succeeding events.[38]

Weeks passed during which Captain Herrera abandoned the *María Luz* and set out for Peru via Hong Kong. In the same period the Japanese Foreign Office invited DeLong's deeper identification with the case. Indicating that the Peruvian bark was under no restraint whatever, Minister Soyeshima said, "If you, in the capacity of extending your good offices on behalf of Peru . . ., see fit to do so, there would seem no objection to your taking such charge of the vessel as you may think advisable."[39]

While DeLong mulled over that matter, the Peruvian government, unknown to him, was informing Washington of the steps it contemplated taking. Without any specific reference to the *María Luz,* Minister Manuel Freyre had informed the American secretary of state that his government proposed "very soon to accredit a Legation of the first class to China and Japan, with the double object of concluding treaties of friendship and commerce with those Empires, and of entering into other negotiations of great importance." Seeking the aid of American diplomatic representatives in those countries, the Peruvian further indicated, "Said Legation will leave Peru at the close of the present month, on board of one of the vessels of our squadron, and will take with it some samples of the natural productions and manufactures of the Republic."[40] The merchandise possibly sparked mild curiosity; the use of a naval unit contributed to wild rumor.

Simultaneously with Freyre's note to Fish, a shorter, less informative one by Foreign Minister J. de la Riva Agüero went to DeLong. Acknowledging receipt of DeLong's dispatch of August 19, the first such received in Lima, the Peruvian official simply thanked him for his "intervention in favor of the affairs of Peru," saying nothing about the proposed Peruvian mission.[41] It would be 1873 before the American diplomat received this communication from Lima. In the meantime the *María Luz* was inspiring a flurry of activity.

Acting upon Minister Soyeshima's invitation, DeLong promptly put fellow American Benjamin C. Trask aboard the vessel as master. Indicating expenses that approximated $400 monthly, Trask suggested the discharge of the crew and the substitution of a skeleton force at a cost of $140 per month. Something else that commended his report to DeLong was Trask's statement that the departing crew members would willingly pay their own passage to Hong Kong.

When DeLong informed the Japanese authorities of this, Taku Oye replied, "The reason given for the discharge of the crew seems to be good, and the course suggested therefore approved." DeLong next instructed his agent to "see the crew on board the *China* to-night or early in the morning to-morrow, and just before the steamer sails give each man his passage-ticket and the money due him." Informed of events, Minister Soyeshima wrote DeLong, " . . . I am gratified to learn that you have sent the riotous crew of the *María Luz* beyond the limits of this empire."[42] Despite the departure of the Chinese, Captain Herrera, and the crew, the case of the *María Luz* remained alive and threatening.

During this time certain of Minister DeLong's communications to the Peruvian Foreign Office, plus at least one by the Belgian Eduard Seve, had inspired activity in Lima. Foreign Minister J. de la Riva Agüero vaguely informed DeLong of the mission which, he said, "was ready to leave when the news of the *María Luz* affair reached here." Indicating that the "main object is to enter into relations of amity and compass treaties of commerce and navigation with China and Japan," the Peruvian continued, "This mission is absolutely one of peace."[43]

The lengthy instructions supplied emissary Captain Aurelio García y García following his appointment by President Manuel Pardo included the following directives: 1) the treaties with Japan and

China, the primary reason for the mission, should include extraterritorial and most-favored-nation stipulations; 2) the freedom of the citizens of all signatories to emigrate must be maintained and special conventions with China on that score were desired; 3) for the harmonization of the Chinese migration to Peru it was hoped that China would send an agent there; and 4) the right of all signatories to establish consulates would be observed. Finally it was hoped that friendly assists in Japan would come his way from the representatives of the United States and France.[44]

While García traveled toward Japan, messages from the Peruvian foreign minister and the American secretary of state left DeLong both relieved and confused. The coming of the Peruvian emissary obviously relieved him. At the same time Fish's statement, "It does not appear that the Peruvian government had in any way entrusted to your charge the case of the 'Maria Luz' or . . . had made any communication to you with regard to any occasion that might arise for the exercise of your good offices," suggested that DeLong's past identification with the case had been beyond the call of duty. Meanwhile both García's instructions and the Peruvian foreign minister's direct correspondence with DeLong implied a continuing role for him. He informed Japanese authorities of the coming of Captain García and he wrote Lima of his willingness to aid that mission.[45]

Meanwhile, at least one piece of chauvinistic writing out of Lima was disturbing the Japanese. An account of the *María Luz* case insisted that "The Peruvian government is more than indignant," adding, "Captain García will sail in the *Independencia,* a formidable iron-clad frigate, mounting sixteen heavy guns. . . . We are here unaware of the force of the Japanese navy; but, should the matter prove serious, it is said that the intrepid '*Japs*' will find a tough antagonist in the frigate." When Foreign Minister Soyeshima asked what would be the American response if the Peruvians came with hostile intent, DeLong offered comforting assurances.[46]

Arriving in Yokohama on February 27 and immediately contacting DeLong, Minister García was received by the Japanese with marked signs of hospitality, among which the temporary use of a palace as his residence and the entry of his coach into the inner courtyard of the imperial palace constituted "firsts" for foreign diplomats. Assisted by documents supplied by DeLong, García readied his presentation of the Peruvian case regarding the *María*

Luz. On March 31, 1873, his detailed statement, made lengthier still by a dozen annexes, went to the Japanese Foreign Office. First, however, García asked DeLong to read and react to his statement.

"Both Mr. Mjeno [Uyeno] and Señor García," DeLong wrote Fish, "have since conferred with me as to whom I would suggest as an arbitrator, provided they could not agree." Weeks elapsed and García, in an unsuccessful bid to speed the Japanese response, declared that he could not remain in Japan much longer, which he nonetheless did.[47]

The Japanese reply supported their every prior act and decision, repudiating completely the Peruvian line of argument. The two parties, poles apart, immediately signed a protocol which provided for arbitration. After brief diplomatic sparring which included the Peruvian proposal of the emperor of Brazil as arbiter and the Japanese refusal on grounds that Japan and Brazil did not maintain diplomatic relations, they agreed upon the czar of Russia.

The protocol provided for the submission to the arbiter of all relevant documents within twelve months of his acceptance of that role. Each country could and did name an agent to represent it before the arbiter. The czar had to determine whether Japan bore responsibility in the handling of the *María Luz* and the Chinese laborers and, if so, to indicate the sum owed Peru as indemnity.

Inasmuch as the value of the ship could affect the payment of any indemnity, both parties agreed to her sale. DeLong assumed that neutral function and prepared, by means of inventory and advertisements, for the public auction which took place in Yokohama. The sale of the *María Luz* realized $7,250 (Mexican). After deducting certain expenses and creditors' claims, $4,713.28 were deposited in a designated bank, awaiting possible assignment by the arbitrator.[48]

Minister García next turned to treaty talks—the second phase of his Japanese mission—and immediately encountered delay. The Japanese desire to revise the unequal treaties under which foreign powers enjoyed rights of extraterritoriality had recently prompted the sending of a special embassy to Europe and the United States, and the return of that mission was being awaited. Nonetheless preliminary conferences did get underway. When Japan came to realize that Peru refused to be the first country denied extraterritorial rights, the negotiations proceeded more smoothly and swiftly. Nevertheless, between the signing of the preliminary and definitive drafts of the emerging treaty, Japanese concern about the coolie traffic led Soyeshima to tell García that he was disposed to propose a clause to the effect that all difficulties occurring aboard Peruvian vessels transporting Chinese emigrants would be under Japanese jurisdiction. However, to facilitate García's departure for China, the Tokyo authorities, while not insisting upon the treaty alteration, did reserve freedom of action in all such cases.[49]

On August 21, 1873, the negotiators signed a ten-article treaty. Article one pledged peace, friendship, and the protection of both nationalities' persons and property. The next article gave each country the right to appoint diplomatic and consular representatives as well as promising most-favored-nation treatment and freedom of movement anywhere in the respective countries. The third article permitted Japanese to reside anywhere in Peru while limiting Peruvian residence in Japan to those cities which had been or might be opened to foreigners. The case of the *María Luz* influenced article four, which pledged assistance and friendly treatment for vessels and men stranded or wrecked on the coasts of the two countries. The insistence, in the fifth article, that the duties applied to the exports and imports of other nationalities would be effective amounted to an underscoring of the pledge of most-favored-nation treatment. Instead of spelling out the nature of extraterritorial jurisdiction, as in many other Japanese treaties, the sixth article arrived at the same meaning by indicating that the Peruvians would enjoy every privilege, immunity, jurisdiction, and advantage granted other nations. Both governments promised not to restrict the employment of citizens of the other country. The Japanese pursuit of treaty revision, introduced in the preamble of the document, was reiterated in article eight which stated that when Japan's treaties were revised, Japan and Peru would conclude a new treaty and this present preliminary one would be terminated. Plagued by the problem of language, the signatories agreed upon the English text of the treaty as the decisive one. The tenth and last article, after providing for the exchange of ratifications in Tokyo as soon as possible, indicated that the treaty came into force at the date of signing. On instructions from Minister García, that same day witnessed the earliest activity by Peruvian Consul General Oscar Heeren.[50] The treaty ratifications were exchanged May 17, 1875.

Twelve days later the czar handed down his arbitral award concerning the *María Luz*. Despite the detailed exposition of the

Peruvian case, and the eighty-two supporting documents presented by José A. de Lavalle in St. Petersburg, that award, which was absolutely decisive and final and was to be executed without objection, evasion or delay of any kind, totally favored Japan. In the meantime the Portuguese decree of December 27, 1873, had stopped the emigration of Chinese to Peru via Macao.[51] Tempering Peruvian disappointment was the realization that the future would be free of cases resembling those of the *Cayaltí* and *María Luz*.

Acrimony and delay had marked the case of the *María Luz* but brevity and cordiality keynoted the negotiation and content of the Japanese-Peruvian treaty of 1873. This first treaty between Japan and a Latin American state did more than establish political ties and eliminate shipping incidents as sources of friction. Certain portions of it, touching on trade and migration, reflected areas of interest which the Japanese, in particular, would later pursue. Meanwhile neither government hurried to send officials, immigrants, ships, goods, or anything else to the other. Time would underscore the truth that the settlement of a peculiar and negative problem, the case of the *María Luz,* rather than an accumulation of ordinary positive interests had inspired this initial diplomatic arrangement. Minister García's efforts to promote trade between the two countries, centering about his successful moves to have the Japanese put both nitrates and guano on the list of duty-free commodities, proved totally unproductive.[52] After the settlement of the *María Luz* case, no real basis for a continuing relationship existed and none developed.

For a decade and a half the two countries lacked meaningful contacts. These were years during which Peru's meager merchant marine scarcely included transpacific voyages in its operations, and when the small but growing Japanese merchant marine plied sea lanes in the northern hemisphere to Japan's major trading partners, the United States and Western Europe. Related to the absence of ship movements between Japan and Peru was the fact that neither country could significantly interest the other commercially. In the last third of the nineteenth century, when guano commonly was a leading export of Peru, Japanese farming developed no need for, much less dependence upon, that Peruvian fertilizer, nor did Peruvians generate much demand for the silk, tea, and rice of Japan. Both countries had large percentages of their populations living close to the level of bare subsistence, lacking the money income that might have prompted widening trade between them. The conjunction of such negative factors as low per capita incomes, the failure of each country to produce goods needed by the other, and the absence of shipping, with certain Peruvian political and economic realities—administrative instability, depreciated currency, flight of capital, and national bankruptcy in the wake of the War of the Pacific—and the unproductive nature of Japanese-Peruvian commercial relations appears logical and natural. Added to all this was the sometimes rapid, sometimes cautious Japanese formulation of basic economic outlooks which included a shift from state control to private enterprise in the early decades of the Meiji era.

Meanwhile Peruvian insistence upon exercising extraterritorial rights in Japan led a later foreign minister of the South American country, Alberto Ulloa, to remark, "that period is simply marked by an arrogant attitude on the part of our country." The first call at a Peruvian port by a Japanese vessel occurred in May 1883. However, no importance attached to it beyond the fact that a dead seaman was carried ashore at Callao for burial in the English cemetery.[53]

Japanese interest in Peru began in 1889, when Korekiyo Takahashi's urge to engage in silver mining there, stimulated by Peru's consular representative Oscar Heeren, led to the formation of a short-lived Japanese company. However, the former director of the Japanese Patent Bureau and his colleagues, discouraged in the course of their personal inspection of the mining site which they found to be an abandoned one, quickly returned to Japan, disabused of the idea of investing in the Cerro de Pasco area.

The next Japanese identified with Peru was a widely traveled, well-read romantic named Ikutarō Aoyagi. This graduate of the University of California and student of the Incas spent half of 1893 in Peru. While there he visited two colonization projects. At one of them, Perené, he discussed with a Briton named McKenzie the idea of Japanese migration to Peru. McKenzie, expounding grandiose proposals that would welcome Japanese labor, promised Aoyagi additional information which he never provided. Nonetheless Aoyagi returned to Japan and occupied himself with emigration activities, especially in reference to Brazil.[54]

Meanwhile Japan and Peru had moved toward treaty revision. For the Japanese it represented but a minor facet of a general policy which specifically concerned tariffs and judicial jurisdiction. Peru had no equivalently strong motivation but authorities in Lima could easily conclude that the treaty of 1873 had failed to foster significant ties between the two nations. Also, both governments, in their renewed awareness of one another, reflected the widening international outlook then beginning in numerous countries.

Inasmuch as neither country had diplomatic or consular representatives in the other's territory, the Japanese and Peruvian ministers to the United States, Munemitsu Mutsu and Felix C.C. Zegarra, handled their countries' mutual affairs in Washington. On July 29, 1889, Mutsu's note included the proposed text of a new treaty. However, a combination of circumstances tempered Peruvian willingness to discuss treaty modification. Repeated personal shifts in the administration of President Andrés Cáceres, plus the imminent election of 1890, reduced the prospective consideration of such a marginal matter as Peruvian-Japanese relations. The withdrawal of Mutsu from the legation in Washington injected another disruptive element. Most importantly Peru, jealous of the extraterritorial rights which made her the legal equal of the major powers in her relations with Japan, was unwilling to surrender those rights before any major power did so.

The Japanese had based their overture to Peru, in part, on their negotiation with Mexico in 1888 of a treaty favorable to their revisionist outlook, but Peru readily noted the difference between the two Latin-American republics in their relations with Japan. Mexico, lacking previous treaty ties with Japan, was surrendering nothing. On the other hand Peru, because of the treaty of 1873, would not only be surrendering something in her relations with Japan but also in reference to the major powers.

Five years after those unproductive contacts between Mutsu and Zegarra, changed circumstances conferred better prospects upon a renewal in Washington of the treaty-revision effort. In September 1894, by which time a new Anglo-Japanese treaty had been written, ratified, and exchanged and Japan was likewise well advanced in negotiations with other leading powers, Minister Shinichirō Kurino's note to Peruvian Chargé José María Irigoyen enclosed the text of a proposed treaty and invited Peru to name a negotiator. Chargé Irigoyen promptly contacted Foreign Minister Manuel Irigoyen.[55]

In Washington Kurino's repeated visits to his Peruvian colleague reflected not only Japanese interest in treaty revision but also a desire to overcome Peruvian procrastination. Some of the latter, however, derived from the shaky state of Peruvian affairs in the aftermath of the death of President Morales Bermúdez, the return to power of Cáceres, and subsequent revolutionary rumblings. Under the circumstances the Japanese, having initiated the move for treaty talks, applied pressure repeatedly to bring about negotiations. Early in 1895 Minister Irigoyen received the desired full powers and he and Kurino entered upon the discussions which produced the treaty of March 20, a nineteen-article document which replaced the "preliminary" one of 1873.[56]

The new treaty was largely economic in tone, featuring most-favored treatment in reference to goods, property, taxes, duties, and shipping charges. Considering both countries' almost nonexistent commercial awareness of each other, this emphasis optimistically looked toward the future. The treaty also denied Peru the privilege of extraterritoriality—Japanese courts and law were to be used in the dispensation of justice. Balancing, as it were, that concession to Japanese sovereignty was the acquisition by Peruvians, exceedingly few of whom had set foot in Japan, of the right to reside anywhere in that country.

This treaty, like all others then being negotiated by Japan, was scheduled to become effective in mid-1899. Meanwhile the signatories had until November 20, 1895, to effect an exchange of ratifications. On occasion Kurino politely nudged the Foreign Office in Lima but delay nonetheless set in. In the meantime turmoil had altered the Peruvian leadership: Nicolás de Piérola assumed the presidency and the duties of foreign minister were passed on to Ricardo Ortíz de Zevallos who proposed a new date for the ratification formalities.

While Peru was floundering and recovering, Japan hoped that her additional treaty-negotiating successes with the United States, Russia, and Italy would encourage a Peruvian response. Tōru Hoshi, Kurino's replacement in Washington, maintained diplomatic pressure upon Peru. Finally word came that the Peruvian Foreign Office had submitted the treaty, accompanied by a recommendation of prompt action, to the congress. All went well, the congressional approval permitting the exchange of ratifications, as rescheduled, on December 24, 1896, in Washington.[57]

In view of the meagerness of past Japanese-Peruvian relations and of the tardy exchange of treaty ratifications, it might be wondered whether this second document constituted another response to accidental circumstances rather than being a harbinger of changing times. On the other hand, four weeks after the conclusion of the treaty between Peru and Japan, hostilities with China were terminated by the Treaty of Shimonoseki. The Japanese possessed both the freedom and energy to turn to new undertakings in other regions. A measure of postwar readjustment for Japan would bring Peru within the range of Japanese interests.

2

The Japanese Immigrants, 1899-1941

In the late 1890s, for the first time in decades, Peru faced the future with hope. Following the collapse in the 1870s of an economy overly dependent on guano revenues which had benefited only a tiny minority, the nation experienced a combination of political discontinuity, economic distress, and military humiliation. The last came at the hands of Chile in the War of the Pacific. Early in the 1890s civil war compounded the nation's economic woes and political frustrations. However, at long last, the fortunate coincidence of political stability and economic improvement during the decade following 1895 offered opportunities to native Peruvians and foreigners alike. Some of the latter—Britons, Americans, French, Germans, and Italians—came as investors in plantation agriculture and mining enterprises, others as participants in a nascent industrialization. A second category of foreigners consisted of individuals seeking work as unskilled laborers.

The Peruvian need for labor stemmed from a complex of circumstances. The desert coastal stretches which, due to expanding irrigation systems, were blossoming as domestic and foreign-owned corporate ventures in plantation agriculture lacked a local labor supply. Neither the government nor the plantation operators succeeded in luring significant numbers of Indians from the Sierra region. Hence the need for immigrants not only existed, it grew. During the quarter century between 1849 and 1874, Chinese had come to Peru and for a longer time, during and after that period, Peruvian immigration policy tried to draw white immigrants from Europe. However, both the Orientals and the Europeans proved disappointing. To the smallness of their numbers they quickly added a preference for urban, not rural, life. Accordingly the need for agricultural laborers persisted. Even though the government stressed the "white" factor in pamphlets aimed at Europeans, it failed to produce the desired results. Meanwhile Peru directed no effort toward Japan but interest nonetheless arose there.

Thirty years earlier the first Japanese laborers to migrate eastward had gone to Hawaii. This emigration was initiated early in 1868 in moments of turmoil as the new Meiji government replaced the Tokugawa shogunate. The flow of workers to Hawaii was soon systematized in an 1871 treaty between Japan and the Hawaiian kingdom. Two decades later the so-called government contract emigrants yielded to "private contract emigrants." At the turn of the century "free emigration" would become the order of the day.[1]

Japanese emigration to Peru would lean heavily on this Hawaiian experience. As upset economic conditions in the wake of the Meiji Restoration had induced departures, so unsettled economic conditions in the aftermath of the Sino-Japanese War prompted a similar movement in the mid-1890s. In addition the successful precedent whereby Japanese workers had fitted into plantation agriculture in Hawaii suggested the same could happen again in Peru. Profit-minded shippers and emigration agents further promoted the idea of bringing Peru to the attention of would-be emigrants. Two other factors joined all else: agricultural Japan was overcrowded and some ex-servicemen represented a highly restless element amid cramped living conditions and limited opportunities. However, despite unofficial Japanese and Peruvian interest, the absence of official Peruvian consideration of Japanese immigration meant that any such move would be primarily Japanese in origin and private in nature.

Almost accidentally a pair of business-minded civilians initiated the contacts which were soon to result in substantial Japanese immigration to Peru. In 1898 Teikichi Tanaka, an official of the Morioka Emigration Company, arrived in Brazil, where he intended to promote Japanese immigration. Shortly after his arrival he was contacted by Augusto B. Leguía, the Peruvian sugar producer then laying the basis of the economic power which helped catapult him into the presidency in 1908. Tanaka hurried to Peru to see Leguía, whom he had previously met in the United States. The Peruvian magnate and his fellow-investors in large-scale sugar and cotton plantations needed and wanted a large, hard-working, dependable labor force. Leguía and Tanaka tentatively agreed on terms which were submitted to the Morioka Emigration Company.

That company, then limited to Brazil in its operation, promptly sought from the Foreign Ministry in Tokyo the right to transport emigrants to Peru. Because of their sketchy awareness of that part of the world, the Japanese authorities hesitated. At that time the only Japanese diplomatic mission in Latin America, headed by Yoshibumi Murota, Minister to Mexico, had but recently been enlarged to include Peru. In response to the Morioka request, the Foreign Office instructed Murota to proceed to Peru to present his credentials and to conduct an investigation regarding immigration prospects.

In May 1898, Murota and Clerk Zōji Amari, the latter destined to long identification with Japanese diplomacy in Latin America, reached Peru. They found the prospects favorable and immediately entered into negotiations with the Peruvian government. Meanwhile Leguía and others had brought their influence to bear upon Peruvian officials. A presidential decree later that year permitted Japanese immigration and led to a four-year contract. According to the specific terms, the ideal recruits were male, between twenty and forty-five years of age, experienced in agriculture, and of sound moral character. The agreement called for labor on sugar plantations, ten hours daily in the field, or twelve hours in the mill. The contract additionally set the wage and listed the employers' responsibilities regarding travel expenses, housing, medical facilities, and the schedule of deductions whereby the Morioka Company could amass the sum sufficient to cover the homeward passage of the worker at the end of four years.

In April 1899, 790 Japanese settlers arrived at Callao aboard the *Sakura Maru* of the Nippon Yūsen Kaisha ("Japan Mail Line"). Recruited by the Morioka Emigration Company, these agricultural workers came principally from Yamaguchi, Hiroshima, Okayama, and Niigata prefectures. From Callao the *Sakura Maru* began a coastwise voyage to distribute laborers to the contracting plantations. At Ancón 130 Japanese went ashore to work on the plantations of Puente Piedra, Caudevilla, and Estrella. At nearby Chancay 30 landed to labor on the Palpa plantation. To the north, at Supe, 150 disembarked for San Nicolás plantation and 50 for Huaito. From Salaverry 50 proceeded to Pampas plantation. Another 50 landed at Pacasmayo for service at Rurifuiko plantation. Eten, the northernmost port visited, saw 50 go to Cayaltí and an equal number to Pomalca plantations. Doubling back southward, the ship deposited the remaining 226 Japanese at Cerro Azul for the Casa Blanca plantation, the British operation with which Leguía was associated. Four of this initial shipload of Japanese became houseboys for Peruvian families.[2]

Discontent speedily arose. In less than three months circumstances impelled emigration agent Tanaka to telegraph Minister Murota in Mexico. "Feeling against immigrants strong. Contracts broken on flimsy grounds. Many have returned to Callao. Have been clashes with Peruvians. Situation out of control. Desire help of American consul at Callao."[3] The language barrier, compounded in instances in which even the Japanese supervisors did not know sufficient Spanish, contributed not only to misunderstandings but also to physical violence. Failure to communicate produced confusion about work assignments, the faulty or tardy completion of which, in turn, invited disputes about the downward revision of wage schedules.

From Mexico, Minister Murota referred Tanaka to Guillermo Espantoso, whose service as honorary Japanese consul in Lima dated from late December 1898. Soon both Espantoso and Tanaka reported dreary details. At San Nicolás plantation, site of the first incidents, the plantation officials had tried to prevent the Japanese from purchasing goods at lower prices from Chinese shops. A rumor that the Morioka Company had introduced 800 Japanese soldiers in the guise of farmers encouraged the plantation operators to arm themselves and to request a contingent of soldiers. Relations further deteriorated and finally the dissatisfied Japanese were told they could depart. More than two-thirds seized the opportunity and set out for Callao. Others drifted there from Cayaltí, Pampas, and Rurifuiko plantations. By late summer 321 workers had made their way to Peru's major port.

During these first months in Peru, on and off the plantations, the Japanese suffered a frightening incidence of severe illness. Malaria, typhoid, yellow fever, and dysentery exacted heavy tolls, one account reporting 143 deaths during the first year.[4]

Simultaneously the growing number of discontented workers in Callao posed problems for Tanaka, who had to find temporary housing for them while trying to reassign them to other jobs. Some, going to coffee plantations on the eastern slopes of the Andes and to Bolivia, soon learned they had gone from bad to worse. Meanwhile, in Callao, anti-immigrant sentiment focused specifically on the

Japanese and ugly incidents of violence took place. Tanaka's efforts, like his problems, were unceasing. Japanese shipping, which might have lightened both, did not appear.

At Casa Blanca, the plantation for which Leguía had requested the largest contingent of workers, the problems of the Japanese mounted. Their pay remained unchanged despite a doubling of the work load that provoked trouble on four occasions. Sickness among the workers, who were ill-quartered in old factories devoid of partitions, assumed such epidemic proportions that at times fewer than 15 percent of them could work. In one sixty-day period more than 15 percent of the immigrants died. Discouraged survivors begged Tanaka to send them home but the absence of shipping kept them in Peru.[5]

The activities of two men mirrored the depression and frustration of the Japanese workers in Peru. At odds with the Morioka Emigration Company, agent Tanaka surrendered his post, returned to Japan, and died. In the same troubled period the Japanese government ordered Ryōji Noda, another lower echelon diplomat destined to long service in Latin America, to proceed to Peru from the legation in Mexico. In September 1900, he recommended the return of all the settlers to Japan. However, two months later Noda reported changes for the better, including a general agreement on wages.

The humanity of Noda's proposed repatriation succumbed to economic considerations. The Morioka operation, already suffering crushing expenses, could not shoulder the cost of returning the settlers. Furthermore neither the home office nor its new agent in Peru, Ryōsuke Isomura, cared to sound the death knell of an entire operation. Instead, as time passed and the absence of ships made repatriation impossible, the number of complaints lessened. More people in Japan considered emigrating from the homeland, and it appeared that a second contingent might reverse the record compiled by the emigrants of 1899.

In July 1903, approximately 1080 settlers, recruited by the Morioka Company in more than a half-dozen prefectures, arrived in Peru. Leguía, still closely identified with sugar production, was a leader among Peruvians arranging for this group. In the course of time his persistent identification with Japanese immigration led to wide-ranging estimates of the future president as a greedy entrepreneur and benefactor of foreigners, among other unflattering designations.

This second contingent of Japanese both resembled and differed from their predecessors. As diligent, honest, skillful workers they approximated those who had preceded them. They differed, however, on two counts: more than 15 percent of them were free, noncontract laborers and secondly, the group included more than one hundred wives. The noncontractual status of these immigrants helped them in finding work to their liking, hastened adjustment to their new country, and reduced complaints. The presence of the wives promised a measure of social stability and satisfaction that the first lot of immigrants conspicuously lacked. A much higher percentage of this second group completed the four-year term of service, fulfilling their contracts.

Some friction and frustration continued, but so did the flow of Japanese immigrants. In November 1906, the third Morioka-contracted group, totaling 774, reached Peru. The contract period, considered unduly long at four years, had been shortened to a scant six months. Whereas four years had provided opportunity for adjustment, including the acquisition of some Spanish, the six-month interval was too brief for this. Without a skill, other than that which, as farmers, they had brought to their initial contract work, many Japanese, free after six months, drifted into service as household servants. Although neither dignity nor good income attached to this work, the immigrants enjoyed opportunities to learn Spanish and to study the urban scene and its prospects. For contracting landowners the six-month labor contract proved a great disappointment; for many Japanese it provided premature mobility; for all it signalled changing times.[6]

The physical mobility that, from the beginning, was characteristic of so many of the Japanese in Peru derived from numerous circumstances. Malaria and other health problems often hastened their exodus from plantations. Another factor was the frequent failure of Peruvian landowners and managers to adhere to the financial terms of the contracts. Some were simply unscrupulous while others rationalized their insistence upon lowering the wages. Many Japanese, slight of build, were miscast as cane-cutters. Peruvian employers also insisted they could not make flagrant distinctions, in the payment of wages, between their native Peruvian and Japanese workers, even though such operators, in their haste to increase the number of the latter, readily admitted their preference for the foreigner.

For various reasons it followed that Peruvian employers preferred to shift their Japanese workers from relatively high and fixed wages to the piece-work *(tarea)* system. Unlike an established daily wage, any alteration of which would be readily recognized, the tarea varied widely, inviting manipulation and abuse by landowners as workers became more proficient. Inasmuch as most Japanese planned to save money for their return to Japan or for the passage of relatives to Peru, any blow to those plans fed the discontent which quickly moved them from rural to urban settings.

Meanwhile additional factors hastened emigration to Peru. Japanese readjustment following the Russo-Japanese War, during which Peru had declared its neutrality, included an urge to emigrate on the part of many footloose ex-servicemen. During one of the periodic disputes regarding the Peruvian-Ecuadorian boundary, a number of Japanese ex-soldiers became parties to a propaganda barrage. Dissatisfied with their work assignments, they went to the Ministry of War and volunteered their services. While awaiting information, they were hailed by nearby Peruvian soldiers, to whose *"Viva japoné*s," they responded with *"Viva Perú."* This episode involving would-be volunteers received wide publicity. Momentarily, at least, it promoted friendlier relations between Japanese and Peruvians. How much the specter of fierce Japanese warriors eventually contributed to the peaceful resolution of the international incident is open to question.[7] Likewise uncertain is the contribution this episode made to the later Peruvian view that the Japanese among them were armed, trained, and a threat to Peru.

Also spurring emigration was the fact that the first three groups had come from a dozen widely separated prefectures in Japan, thereby increasing awareness of Peru in that country. In addition, early in the term of President José Pardo, messages from the Japanese emperor, as well as the appearance in Lima of Minister Toraichi Sugimura who, like his predecessors, was serving both Mexico and Peru, indicated an intensification of Japanese official interest. In addition, the Meiji Colonization Company began to compete with the Morioka operation.[8]

Behind the entry of the Meiji Colonization Company as a supplier of workers for Peruvian enterprises was an effort to exploit the wild rubber industry then booming in the Amazon basin. Because of hardships encountered in the jungles by dozens of Japanese, the request for additional workers in October 1905 by the general manager of the Inca Rubber Company won approval only after an investigation of conditions in the area. Then the agent of the Meiji Company contracted to supply five hundred rubber gatherers.

When the first contingent of that company's immigrants arrived in February 1907, one hundred men proceeded to the rubber enterprise in the Tambopata River region of southeastern Peru. The journey was itself an ordeal, a sequence of travel by steamer, train, horseback, and hiking. Although five workers later fled the area, most of them relished the daily wage of two yen fifty sen despite the high cost of food, the heat, the insects, and other inconveniences. These workers, remitting sizable sums to Japan, represented the first successful trans-Andine move by Japanese into the Amazon basin.

Next Michitarō Shindō, a representative of the Meiji Company who had accompanied the one hundred workers to the Tambopata region, negotiated a second contract with the Inca Rubber Company, pledging five thousand Japanese workers within five years. In less than a year, however, it became evident that five hundred men would meet the immediate needs of the company—information which no one shared with the prospective emigrants.

When 754 workers arrived in Peru, they learned there was no contract for their services, either in the lucrative rubber region or in less well-paid agricultural work. Embarrassed by the arrival of these enraged Japanese, the agents of the Meiji Company did the best they could under the circumstances. Both the agents and the immigrants had to settle for labor contracts so overwhelmingly favorable to the landholders as to guarantee future complaints. Although the final distribution of the unhappy Japanese to more than a half dozen sites, where their daily wage was seventy sen, not two yen fifty sen, lessened the impact of their complaints, the failure of the Meiji Company to place them in accordance with contracts constituted a violation of the Emigrants' Protection Law. This prematurely heavy dependence upon the rubber industry to absorb Japanese immigrants ended not only in a fiasco for the workers but also for the emigration company which ceased operations.[9]

Despite the collapse of the Meiji Colonization Company and the adverse reports that disappointed emigrants surely sent home, the years 1906-1909 constituted a peak period of early Japanese emigration to Peru (see table 1).

At the end of 1909, of the total of 6,295 immigrants to Peru, 5,158 still lived there. The death rate, once astronomical, had been

TABLE 1

Emigration of Japanese to Peru, 1906-1909

Year	Morioka Co.	Meiji Co.	Total
1906	774		774
1907	203	250	453
1908	1,688	754	2,442
1909	661		661

reduced considerably and furthermore very few immigrants had returned to Japan. By this time the immigrants were arriving from more than two dozen prefectures and their distribution in Peru, from Eten to Tacna and from coastal plains and port cities to *montaña* and Amazon basin, was similarly widespread.

Sugar plantations still afforded most of the Japanese their livelihood. Wages continued low and troubles repeatedly surfaced. Although some workers deserted, a high percentage did complete their original contract obligations. At the same time increasing numbers found their way to urban areas. The example of Kenkichi Nakao, who served as office boy for President Pardo, inspired restless agricultural laborers. Approximately forty-five of the unwanted Meiji Company immigrants of 1908 finally located in Lima.

Hardships and disappointments notwithstanding, many saved the small sums that spelled economic mobility and with this modest capital rented farm land or initiated small business ventures in the urban areas. At the end of the decade Consul Keiichi Itō could report no success stories but Japanese adaptability, persistence, and intelligence had given the emigration an air of both hope and permanence. This despite the fact that an unusually high percentage of the emigrants, more than 96 percent, had been male—a circumstance that posed questions and problems.[10]

Representative of the Peruvian endorsement of this immigration was the case of Eusebio Figueroa y Parra, owner of forty thousand *hectares* of land to the east of Lima which he said could produce sugar, coffee, coca, corn, and fruits. For the operation that he envisioned, he desired eight to ten thousand Japanese men and their families. Directing his request to the Japanese Foreign Office, Figueroa y Parra stated that he preferred Japanese workers because "they are intelligent, of simple habits, industrious, enterprising and tenacious at work." The Foreign Office replied that he must make such arrangements through emigration companies, and not directly with the Japanese government.[11]

While certain moneyed men eyed the Japanese as cheap and dependable labor, other Peruvians saw them differently. Gradually much of the animosity long directed at the more numerous Chinese, who had preceded them by a half century, began to rub off on the Japanese. During the springtime that landowner Figueroa y Parra was trying to obtain thousands of Japanese, a Lima newspaper was proclaiming, "Public sentiment rejects the entry of yellow laborers."[12] Although this outburst paralleled the arrival of another shipload of Chinese, the reference to "yellows," not "Chinese," ominously included the Japanese in the denunciation. Some might see in this "anti-yellow" sentiment a Peruvian endorsement of the United States outlook that prompted the Gentlemen's Agreement of 1907-1908; others might judge it to be purely and completely Peruvian in origin. Difficult though it is to assess the various motivations producing anti-Japanese sentiment in Peru, its numerous manifestations became crystal clear.

Although the press increasingly lumped together all Orientals, Peruvian officials, in response to pressure exerted by Tokyo authorities, differentiated between Japanese and other Asians, as is seen in the matter of the sanitary passports. When Peruvian Consul E.C. Davis notified prefectural and national officials in Japan that Peru intended to collect one hundred yen for each sanitary passport issued to an Asian immigrant bound for Peru, a flurry of inquiry resulted in the Peruvian ruling that "Japanese are exempt from the Sanitary Tax."[13]

As the number of Japanese entering Peru rapidly increased, those desiring their services pressed for a renegotiation of the time-span of the basic contract. The pendulum, swinging from the four-year to the six-month term, had moved from one extreme to the other and they now sought an intermediate position. A leading advocate of a contract to run "about two years" was Edward L. Houghton, General Manager of The British Sugar Company, Ltd., one of the first and most consistent users of Japanese labor. Significantly, Augusto B. Leguía, who by this time had become president of Peru, continued to possess a major interest in this firm. The Japanese Foreign Office readily authorized the extension of the contract to two years. Pleased, the employers of Japanese farm laborers, again led by The British Sugar Company, next objected to official

Japanese insistence upon a daily wage of 1.20 *soles,* complaining that it was 20 percent above the maximum paid Peruvian labor.[14]

In this transpacific population movement, Okinawans, due to a number of economic and social factors in Japan, soon constituted a majority. Following Japan's acquisition of Okinawa in the nineteenth century, politicians and businessmen from the main islands had swept into Okinawa and the rest of the Ryūkyū Islands like so many parasitical carpetbaggers. There, in their own homeland, the Okinawans were economically and politically exploited. Quickly the islands, characterized by dense population, sparse resources, and widespread poverty, assumed the status of a quasi-colony within the Japanese Empire. To all else, their language, dress, and other marks of a distinctive culture were denigrated by the main islanders who customarily looked upon Okinawans "as rustic, second-class cousins within the Japanese nation-family." In the dawning years of the twentieth century, when emigration became a persistent expression of the Japanese search for economic opportunity on many world fronts, Okinawans crowded the ranks of the discontented.[15]

A mid-1910 report to the Japanese Ministry of Foreign Affairs indicated, by their distribution, the restless questing of the Okinawans and all others in Peru. It listed every community, hacienda, and rubber-gathering enterprise with which Japanese were identified.[16]

TABLE 2
Distribution of Japanese
in Peru, 1910

Department	*Cities and Towns*	*Haciendas*
Lima	19	52
Ancash	10	15
Libertad	10	20
Lambayeque	6	8
Piura	3	0
Loreto	1	0
Junín	8	1
Ayacucho	1	0
Ica	5	5
Arequipa	3	8
Tacna	0	4
Puno (5 rubber enterprises)	0	0

Some discontented Japanese, repelled by all, responded to opportunities elsewhere in Latin America. Mexican advertising lured 179 Peruvian Japanese northward, principally to the Tabasco Plantation Company which, despite its name, was located in the Mexican state of Veracruz. In addition to a daily wage of $1.50 (Mexican) for eleven hours labor in the cane fields or twelve hours in the mill, individuals who signed for a term of three years were to receive housing, water, and fuel free of charge and the cost of passage from Peru to Salina Cruz, Mexico would be reimbursed. Some who made this move honestly intended to remain in agricultural work and comply with the terms of the agreement. Others, engaging in a kind of international leap-frog, left Peru for Mexico with the idea of stealing into the United States.[17]

Meanwhile the emigration to Peru also experienced changes. Following the demise of the Meiji Company, The Tōyō Emigration Company began to compete with the Morioka Company which continued its interest in Peru. However, when the Overseas Development Company was formed late in 1917, the Tōyō Emigration Company merged into it. In October 1920, the Overseas Development Company attained a monopoly position by absorbing the Morioka Company. For the next three years, until November 1923, when Japanese migration to Peru by contract was abolished, all emigrant contracts involved the Overseas Development Company (see table 3).

The quarter century of contract-dominated Japanese emigration to Peru had produced the following results:

TABLE 3
Emigrants and Emigration Companies, 1898-1923

	Total Emigrants to Peru
Morioka Emigration Company (1898-1920)	14,829
Meiji Colonization Company (1907-1909)	1,003
Tōyō Emigration Company (1910-17)	878
Overseas Development Company (1917-23)	1,054
Total	17,764

As for the demise of the system, aside from irregularities, more than a few of which had justifiably been charged against the Meiji Colonization Company, the idea of agreements that fixed wages for definite periods of time and required the reimbursement of transportation costs smacked too much of the indentured servant concept to survive in the postwar world.[18]

Despite the constantly shifting structure of the emigration companies, the hardships attending the emigrants, and the changing international forces of the 1910s, Japanese emigration had proceeded with considerable regularity (see table 4).

TABLE 4
Emigration of Japanese to Peru, 1910-21[19]

Year	Male	Female	Total
1910	425	14	439
1911	322	12	334
1912	550	73	623
1913	980	179	1,159
1914	909	169	1,078
1915	877	203	1,080
1916	867	135	1,002
1917	1,137	318	1,455
1918	1,013	346	1,359
1919	1,319	177	1,496
1920	583	74	657
1921	546	77	623

While many new contract laborers suffered limitations and frustrations, as had their predecessors, numerous earlier immigrants not only demonstrated mobility in this period but also achieved genuine economic well-being. While the newly arrived contract laborer resisted the opportunities presumably present in recently acquired Korea and turned his back on wartime opportunities in Japan proper in favor of rural Peru, the ex-contract laborer there found the pull of the cities irresistible. The sequence of economic opportunity thus involved three steps: repudiation of East Asia, temporary adoption of rural Peru, and finally permanent identification with urban Peru. In the 1910s, significant percentages of the Japanese-Peruvians were taking this final step. The results included more Japanese-owned and operated barber shops, grocery stores, general merchandise outlets, and restaurants.

Reflecting the mobility that led many toward Lima were the early Peruvian experiences of two Okinawans, Kame Kina and Sobuku Yamekawa. In mid-1918 Kina and his wife contracted through the Morioka Emigration Company to work for one year at the Chiclin hacienda near Trujillo. Although pleased with their work and able to save a sizable sum, they moved south at the end of twelve months to another hacienda, this one quite near the Peruvian capital. Within a few months, during which they added to their savings, the lure of Lima increased, buttressed by an offer of employment in a cousin's cafe. Again man and wife worked as a team, he as waiter, she as cook. After three months Kina purchased the business outright from his kinsman and the trek from rural to urban Peru seemed complete. Soon, however, the Kinas, realizing they preferred farm life, returned to it. Nonetheless the experience clearly indicated the magnetic pull of urban Peru, even for those who preferred farming.

Sobuku Yamekawa, seeking to escape the poverty which even forced him to leave his wife in Okinawa, arrived in Peru in mid-1919 and proceeded to a malaria-ridden plantation from which he immediately fled. In Lima he, like Kina, was assisted by fellow Okinawans. Five years passed before he could pay for his own passage and finance his wife's journey to Peru. Work in a cafe owned by a relative increased the savings which enabled him to purchase the business. Prospering, he undertook other business operations and investments, wedded permanently to urban life. In many instances, as the experiences of Kina and Yamekawa attest, the presence there of friends or relatives augmented the urban attraction.[20]

During the wartime years Japanese mobility, plus a capacity for hard work, growing indications of their economic success, and the continuing disembarkation of fresh contingents from Japan, also nurtured Peruvian racial prejudice. When the *Senjō Maru* docked at Callao in January 1916, the hundreds of Chinese and Japanese had scarcely set foot ashore before newspapers attacked the rising tide of "yellow" immigrants.[21]

During the 1920s, even while segments of the Peruvian press denounced as excessive the number of Japanese then in Peru, the Peruvian consulate in Yokohama was outlining the advantages offered immigrants by the Peruvian government: (1) free room and board for eight days upon arrival at Callao; (2) aid in finding work which included government willingness to give farmers ten hectares of land in the montaña region around the Masamari River; and (3) loans up to fifty dollars (Peruvian) to farmers. A check on these matters by the American embassy produced a report which labeled the Peruvian statements about the immigrant hotel, the loans, and the availability of land as sheer propaganda, totally removed from reality. Climaxing all else, the Peruvian Director of Immigration reportedly said, "Peru did not wish Japanese immigrants."[22]

Statistics of the period, however, belied that remark of 1926 (see table 5).

TABLE 5
Emigration of Japanese to Peru, 1924-30[23]

Year	Via Emigration Companies	Independently	Total
1924	335	416	751
1925	306	731	1,037
1926	496	866	1,362
1927	392	1,031	1,423
1928	312	841	1,153
1929	222	1,105	1,327
1930	139	741	880

These figures prompt a variety of conclusions. Japanese emigration to Peru remained small despite that country's stability during the Leguía dictatorship and peace on the international scene. Obviously the abolition of worker-contracts in 1923 did not scuttle the Japanese desire and capacity to move to Peru. Just as unsavory reports about contracts had led to their abolition, so ugly rumors about emigration companies encouraged many to emigrate on their own.

During the 1920s the practice of "calling" increasingly accounted for the movement of Japanese immigrants into Peru. By this procedure a Japanese who desired to emigrate there was, in essence, sponsored by a relative or friend already in that country. The Japanese-Peruvian who initiated the proceedings assumed a measure of responsibility and had to meet certain financial requirements. After the prospective immigrant won the approval of the Central Japanese Association of Peru, an application for his entry went to the Japanese consulate in Lima which, in turn, concerned itself with passport and other legal formalities. Inasmuch as the "callers" generally were urban businessmen, this practice frequently meant that Japanese newcomers of the 1920s and 1930s began their Peruvian experience in urban settings. The case of Ryōshin Onaga illustrates several aspects of this practice. "Called" by a brother in Peru, Ryōshin willingly exchanged the farm work he detested in Okinawa for employment as a waiter in his brother's cafe in Lima. Never in succeeding years in Peru did the ex-farmer feel any urge to return to rural life.[24]

One of the periodic surveys of the overseas Japanese, that compiled by the Bureau of Commercial Affairs of the Japanese Ministry of Foreign Affairs as of October 1, 1927, revealed the following:

TABLE 6
Economic Survey of the Japanese in Peru, 1927

Areas	Employed males	Employed females	Dependent males	Dependent females	Total
Lima	5,866	9	2,641	4,226	12,742
Remainder of Peru	1,341	0	393	731	2,465

More than 47 percent of the Japanese were gainfully employed, those in the Lima area pursuing thirty-six different occupations, while those elsewhere in the country engaged in twenty-eight different lines of work. The report of the American embassy in Lima concerning the 3,345 commercial establishments inspected by Peruvian authorities during 1927 indicated that of the 746 owned by Japanese, who led all foreigners, not more than twenty were of substantial commercial importance.[25]

Events of the 1930s affected the movement of Japanese in a variety of ways. Economic depression simultaneously encouraged some to leave their homeland for Peru while others were leaving Peru for Japan. The impact on emigration of the Manchurian episode at the beginning of the decade is unclear. However, the outbreak of hostilities with China a few years later distinctly curtailed Japanese emigration. Meanwhile restrictive legislation lessened the welcome accorded Japanese in many countries. Aside from Peru, the legislation within Latin America that most affected Peru was the Brazilian action of 1934.

The Brazilian constitution of July 16, 1934, stated that the number of immigrants allowed to enter Brazil from a given country would be restricted to a yearly maximum of 2 percent of the total number that nationality had sent to Brazil during the preceding fifty years. Since their initial entry in 1908, some 142,457 Japanese had emigrated to Brazil. Accordingly their annual quota was 2,848, a figure that was but slightly more than 11 percent of the 24,494 that arrived in Brazil in 1933. A decade earlier, when United States legislation closed the door completely on would-be Japanese immigrants, many emigrating Japanese simply changed their destination, witness the 137 percent increase in the number of them entering Brazil during the first full calendar year following the passage of the Washington legislation of 1924. In view of the small quota set by Rio de Janeiro authorities, Peruvians feared, in 1934, that the curtailment of the flow of Japanese to Brazil would similarly cause their country to become the objective of increased numbers of Japanese.

TABLE 7
Movement of Japanese in and out of Peru, 1931-37[26]

Year	Entering Peru	Leaving Peru
1931	299	498
1932	369	672
1933	481	634
1934	473	634
1935	814	?
1936	593	?
1937	116	?

The Peruvian immigration law of June 1936 became the harbinger of troubles for the Japanese. Of greatest concern to them were the following parts of the decree: a) the annual immigration could not exceed sixteen thousand, which was presumed to represent two-tenths of 1 percent of Peru's total population; b) immigration by racial groups was prohibited; c) foreign residents who returned to their native lands and then desired reentry into Peru could do so only within the established quotas; d) the 80 percent employment rule established by Law No. 7505 was extended to include the enterprises, meaning that no more than 20 percent of those practicing the professions and operating businesses could be foreigners; and e) although those foreigners already so occupied were permitted to continue, they could sell or transfer their operations to another foreigner only if in compliance with this percentage rule. Fortunately the transfer of titles to businesses from Japanese citizens to their nisei sons lessened the intended impact of this provision. However, the appeal of the Peruvian legislators, as they enacted the immigration provisions, to five articles of the Peruvian constitution suggested their stance would be an unyielding one.[27]

Japan immediately protested but Foreign Minister Alberto Ulloa, declining the protest, indicated that the provisions applied generally, not uniquely to any one country or people. Some

Japanese-Peruvians, sensing their disabilities, hastened to be naturalized, something previously done by very few Japanese. Peruvian officials, in turn, concluded that this amounted to a loophole in the legislation. To correct it a new decree, that of July 11, 1936, temporarily suspended the authorization of letters of naturalization.[28]

By midsummer 1936, Japanese relations with Peru were approaching a shambles. More important to Japan than the emigration of additional Japanese to Peru was the maintenance of unrestricted opportunity for those already there. Whereas the immigration law was but one of several factors affecting Japanese emigration to Peru, that legislation singlehandedly could lessen the economic power that Japan wanted to expand in Peru. Accordingly, Japanese opposition to the law was overwhelmingly economic and only secondarily based on social grounds.

The climax of the consistently worsening position of the Japanese came on May 13, 1940, in the form of anti-Japanese demonstrations in Lima. Numerous Japanese business establishments came under attack by Peruvian mobs. Journalists, touring the area of greatest unrest, noted "various groups were beating the shops of the Japanese with sticks, wooden rams and anything that came to hand." Scores suffered injury as their property damage mounted.[29]

When Peru, less than a week after the rioting, promulgated a decree suspending temporarily the entry of immigrants, the two governments interpreted it differently. To the Japanese it represented oppression and restriction; to the Peruvian it promised to simplify the taking of the national census scheduled for June. Peruvian authorities also instituted stricter surveillance over foreign residents.

The census of June 1940 afforded an unusually clear and multifaceted glimpse of the Japanese in Peru (see table 8).[30] That total of 17,598 Japanese in Peru, counted in tense moments when Peruvians were not disposed to overlook one of them, was considerably below estimates that had long been and would continue to be bruited about in the Peruvian and world press.

TABLE 8
The Japanese in Peru, by Department and Sex, 1940

Department	Male	Female	Total
Amazonas	0	0	0
Ancash	161	46	207
Apurimac	1	0	1
Arequipa	43	10	53
Ayacucho	14	1	15
Cajamarca	9	7	16
Callao	1,253	763	1,996
Cuzco	17	2	19
Huancavelica	3	2	5
Huánuco	20	5	25
Ica	179	61	240
Junín	360	149	509
La Libertad	303	138	441
Lambayeque	139	42	181
Lima	8,983	4,574	13,557
Loreto	27	8	35
Madre de Dios	31	6	37
Moquequa	2	0	2
Piura	197	34	231
Puno	9	3	12
San Martín	7	0	7
Tacna	7	2	9
Tumbes	0	'0	0
	11,745	5,853	17,598

The economically active Japanese supported themselves as shown in table 9.

TABLE 9
Economic Activity, 1940

Activity	Male	Female	Total	%
Commerce and credit	3,236	439	3,675	32.4
Professionals & domestics	2,508	330	2,838	25.0
Agriculture	2,272	195	2,467	21.8
Processing industries	1,467	107	1,574	13.9
Ranching, fishing & hunting	199	12	211	1.8
Public administration	140	36	176	1.5
Mining	24	1	25	.2
Construction	8	0	8	.07
Unclassified	328	12	340	3.0
	10,182	1,132	11,314	

Maritally the social structure of the Japanese colony appeared as follows:

TABLE 10
Marital Status, 1940

Condition	Male	Female
Married	6,127	4,472
Mate dead	423	172
Divorced	21	6
Cohabiting	369	59
Unmarried	4,801	1,144
Undeclared	4	0

By age groups and sex the Japanese were constituted as follows:

TABLE 11
Age Groups and Sex, 1940

Group	Male	Female
Under 14	69	67
15 to 19	156	119
20 to 24	608	591
25 to 34	3,228	2,090
35 to 59	7,295	2,876
60 and over	387	109
Age unknown	2	1
	11,745	5,853

* * * *

Once all the Japanese in Peru were males of vigorous working age. Four decades later they were male and female, infant and aged, and in-between.

Once all the Japanese were farmers, working on coastal plantations owned by others. Four decades later they lived in all regions of Peru, gaining their livelihoods in scores of ways.

Once all the Japanese came shepherded by agents of emigration companies. Four decades later they did so on their own.

Once most Japanese came anticipating eventual return to Japan. Four decades later they and their children and grandchildren were rooted in Peru.

Once all the Japanese who came were wanted. Four decades later their entry was limited, their welcome curtailed, their presence resented.

3

Early Diplomatic and Commercial Relations

For decades, in the absence of meaningful and persistent contacts between the two peoples, Japanese-Peruvian diplomatic relations scarcely existed. Although the *Cayaltí* and *María Luz* incidents made the two governments aware of each other, no follow-up movement of people or products provoked the establishment of legations or consulates. However, once Korekiyo Takahashi and Ikutarō Aoyagi, along with other Japanese businessmen and travelers brought Peru within the range of Japanese consciousness, mutual indifference gave way to diplomatic conversations in Washington. The treaty of 1895 derived from circumstances totally unlike those which prompted the treaty of 1873. Overweening emphasis on domestic affairs, characteristic of the earlier time in both countries, had yielded to widening world-mindedness. The political, economic, and military progress of Meiji Japan, in addition to her desire to modernize and play a role on the world stage—as evidenced by her victory over China—readied the island nation for significant international relationships. Somewhat similarly, political stability and multiple economic ambitions had prepared Peru for wide-ranging international contacts. Diplomats did little to promote the initial Japanese emigration but the persistent identification of more and more Japanese with Peru fortified the need for diplomatic channels between Tokyo and Lima.

However, those official channels developed slowly. For more than a decade the Japanese Foreign Office continued to meet its Peruvian needs via ministers residing in Mexico. Only briefly had Minister

Early Relations 43

Murota gone to Lima, to present his credentials and to survey immigration prospects. His three immediate successors in Mexico City, likewise responsible for Peru, gave the country but passing attention. Meanwhile in the wake of Murota's visit there, and several months before the first group of Japanese immigrants arrived, Guillermo Espantoso became honorary Japanese consul in Peru. When other non-Japanese succeeded to that role, Japan signified that its need for representation in Peru was minimal. Peru, in this period, similarly relied upon foreigners as honorary consuls in Japan.

By 1908, however, the numbers and problems of immigrants in Peru provided sufficient reason for Japanese diplomatic and consular concern. The Peruvian diplomatic assignment was detached from the legation in Mexico and transferred to Santiago, Chile. In doing so, the Japanese ignored the historical enmity between Peru and Chile. This arrangement, which continued for more than a decade, suggested to Peruvians that Japan considered their country inferior to Chile, a notion sure to infuriate any Peruvian. When Minister Eki Hioki presented his credentials to diminutive President Leguía, the Japanese diplomat indicated that one of his most important official and personal interests was "taking care that the Japanese immigration in this country continue to develop the economic production and potential of the Republic."[1] From a consular standpoint Japan distinctly improved the situation, in 1909, when it closed the honorary consulate and installed an imperial consulate general in Lima.

As Japanese contacts with Peru increased, so did United States concern. Real and imagined Japanese interest in land repeatedly focused the attention of American diplomats on the Japanese from the Rio Grande to Cape Horn. Late in 1916, Minister Benton McMillin informed Washington that Tambo Real, a fine French-owned estate on Chimbote Bay, back of which lay immense coal deposits, was the object of Japanese negotiations, "presumably more for a naval base, harbor control and coaling station than sugar production." If uncertainty inspired that dispatch, gross ignorance spawned an instruction from Secretary of State Robert Lansing to the American embassy in Mexico. The fact that the Japanese consul at Lima was sending telegrams in code "addressed to Koshi Mexico" led Lansing to say, "Please investigate and report."[2] Apparently American diplomats in Washington and elsewhere did not know that "kōshi" simply meant "minister" in Japanese.

An early evidence of the impact of Peruvian anti-Japanese sentiment upon diplomatic negotiations also occurred in that wartime period. In December 1916, Japan recommended that the two governments reciprocally permit physicians and dentists of the other nationality to practice their professions. Peru had such arrangements with other countries, as did Japan whose latest such agreement was with Mexico. However, that which seemed routine and desirable proved, from the Peruvian standpoint, to be neither and Foreign Minister Enrique de la Riva Agüero scuttled the idea.[3] In addition to any anti-Japanese feelings behind the Peruvian decision was their realization that the agreement would be reciprocal in name only, there being no Peruvian physicians or dentists in Japan or desirous of going there.

On other occasions official Japanese proposals won the respect and cooperation of Peru. For example, Peru readily assented when Japan requested that commercial ships armed against submarine attack be allowed in Peruvian harbors. Economic necessity caused by the interruption of normal commercial ties with Europe might have influenced that decision but, a little later, some measure of admiration must have prompted Peru to ask permission to send an army commission to study Japan's military organization.[4]

While Japanese-Peruvian relations fluctuated, American interest in that relationship persisted. Learning of a rumored Japanese land purchase near Huánuco, Lansing instructed the American legation in Lima, "Investigate and report, giving your opinion as to attitude of present government toward these transactions."[5]

At the close of World War One the Peruvian Congress was considering an anti-Asian bill which would plague Japanese-Peruvian relations long thereafter. Minister Shichita Tatsuke, serving Peru from Chile, addressed a vigorous note to the Peruvian Foreign Office. First he attacked the Peruvian assumption that the presence of the Japanese contributed to "ethnic degeneration." In addition to citing the vigor of the Japanese people, he pointed out the readily evident truth that little intermarriage had occurred between Japanese and Peruvians. To the argument that Asians in Peru had contributed to the economic misery of the native working class, he also offered stout denial. Foreign Minister Elguera's note, penned some six months later, constituted acknowledgment of receipt rather than a reply to Tatsuke's communication.[6] Peruvian avoidance of the substance of the protest suggested an unbridgeable chasm was in the making.

Increased interest in Peru in the postwar years required an upgrading of the Japanese mission there. Between 1908 and 1921, while the minister to Peru resided in Chile, the status of the Lima mission was that of a diplomatic stepchild. Early in 1921, when a training cruise brought the Japanese navy ships *Iwate* and *Asama* to Peru, President Leguía declined to entertain the commanding admiral on the grounds there was no Japanese minister in Lima. Almost simultaneously a petition signed by 860 Japanese-Peruvians put additional pressure on the Japanese Foreign Office. Late in 1921 Tokyo named Seisaburō Shimizu its first resident minister in Peru.[7]

Multiple issues awaited Shimizu. The problem of Peruvian prejudice and discrimination born of social and economic circumstances deserved constant attention. Any information program—perhaps better termed a counter-propaganda campaign—could best be executed by a well-directed legation staff. Besides the well-being of the Japanese already in Peru, the legation concerned itself with the persistent urge to emigrate which inclined still more toward Peru. Recent arrivals, facing a strange culture, frequently turned to Japanese officials for assistance. To all else the Japanese desire to increase trade between the two countries guaranteed a visit, in 1922, by a commercial mission to Latin America.[8]

The 1920s provided several coincidences which the Japanese exploited diplomatically. All that decade Augusto B. Leguía, whose cultivation of foreigners prominently included Japanese, controlled Peru. Exchanges of decorations and state dinners led an American diplomat to report that the Japanese official "appears to be launching an energetic social campaign here." In short order Peru similarly upgraded the importance of its mission in Tokyo.[9]

Peruvian celebration of the centenary of their independence presented the Japanese with opportunities which they, like other foreigners, seized. The legation joined the Japanese community of Lima in the cornerstone ceremony which promised another monument for the capital. Special ambassadors from Tokyo attended centennial festivities and a squadron of training vessels included Callao among its ports of call.[10]

However, the clash between an old treaty and new laws indicated all was not harmonious in official Japanese-Peruvian relations. An executive decree identified Leguía's administration with a racial stance that insulted the Japanese. Citing the scarcity of good farm laborers in Peru and encouraging immigrants by paying the cost of their transportation, Peru directed her offer to "any immigrant of the white race." The following year the Japanese challenged, as a violation of the treaty of 1895, a Peruvian law which subjected all foreigners to a special tax. Peru modified the decree but not long thereafter she also denounced the treaty of 1895.[11]

If the termination of immigrant contracts in 1923 closed out one phase of their relations, the negotiation of the treaty of friendship, commerce, and navigation of September 30, 1924, presumed to usher in a new era. Some measure of Shimizu's success might be shared by his wife, Miyoko, whose hand-in-hand strolls with President Leguía did not go for naught. The treaty of 1924, without use of the specific term, retained the most-favored-nation provisions of the previous treaty concerning import and export duties, harbor charges, warehousing, drawbacks, and related commercial matters. The new document also resembled the old one concerning the handling of wrecked or stranded ships, equality of treatment in the courts, and exemption from compulsory military service. In view of the tensions, economic and otherwise, that had occasionally surfaced, two articles of the new treaty possessed special relevance. The pledge, in article one, of "perpetual peace and amity" was not limited to the two countries; it also included "their respective subjects and citizens." In other words, the injury or death of nationals of either state by mob action would constitute a breach of the treaty. Article three, stating that "They [subjects and citizens] shall in all that relates to the pursuit of their industries, callings, professions and educational studies be placed in all respects upon the same footing as the subjects or citizens of any European or North-American nations," conceivably represented a refuge for Japanese businessmen who had previously encountered discrimination and boycott. Suffering interminable delays, the exchange of treaty ratifications did not occur until February 1930.[12]

The Japanese hoped to counteract Peruvian ill will, some of which was influenced by United States-Japanese relations, especially in reference to the Washington Conference and the immigration legislation of 1924. Illustrative of that relationship was an exchange in Kobe between the Peruvian and American consuls stationed there. On instructions from Lima, Consul José B. Goyburu Elias asked Consul E.R. Dickover for copies of the American legislation or regulations restricting the immigration of Japanese. In addition he sought "an extra-official opinion as to the probable action of the

American Government, in view of the Monroe Doctrine, should the Peruvian Government prohibit the further entry of Japanese and should the Japanese Government thereupon threaten Peru."[13]

Almost simultaneously, in Peru, a memorandum prepared by Wallace Thompson following an interview with President Leguía cast additional light on the role of the United States in Peruvian-Japanese relations. After asking whether the United States might revise its newly enacted exclusion law, Leguía stated that the Japanese were unwelcome and unpopular in Peru. Although Peru had taken action against the Chinese, she could not proceed in the same manner against Japan, he added, because "Japanese exclusion without the support of the United States would have meant war." Leguía hinted at joint action by west coast South American governments against the Japanese if the United States pledged support of their stance. His hint that Minister Shimizu's visit to Chile might lead to a naval base there for the Japanese led State Department officials to pursue the matter in Chile. There the Americans learned Leguía's rumor stemmed from the historic enmity between Peru and Chile rather than from contemporary reality.[14]

"The question of further Asiatic immigration to South America, and especially to Peru," Washington's man in Lima wrote, "will depend largely on the action taken by the Government of the United States." A few months later, editorially disapproving any extensive immigration of Japanese laborers to Peru and terming it ridiculous to welcome unassimilable people, *El Tiempo* continued the show of anti-Japanese sentiment. Rooted in the Peruvian past, the newspaper also reflected the contemporary outlook in the United States.[15]

When the Peruvian attack continued, Japan sent an able propagandist, Spanish-speaking Kinta Arai, to Peru to help counteract it. One is left to wonder, however, about the impact of his series of lectures, with lantern slides, entitled "Japan of Today." Arai's Spanish translation of the aims and regulations of the Central Japanese Association also sought to allay Peruvian suspicions and fears.[16]

When newly appointed ministers presented their credentials to President Leguía, his response made strikingly obvious the gap between Peruvian officials and the public concerning the Japanese. In July 1925, as Keiichi Yamazaki replaced Shimizu as minister to Peru, Leguía "expressed himself, at least by implication, as strongly favoring Japanese emigration to Peru." That same summer native commercial interests in Lima voiced vigorous complaints regarding Japanese retail establishments in the capital.[17]

On May 31, 1929, Saburō Kurusu presented his credentials to President Leguía as the new Japanese minister. Like his immediate predecessors, Kurusu was a career diplomat. Although Peru, like the remainder of Latin America, remained low on the Japanese scale of diplomatic priorities, ably trained career diplomats received the appointments to Lima. Behind Kurusu were consular duty in Asia and the United States, and diplomatic assignments in Europe and Latin America. Distantly ahead was a dramatic moment in Washington, D.C. on December 7, 1941.[18] In the meantime he faced problems in Peru.

An accidental opportunity quickly enabled Kurusu to demonstrate his ability and to ingratiate himself with Leguía's government. Serving as arbitrator for a long-standing dispute concerning a contract between the Peruvian government and a British company regarding the exploitation of guano deposits, he rendered a compromise decision which became an acceptable basis for settlement and won for himself the trust and respect of the Lima authorities.

However, as the mid-1930 revolution led by Luis Sánchez Cerro gained the momentum that toppled Leguía, it readily generated an anti-Japanese thrust. Leguía's enemies could recite a long list of his pro-Japanese inclinations: he had led the initial movement to bring Japanese to Peru; never had he responded to Peruvian urgings to curb their entry; he had accepted Tokyo's decorations; walked hand-in-hand in public with the wife of a Japanese diplomat; and had applauded the erection of a bronze statue by the Japanese colony. To Peruvians caught up in the deepening economic depression of the 1930s to which their export economy made them so susceptible, the relative well-being of so many Japanese was doubly distasteful. Much as in Mexico twenty years earlier, when anti-Díaz forces claimed that Mexico was the mother of foreigners and the stepmother of Mexicans, Peruvians leveled similar charges against Leguía.

So it happened that the revolutionary upheaval that dislodged Leguía easily included incidents in which Japanese were roughly handled, their property damaged, shops plundered, and their lives endangered. Forcefully depicting the plight of his countrymen,

Kurusu insisted that the Peruvian revolutionists approve the organization among the Japanese of an armed vigilance committee. When this firm stand was publicized, the attacks quickly subsided.[19] The vigilance committees definitely helped to restore calm at that time but their performance quite possibly fed later Peruvian fears that the Japanese community constituted a veritable military organization.

In the aftermath of the revolution of 1930, claims, violence, and rumors underscored the need for action. When one Lima newspaper exaggerated the claims filed by Japanese, Consul Yodogawa attacked it for spreading false rumors, prejudice, and encouraging lawlessness. When another newspaper attempted to divorce Peru from any responsibility for the breakdown of law and order, Yodogawa stamped it strange that victims of assault, not the perpetrators, received condemnation.[20]

In the meantime, the journalistic tilt resolving nothing, Kurusu hit upon an idea to mollify the Peruvians. Winning from Tokyo authorities a $97,700 subsidy for his proposed program, the Japanese minister, in March 1931, established the Peruvian Colonization Association (Perū Takushoku Kumiai), the purpose of which was the dispersal of some of the urban Japanese. With the slogan "Go to the montaña" the association hoped to lure city-dwellers to the Chanchamayo Valley along the Punizas River on the eastern slope of the Andes. This officially sponsored movement to the montaña, like private ones earlier, failed to attract sizable numbers of volunteers. One of the primary factors that had long discouraged Peruvian exploitation of the montaña, namely the slow, difficult, and expensive transportation, also denied to the Japanese any economic opportunity in that remote region. However, the purchase of 2,450 acres of land in the Chanchamayo Valley did induce sixteen families to attempt the well-nigh impossible. They migrated to the montaña the same month, June 1932, that Kurusu, the ablest prewar Japanese diplomat in Peru, relinquished his post.[21]

Following Kurusu's departure the unity of purpose and harmonious cooperation which had characterized the labors of Japanese diplomatic and consular officials in Peru quickly disintegrated. Early in the administration of President Oscar Benavides a new Peruvian constitution modified the terms concerning naturalization by adding the phrase "that they renounce their nationality." Although previously naturalized Japanese were not the only immigrants enjoying dual citizenship, the rise of their associations and schools, tending to accentuate the continuation of their culture, at least partially inspired this stronger demand for loyalty to Peru.[22]

The new minister, Yoshiatsu Murakami, faced not only the mounting discouragement of the Japanese-Peruvians but also the relentless hostility of the Peruvian press. His protest concerning the latter evoked no response from Foreign Minister Solón Polo.[23]

During this time another crisis faced the Japanese residents, the requirement that 80 percent of the workers in any business establishment be native Peruvians. When the government announced regulations to implement that legislation, the Japanese were in disarray because Minister Murakami and the leaders of the powerful Central Japanese Association held different opinions.

Peru compounded the confusion when, on October 5, 1934, it denounced the 1924 treaty which had only become operative in 1930. One summary of reasons for the denunciation mentioned Japanese espionage of monumental proportions, rigid orders emanating from mysterious organizations, secret mobilizations, the movement of funds from Peru to Japan through irregular channels, and much more—most of which represented completely unsubstantiated rumor.[24] Desiring a treaty that reflected the economic realities of the mid-1930s, Peru fruitlessly proposed the negotiation of a new document.

To cope with the problem of rising unemployment, Peru quickly supplemented the law calling for an 80 percent native work force with legislation that established import quotas. A wide-ranging decree of May 10, 1935, set quotas for the importation of cotton goods. Ostensibly, by this measure, the Peruvians hoped to salvage many domestic textile manufacturers which in terms of technology, size, and working capital could not compete with foreign producers. After all, the 80 percent labor regulation meant nothing if the very businesses collapsed. However, the idea of quotas, totally new to Peruvians, raised so much complaint that the government on December 31, 1935, scrapped this general legislation regarding cotton quotas. At the same time awareness that Japan, the leading supplier, constituted the biggest threat to the domestic cotton industry led Peruvian authorities to seek a "Gentlemen's Agreement" whereby the Japanese would freely and significantly reduce the level of their exports to Peru. This approach failed because by the mid-1930s Japan had long since realized that such agreements violated her most-favored-nation status in addition to treating her as an inferior. Next the Peruvian government issued, on the same day it discarded the general one, a decree that specifically fixed quotas on Japanese cotton cloth and cotton articles. Shortly thereafter, when necessity reintroduced some cordiality into Japanese-Peruvian relations, an exchange of notes in March 1936 limited the annual entry of Japanese cotton products into Peru to 612,714 kilos.[25]

Even less diplomatic success attended Japanese efforts to protest the immigration legislation of June 1936 which, with its quotas, especially affected the Japanese, who made up the majority of immigrants then entering Peru. As previously indicated, when some Japanese-Peruvians sought added security through naturalization, Peru temporarily suspended that procedure. Categorical negatives from the Peruvian Foreign Office so upset Japanese officials that, in frustration, they indulged in questionable diplomatic activity. Apparently believing that no unanimity of outlook prevailed in the Benavides administration on the immigration issue, Japanese officials held conversations with the Ministers of Education, Government, and Justice. Learning of this, Foreign Minister Ulloa reminded the Japanese that the Peruvian Foreign Office constituted the regular and exclusive channel for the conduct of business between a foreign mission and the government of Peru.[26]

The mid-1930s had had a chilling effect on Japanese-Peruvian relations: the 80 percent labor law, the denunciation of the treaty, the imposition of import quotas, the promulgation of an immigration decree, and suspension of the naturalization procedure. Nonetheless efforts to promote as much harmony as possible occupied representatives of both countries. In 1937 a group of Japanese astronomers used Libertad Department as their base for the observation of a solar eclipse. That same year Chargé Nobuo Fujimura helped to establish the Japan-Peru Cultural Association. In mid-1938 a Peruvian cultural and economic mission journeyed to Japan. Fujimura also arranged to send three Peruvian students to Japan to study for three years. Indeed he dedicated his every effort to closing the breach between the two countries and to promoting understanding between their peoples.[27]

Unfortunately the two years between mid-1938 and mid-1940, the period of Minister Masamoto Kitada's tenure in Lima, witnessed divisions and strife among the Japanese-Peruvians that seriously weakened their position. Kitada failed to give the Japan Association of Peru, the hub of the thirty-seven Japanese-Peruvian associations, the leadership it required. He also shelved the program of the Japan-Peru Cultural Association which Fujimura had initiated, doing nothing to follow up the possibilities offered when Peruvian visitors to Japan returned home. To all else Kitada contributed greatly to the division and conflict between Japanese diplomatic and consular officials in Peru; his jealousy, timidity, and incompetence undermined the desired cooperation and unity of outlook.[28]

Ironically two Japanese barbers magnified enormously the divisiveness within the Japanese colony as well as that between the Japanese and Peruvian officials. A bitter rivalry between Shinzō Kurimoto and Tokijirō Furuya, both of whom had the new hair-dressing machines that produced the popular "permanent wave," culminated in a bizarre episode. Exercising his power as leader of the Association of Barbers, Kurimoto induced certain Japanese consular officials to kidnap Furuya and ship him back to Japan. When the Peruvian woman who lived with him resisted, she, too, was seized. Peruvian authorities intervened while she was confined at the Japanese consulate and Furuya was being held aboard a ready-to-depart vessel. Their return of Furuya and the unexplained death of the woman, plus official Japanese implication in the affair, in barefaced disregard of Peruvian sovereignty, further inclined the Peruvian public toward anti-Japanese sentiments while hastening the departure of consular officer Hayasaka.[29] At a time when anti-Japanese feeling in Peru and the China Incident in East Asia called for maximum unity within the Japanese colony, the divisiveness produced by the stupidity of the Furuya affair and the attendant ineptness of Japanese officials only accentuated the worsening crisis.

In early May 1940, any level-headed observer of Peruvian public opinion might have concluded that the rising tempo of anti-Japanese sentiment could produce no good, but no one anticipated the bitter events that erupted on May 13. For some time, rumors fed by fiercely nationalist journalists and gossips had persistently insisted that the Japanese-Peruvians engaged in activities that threatened Peruvian sovereignty. The anti-Japanese demonstration that began in Lima shortly after 11 A.M. quickly developed into full-scale rioting. From then until the evening of the next day, by which time Peruvian troops had suppressed the rioting, roving bands assaulted Japanese-owned businesses of metropolitan Lima. At 5:30 P.M., May 13, Peruvian newsmen saw a group of youths break down the doors of a Japanese store at the corner of San Ildefonso and Viterbo. In the Urbanización Jesús María numerous small mobs attacked Japanese shops with clubs and anything else that came to hand. Opposite the Italian Hospital the journalists watched the mob crash through the doors of a Japanese store. In the wake of the break-ins the rioters turned looters. A Japanese-compiled summary of mid-June listed the following results of the rioting: approximately six hundred establishments suffered damage amounting to $820,050, a figure which later rose to $1,640,100, while scores of individuals were injured and ten Japanese were killed.

Immediately the Japanese, in Lima and in Tokyo, protested the lawlessness and demanded protection of life and property as well as indemnification for the losses sustained. Chargé Satō, heading the Japanese mission in the temporary absence of Minister Kitada, denied a wave of rumors about the Japanese colony—that it was organized militarily, had imported firearms, and had intensified the problem of unemployment for native Peruvians. Regarding the unemployment issue, the legation indicated that since 1938 some 1,466 Japanese had left Peru while only 583 had entered the country.[30]

The Peruvian Foreign Office immediately deplored the rioting and announced measures to block repetition of such events. It likewise extended the fullest guarantees to the Japanese residing in Peru. Meanwhile, as the flurry of diplomatic exchanges mounted, Japan also demanded that Peru assume full responsibility for the calamitous occurrences. The Japanese insisted that Peruvian authorities had ignored their protests about the rising tide of anti-Japanese sentiment fostered by numerous publications. They also declared firmly that once the rioting began Peruvian law-enforcement officials acted indifferently and tardily. To this burden of guilt the Peruvians replied "that the popular outburst had been manifested in an unforeseen manner, that no means were available to block it and that it was impossible to contain it immediately."[31] The more the Japanese blamed the Peruvians for everything, the more the latter sought to avoid full responsibility.

Peruvian authorities countered by proclaiming that the Japanese bore basic responsibility for the state of affairs that had provoked the rioting. They again cited the Furuya affair as a demonstration of the gross disregard of the Japanese community for Peruvian laws and institutions. The Peruvians also hammered away at the evil influence that the monopolistic tendencies of Japanese businessmen represented in many Peruvian towns and cities.

Diplomatic recriminations between the two governments now widened the gulf that had long estranged the two peoples, but mutual desire to maintain international ties led the governments to seek agreement regarding indemnification for damages. Peru approached this by naming a commission presided over by Fernando Wiese, president of the Chamber of Commerce. His group was charged with studying and establishing the value of the damages sustained by Japanese residents in Lima and Callao. On the Japanese side private individuals and government officials spent months assessing the damage. They amassed vast quantities of reports and correspondence on the subject.[32] The Peruvian tendency to declare the Japanese estimates exorbitant and the Japanese inclination to insist the Peruvian estimates were low guaranteed long-term wrangling over the financial issues. This reluctance to agree was reinforced by the state of both the Peruvian economy and the national treasury as well as the fierce tone adopted by jingoistic journalists in Japan.

Reporting the rioting and destruction, *The Japan Advertiser* stated that Peruvian soldiers "just watched the scene smiling, some grinning sarcastically." Another Japanese publication, *Kokumin*, asserted, "It was conducted as an organized movement," to which it added, "Had the incident occurred at a place near Japan, this country would not have stopped with filing a mere protest. . . ." *Nichi Nichi* rattled the sabre even more vigorously, declaring "that if Peru did not hang on the 'skirts' of another Power and were not so far away from this country, Japan would have dispatched a few warships to aid and succor the Japanese as well as take action against the offending country." However, in the spring of 1940, distance was not the only factor limiting Japanese reaction because Japan had many reasons to direct her major attention elsewhere: to the war in China which appeared endless; to the concept of a Monroe Doctrine for the Far East which automatically restricted Japanese inclination to intervene in the Americas; to the German blitzkrieg in the Low Countries which prompted reevaluations of the world scene; and to the resources of the Netherland East Indies so necessary to the wartime economy of Japan. Diplomatically the Japanese, facing bigger issues and problems, could be little concerned about the value of their stake in Peru.

While the Japanese temper was rising and falling, the Peruvians defused the explosive nature of the affair. For one thing, the Lima rioting was quelled within forty-eight hours and the movement of troops into other regions eliminated the prospect of similar disturbances elsewhere in the country. Perhaps the fact that the presumed culprits speedily received punishment in a variety of forms also placated the Japanese. Leading Apristas and Communists, both of which were anathema to the Lima authorities, were conveniently imprisoned or exiled without convincing proof of their identification with the rioting. Sixteen college students and seventy high school students, said to be among the initiators of the disturbances, were expelled from their schools. Eight teachers, charged with inciting students, lost their jobs and two police officers were transferred. The suspension of the publication of the sports magazine *Mundo Gráfico,* which had published articles concerning the military preparedness of the Japanese, represented a slap at the anti-Japanese press. In addition Peruvian publications in general quickly adopted a friendly tone toward Japan and the Japanese.[33] Peru hoped that amends had been made but the social, economic, and diplomatic aftermath of this lawlessness of May 13, 1940, eventually resulted in the rupture of Peruvian-Japanese relations during World War Two.

In mid-November 1940, a secret session of the Peruvian Senate indicated that fundamentally no reconciliation was being effected between Peruvians and Japanese. Senator Diez Canseco declared that the flood of clandestine anti-Japanese papers defied control. His own feelings emerged when he added that while the government was considering indemnification of the Japanese, many Peruvians lacked meat. The senators discussed the "Fifth Column" idea, the social separatism of the Japanese, and their tendencies toward commercial monopolies. Proposing indemnification at a level that would avoid public criticism, which was synonymous with asking the impossible, Diez Canseco additionally urged the government to take steps to control the activities of foreigners, especially the Japanese, Germans, and Italians. Recurring throughout the Senate session was "the Japanese problem that some day we have to resolve."[34]

Trade

For decades Japanese emigration was not only the initial but also the most important reason for Japanese-Peruvian relations. This was a period during which most of the diplomatic issues between the two countries related to those immigrants and their social and economic relationship to Peruvian society, and consequently trade between Japan and Peru played a relatively minor role. The honorary consuls initially employed by both countries never actively promoted transpacific trade.

However, this mutual commercial indifference was somewhat altered in 1910 when Eduardo Muelle, Peru's newly appointed consul in Yokohama, concluded a survey of Japan, Burma, India, and Ceylon. He reported, "For many years trade between our country and Japan has been nil or so insignificant that it scarcely can be taken into consideration."[35] Trade statistics underscored the truth of Consul Muelle's observation (see table 12).

TABLE 12
Japanese Trade with Peru, 1896-1910 (in yen)[36]

Year	Exports	Imports
1896	¥ 1,931	¥ 5,312
1897	7,370	289
1898	1,735	2,984
1899	4,764	2,438
1900	3,426	10,682
1901	5,493	497
1902	2,392	0
1903	12,012	18,089
1904	4,683	2,078
1905	10,408	3,608
1906	49,694	51,676
1907	87,850	483,525
1908	57,560	30,765
1909	44,327	1,006,193
1910	200,378	456,059

Until 1909-10 this trade, almost accidental and relatively trifling, showed no clear advantage for either country. Peru enjoyed favorable trade balances eight of the first fifteen years but never registered that advantage for as often as three consecutive years. After the Russo-Japanese War the total trade volume increased remarkably. Japanese exports to Peru mounted for several reasons: a rapidly expanding industry offered more products for export, and the growing Japanese colony in Peru imported greater quantities of specialty items from the homeland, some for personal consumption, and others for sale in the shops more and more immigrants were opening. By 1910 Japanese exports increased dramatically, and the first Japanese consuls were assigned to Peru. Meanwhile Japanese imports from Peru between 1908 and 1910 fluctuated widely. Expanding Japanese industry wanted more raw materials but competition with other foreign customers of Peru, especially for the nitrates and cotton, the latter additionally subject to the vagaries of differing growing seasons, introduced factors over which Japan had no control. So, too, did occasional flurries of revolution. In addition uncertain shipping schedules also hampered these early transpacific trade prospects.

In 1905, the Orient Steamship Company (Tōyō Kisen Kaisha), aided by a subsidy from the Japanese government, inaugurated scheduled sailings between Japan and Peru via Hong Kong, Honolulu, and Salina Cruz, Mexico. When it developed that its principal business consisted of carrying Japanese immigrants and that the volume of return cargo from Peru was insignificant, it expanded its operations to include Iquique and its nitrate. Increased sugar production in recently acquired Formosa had shattered the Peruvian hope of sending large quantities of that commodity to Japan. Consul Muelle, tempering optimism with reality, thought that Peruvian coffee, guano, and especially cotton had expanding prospects in Japan which, in turn, wanted to sell railroad ties and cement, among other things, to Peru.[37]

Consul Muelle tried to chide his countrymen into promoting trade with Japan by mentioning the growing trade of Chile and Brazil in that area. In 1911, for example, when Peruvian exports to Japan totaled ¥1,668, those of Chile amounted to ¥2,679,493. He urged Peruvian officials to authorize a joint exposition, one which would exhibit Japanese goods in Peru and Peruvian products in Japan. Indulging the refrain so popular in numerous quarters of the world, namely the Japanese lack of raw materials, Muelle insisted that the Japanese market should be especially favorable to Peru. Yet, when all was said, he bluntly informed his superiors, "Unfortunately, every effort to interest our merchants and agriculturists in the study of this market for our national products systematically encountered the most complete indifference on their part."[38]

Peruvian exports to Japan in the first half of the 1910s dismally underscored the truth of Consul Muelle's condemnation of his countrymen's continuing capacity to ignore the Japanese market.

TABLE 13
Japanese Trade with Peru, 1911-18 (in yen)[39]

Year	Exports	Imports
1911	220,211	1,668
1912	193,547	0
1913	117,759	18
1914	137,859	251
1915	134,799	21,997
1916	503,020	489,885
1917	771,316	136,354
1918	2,062,753	686,544

The notable upswing in trade during the second half of the decade leaves one to wonder whether it was the dawning of a new day or simply the accidental and temporary response to artificial wartime conditions.

In the years between World War One and the Great Depression, political stability and policies of economic expansion in both Peru and Japan resulted in less trade fluctuation than in prior years.

TABLE 14
Japanese Trade with Peru, 1919-30 (in U.S. $)[40]

Year	Exports	Imports
1919	$1,401,612	$441,595
1920	1,875,406	245,934
1921	482,400	603,482
1922	593,676	65,008
1923	650,000	271,562
1924	845,837	148,248
1925	681,098	327,009
1926	919,116	81,971
1927	579,824	80,123
1928	828,500	457,319
1929	1,198,801	26,732
1930	1,103,373	125,451

Although still disappointingly small, this trade, with the exception of a single year, regularly presented Japan with a favorable trade balance. Much of the export volume achieved by the Japanese in 1919-20 reflected the windfall enjoyed while normal European suppliers were unable to fill Peruvian needs. In turn, the anticipated resurgence of European industry, plus natural commercial expansion, helped to inspire the successive Japanese commercial missions that visited Peru and other parts of Latin America during the 1920s.[41]

During the 1930s, while economic depression, war, and legislation discouraged Japanese emigration, the movement of Japanese and Peruvian products also responded to special forces.

TABLE 15
Japanese Trade with Peru, 1931-41 (in U.S. $)[42]

Year	Exports	Imports
1931	$ 390,800	$ 8,304
1932	236,405	11,525
1933	999,704	398,189
1934	2,043,751	541,316
1935	1,997,807	3,275,818
1936	1,786,471	3,772,600
1937	1,826,438	1,807,148
1938	1,638,720	561,887
1939	1,580,623	1,802,169
1940	2,899,565	4,496,451
1941	1,727,260	15,473,406

After recovering from the curtailed trade of 1931-32, currency devaluation and the wartime demands of Japan expanded trade despite the persistence of depressed worldwide economic conditions. The surge of Japanese imports from Peru in 1940-41 reflected two things in particular: needs dictated by the continuing war in China, and the fear and uncertainty characterizing United States-Japanese relations that prompted stockpiling.

Occasionally during the 1930s hostility between Peru and a neighbor, as in the revival of tensions with Colombia over Leticia, momentarily introduced a Japanese factor that savored of both the diplomatic and commercial. When Peruvian officials backed the hothead civilians from Iquitos who seized the Colombian river port of Leticia in the upper Amazon basin, the threat of war intensified between the two countries. As purchasing agents hurried to Japan, early in 1933, to buy arms and ammunition, General Sarmiento commented that certain Japanese artillery experts could be utilized in the struggle with Colombia. That autumn, after the reported purchase of $153,840 worth of Japanese military supplies and the likelihood of related Japanese technical assistance, various pressures served to cool the explosive situation. The formal establishment of

Colombian-Japanese diplomatic relations diminished the pro-Peruvian interests in Tokyo, and pressures from the United States and other Western Hemisphere states as well as the League of Nations contributed to defuse the prospect of a war between Colombia and Peru.[43]

In prewar Japanese-Peruvian relations, trade constituted a secondary consideration, at best. The Japanese role in Peruvian foreign trade paled in significance when compared with imports from the United States, Great Britain, France, and Germany. However, the $15,473,406 of imports from Peru in 1941 compared favorably with the $10,401,046 worth from Mexico, $13,077,923 from Chile, $17,217,302 from Argentina, and the $22,447,111 worth from Brazil,[44] the other leading trading partners of Japan in Latin America. A decade of turmoil postponed any possibilities that such trade volumes would herald a greatly expanded transpacific trade.

4

Cultural Collision

Japanese emigration to Peru resulted in multiple collisions between the two peoples. Economic activity spawned much of the conflict. After all, if the Japanese had not managed to establish themselves, they would not have remained in Peru to experience those frictions related to the press and public opinion, diplomacy, social organization, education, and patriotic fervor.

Economic Origins

The initial friction between the Japanese immigrants and the Peruvians was generated in the sugar and cotton plantations where they first labored. The language barrier paralyzed communication between most workers and their employers, inducing doubts, distrust, and disgust. The greed of landowners and plantation managers invited the contract violations that most frequently included lower wage scales than the immigrants expected. Many landless Japanese went to Peru as contract laborers with the intention of earning the capital which, once they returned home, would convert them into landowners. Inasmuch as broken contracts denied many the opportunity to return to Japan, they were obliged to settle permanently in Peru, which many Peruvians protested.

Another early area of friction involved Japanese and Peruvian laborers. The Peruvian resented the Japanese because he was better paid and also because his work habits stamped the average Peruvian as a second-class worker. Made to feel inferior by a foreigner, the ill-educated Peruvian entertained unreasoning and emotional fears that contributed gradually to measures of near hysteria. Like poor whites in the American antebellum South who were brought into economic competition with slaves, the Peruvian workers in their search for superiority emphasized race and culture.

Despite these early frictions it was not easy for Japanese farmers to forego rural life. Although some fled the plantations because of poor working conditions and health problems, others insisted that their upward mobility hinged on land ownership. Such ambitious would-be landowners were dismayed, however, to learn that little desirable land was available for purchase. Land represented many things to a Peruvian, and to the owner of a big estate—much of which routinely lay uncultivated—there was so much social prestige, political influence, and economic power in his landowner status that the diminution of the family estate through sale was unthinkable. Besides this Peruvian love of land, the Japanese often learned that land without water rights, which often were even more difficult to obtain, constituted a mirage of unfulfilled hope. Accordingly the movement to the towns and cities by what originally was a completely rural-based Japanese population derived from countless frustrations.

However, the town, far from being simply the only alternative, possessed positive attractions. There the variety of economic activities offered choices to the person wanting increased income. There the Japanese, better able to learn Spanish, noted that other foreigners, among them the Chinese, Italians, and Syrians, gained acceptance more readily than in less sophisticated rural areas. In the towns, to which many first moved as domestic servants, the Japanese studied other foreign-owned shops, determining, if so minded, how they might best fit into an economic community that promised a personal mobility unattainable on a plantation.

By the close of 1909 a survey conducted by Consul General Kōji Aiba revealed the rising urbanization of the Japanese immigrants. Outside the Lima area there were 441 factory workers, 257 domestics and cooks, 35 carpenters, and 59 small merchants and peddlers. The two cities counting the largest concentrations were Lima, with 741, and Callao with 135, among whom there were scores of small merchants, restauranteurs, grocers, carpenters, coal vendors, gardeners, factory workers, and barbers. Despite this diversity of occupations they rapidly achieved dominance in some fields. One example, barbering, occupied 157 in Lima, 42 in Callao, and 93 more elsewhere in the country.[1] However, whether barbering or doing something else, a preponderance of Japanese in a given activity bred economic antagonisms and racist sentiment. As early as 1910 the seeds of such problems were sprouting in Japanese-Peruvian relations.

On occasion the Peruvian government contributed to this urban drift of the Japanese in a manner that prompted additional friction. The decree of May 27, 1910, regarding colonization in the montaña declared "the colonists can only be Peruvians or Europeans," a candid refusal to admit Japanese to that rural region.[2]

During World War One many of the Japanese in agriculture made a move that brought them economic advancement, while contributing to envy and friction. Wartime conditions had caused a shift in world demand from sugar to cotton. Peruvian cotton proved to be of exceptional quality and its future prospects led many Japanese farmers to lease or buy land for cotton production.[3] In time cotton and cotton products became a focal point for bitter Japanese-Peruvian differences.

In the cities, however, the density of population, the concentration of Japanese, and economic resentments triggered the most unfortunate occurrences, one of which took place in Lima in 1919. A strike of weavers and their sympathizers affected sixty or more industrial plants there, a number of which were Japanese-owned and operated. Worker demands for higher wages and shorter work days soon blossomed into a general strike affecting twenty to thirty thousand workers in the Lima-Callao area. Stores closed, food was difficult to obtain, and anti-foreign feeling mushroomed. As mobs destroyed property, claims ensued, Japanese among them. Diplomats patched up the problem financially but that did not remove the basic resentments. On the heels of a second wave of strikes, rioting and anti-foreign outbursts broke out which again involved the Japanese; a rumor that a Peruvian had sold 800,000 acres of land near Huánuco to a Japanese syndicate nurtured fear of a gigantic colonization scheme.

During the 1920s one Peruvian industrialist, Miguel Lorca, included Japanese workers in the work force of his textile plant El Misti near Arequipa in a manner that guaranteed friction. In order to break strikes among his native workers, as well as to block their organizing, he would import fifty to one hundred Japanese girls who, until their eventual dispersal, constituted a carefully controlled labor force whose diligence and low wages nurtured anti-Japanese sentiments in their fellow workers.[4]

Meanwhile the rapid growth of the number of Japanese barber shops in Lima gave Peruvians grounds for terming the Japanese monopolists, a term applied to them quite frequently as time passed.

TABLE 16
Barber Shops in Lima, 1904-24[5]

Year	Total	Non-Japanese	Japanese	% Japanese
1904	71	70	1	1.4
1910	90	35	55	61.1
1915	130	45	85	65.3
1920	135	40	95	70.3
1924	176	46	130	73.8

In the 1930s one optimistic projection of job prospects related to the implementation of the law requiring that 80 percent of the workers in any establishment be Peruvians suggested that barber shops alone would employ sixteen hundred Peruvian workers.[6]

The Japanese penchant for group action naturally involved numerous kinds of commercial organizations. Indicative of the potential, from the Japanese standpoint, and the threat, from a Peruvian view, of organized Japanese business associations in Lima in 1938 is the following statement of membership:

Japanese Merchants Association	245
Japanese Cafe Owners Association	173
Japanese Barbers Association	121
Japanese Bazaar Owners Association	107
Japanese Charcoal Dealers Association	65
Japanese Chauffeurs Association	63
Japanese Importers Association	35
Japanese Jewelers Association	32
Japanese Restaurant Owners Association	30
Japanese Peddlers Association	26
Japanese Bakery Owners Association	25
Japanese Hotel Owners Association	25
Japanese Building Contractors Association	20

On every economic front the Peruvian faced intense competition, but in no area was it greater than that generated by the Japanese bazaars. These retail establishments not only featured a wide array of textiles, household articles, toys, sporting goods, and other goods but also introduced such merchandising techniques as heavy circular and radio advertising, fixed prices, frequent liquidation sales, and cheap "leaders." Self-financed, instead of being dependent upon expensive bank credit, the Japanese establishments, with stocks that were more than 50 percent Japan-originated, also developed close and profitable ties with their overseas suppliers. Many Peruvians, hating this competition, sought legal safeguards which reemphasized the friction inherent in the circumstances.[7]

Peruvian Discontent

If the frictions that arose between Japanese and Peruvians, workers, employers, and businessmen, had not received the glare of publicity, the collisions that subsequently occurred might never have reached the proportions that they did. Naturally, Peruvian journalists and authors enlarged upon these resentments and animosities thereby influencing wide sectors of the Peruvian reading public.

An early, provocative consideration of problems arising in Japanese-Peruvian relations came from Francisco García Calderón who, discussing the social, political, and economic aspects of the Japanese presence, insisted, "the Japanese is an emissary of imperialistic design. . . . He does not become absorbed into the nation in which he lives; he does not become naturalized under the protection of hospitable laws; he preserves his worship of the Mikado, his national traditions, and his noble devotion to the dead." Sensing that the basic rivalry between the United States and Japan in the Pacific Ocean area could lead those nations to war, García Calderón speculated that "Victorious, the Japanese would invade Western America and convert the Pacific into a vast closed sea, closed to foreign ambitions, *mare clausum,* peopled by Japanese colonies."[8]

In the years following World War One, when anti-Asian feeling in many parts of the world led inexorably toward legislation excluding Oriental immigration, the Peruvian press contributed heavily to the growth of anti-Japanese sentiment in Peru. The protest of the Anti-Asiatic Patriotic League, in mid-1922, not only went to the Peruvian Foreign Office, it also provoked spirited editorial comment.[9] *El Tiempo,* a leader in the anti-Japanese crusade, fired general blasts, as when it termed the Japanese unassimilable, and specific barrages, the latter often tied to economic considerations. During January 1926, it targeted specific types of Japanese business establishments in Lima, insisting that "the Japanese barber shops, bakery shops and cafes constitute a danger for the inhabitants of the metropolis." Behind a screen of concern about public health, the newspapers demanded the immediate closing of all such establishments. Impending monopoly, not sanitary practices, inspired *El Tiempo* to remark, "it can be said that there is not a street in which there is no Japanese barber shop." The ill-will directed earlier at the Chinese fell now upon the Japanese. Peruvian apprehension that Orientals in general were especially susceptible to certain dread diseases, among them leprosy, tuberculosis, elephantiasis, and bubonic plague, embraced the Japanese.[10]

The following year the anti-Japanese journalistic attack, still led by *El Tiempo,* became more broadly based. In February 1927, an unidentified letter-writer from Callao seized on the arrival of the *Bokuyō Maru* and its "new contingent of yellow flesh" (137 Japanese and 160 Chinese) to insist that the continuation of such immigration would convert Peru into "the first and only Asiatic republic of South America." Citing the increasing monopolizing of certain types of businesses by Japanese and Chinese, the enraged nationalist declared "the Asiatic immigration . . . is for the race what cancer or syphilis is for the human body." The newspaper voiced its agreement by heading this letter "Already enough Asians."[11]

Less fury but equal firmness punctuated the sentiment of Ernesto Devéscovi, President of the Unión Regional Tacna, Arica y Tarapacá, whose endorsement of European immigration accompanied the assertion "Asia as a source of immigration is completely undesirable."[12]

To their list of purported Japanese economic and social threats, the Peruvians occasionally added one which invariably sparked official American interest, namely a military threat. From an unnamed Peruvian informant to the American consul general and thence to the ambassador and the Department of State went word in mid-1927 that S.G. Kitsutani of Kitsutani and Company had obtained a twenty-five-year lease on a barren level site to the south of Pisco. Lacking the water that might encourage agriculturists, the coastal strip, it was suggested, "would make an ideal landing field for aircraft."[13] However much such reports, true or false, stirred up government agencies, it was the press of Peru that continued to vex the mass of Peruvian citizenry.

El Tiempo's "anti-yellow campaign" drew applause and support from the Sociedad Internacional de Comerciantes de Lima, S.A. as President Remigio Alcoser of that body urged the Peruvian congress to act to end the "yellow plague" and to fix a 50 percent ceiling on the operation of barber shops; cafes, and some other businesses by Japanese and Chinese. Hailing those proposals, *El Tiempo* urged its readers to express themselves freely in its columns. The newspaper, meanwhile, stressed two themes, the ethnic unity of Peruvians and the economic factor, insisting that 99 percent of the little business establishments were in the hands of Orientals.[14]

Japanese authorities, if possible, had to stem this rising tide of Peruvian hatred. Zōji Amari, an old hand among Japanese diplomats specializing in Latin American affairs, addressed a reply to *El Tiempo*, stressing the advantages Peru derived from its Japanese immigrants. In this same period former Foreign Minister Elguera and five other prominent Peruvians received decorations from the Japanese government; the Japanese colony, hoping to allay Peruvian fears and dampen the anti-Japanese mood, issued a pamphlet which denied that the Japanese were engulfing the land. The impact of the statistics contained in the pamphlet upon the Peruvians can only be surmised (see table 17). For one thing, the rounded-off figures scarcely inspired trust. Furthermore any general emphasis on the total population in Peru did little to alleviate the pressures that certain concentrations, as in Lima and Callao, promoted. While the Japanese suggested that they were hardly more than a needle in the Peruvian haystack, more and more Peruvians eyed them as thorns in their sides.

In 1930, when increased anti-Japanese sentiment accompanied Leguía's ouster, Carlos Vidarte of the Woodworkers' Union of Callao, in a letter to *La Prensa* of Lima, urged the restriction of Japanese immigration. A few days later César Francisco Macera published in the same paper several articles in which he opposed Asian immigration and insisted that a boycott would enable

TABLE 17
The Japanese and Peru, 1925[15]

Total population	12,000
Women	2,000
Children	3,000
Average annual change	
Immigrants from Japan	600
Births	630
Returning to Japan	500
Deaths	200
Net increase	530

Peruvians to cope with those already in Peru. The idea of boycotting Japanese establishments never proved effective for a number of reasons. For one thing, the publications advocating boycott had limited readership among the total population, a considerable percentage of which was illiterate. In addition the continued resort of Peruvians to the Japanese-owned businesses stemmed from the undeniable fact that their generally cheaper prices irresistibly attracted masses of poverty-ridden natives.

The idea of "Peruvianizing" economic activity quickly won adherents. There was a welter of opinion which increasingly emphasized economic issues—for instance, Juan Centeno Bravo urged the establishment of Peruvian cooperatives to replace the Japanese monopolies, and an article by T.A. Rivera Pando insisted that Asian owners of businesses be obligated to hire Peruvian workers. He wanted native Peruvians to constitute 80 percent of the work force of every establishment, a proposal that was later adopted by the government. Although the economic depression persisted as the overriding consideration, some anti-Japanese sentiment embodied fear of ethnic deterioration. A reader, María de Marquina, proposed the assessment of a severe penalty against any Peruvian woman who effected a union with a member of the "yellow" race.[16]

The anti-Japanese outpouring of important sectors of the Peruvian press continued unabated. Insisting that "the Chinese and Japanese are silently conquering Peru," *El Nacional* urged Peruvians to organize their defense while pressuring the Peruvian government to prohibit completely the further immigration of both nationalities.[17] Truth continued to be victimized, as in the article "If the Indian is a problem, the Japanese is a danger" by Alejandro Cruz Montero. He insisted that the six million residents of Peru included six hundred thousand Japanese, a figure which multiplied the true figure more than twentyfold. From that false premise he continued, "Peru has the sad privilege of being the most heavily Japanized country of the world." Leaping to yet another unwarranted conclusion, he declared, "The Japanese will be the Peruvian of the future."[18] Another Peruvian interpreted Cruz Montero's prediction as present reality when he insisted, "Peru belongs to the Japanese and not to the Peruvians. . . . Here the Japanese are living in glory and the Peruvians in hell."[19]

The nationalist-tinged administration of Lieutenant Colonel Luis Miguel Sánchez Cerro (1930-33) did little to alter the conditions spawning such anti-Japanese sentiment. His program to establish "popular restaurants" failed to serve all the needy Peruvians—for whom it was intended—and likewise failed to dislodge the Japanese restauranteurs—against whom it was, in part, aimed. In January 1933, Deputy D. Sotil voiced in the congress the mounting fear and anger of depression-ridden Peruvians as he coupled his request for an investigation of the Japanese Credit Society with a warning that the Japanese were reducing native Peruvians to economic vassalage.

In the 1930s Japanese militarism also excited anti-Japanese feeling in Peru. If, as a growing number of Peruvians concluded, expanding Japanese economic desires had prompted invasion and military conquest in East Asia, would not this pattern repeat itself in Japanese-Peruvian relations? The anti-Japanese campaign of 1937, to which no newspaper contributed more than did *La Prensa* of Lima, amounted to a public debate concerning the "Japanese infiltration." Dr. G. Salinas Cossío advocated "a propaganda campaign directed at awakening public feeling and raising a voice of alarm concerning the terrible danger that Japanese participation in all areas of our economic activity signifies for our national life." Without any supporting evidence, Manuel Romero la Puente insisted that "the production of cotton by the Japanese in Peru is an official activity of the Japanese government." Widening the alleged role of the Japanese government in Peru, he added, "It is the government of Japan that organizes Japanese activity in Peru." Peruvian fear of the Japanese, whether as independent individuals or as collective agents of a foreign government, sometimes expressed itself qualitatively rather than quantitatively, as when one official reportedly said "There are only fifteen thousand Japanese in

Peru—but they count for more than half a million *mestizos* or a million Indians."[20]

On numerous counts Peruvian critics proved quixotically inconsistent, even contradictory. Those who bitterly resented the successful operations of Japanese cotton farmers never bothered to ask why Peruvian landowners sold or leased land to them, or why the Japanese level of production exceeded that of Peruvians. Nor did they inquire whether the Japanese were doing anything illegal. Instead the opposition usually derived from unreasoning and emotional tenets rooted in fervent nationalism. On occasion the physical and cultural separatism of the Japanese was condemned, the reader being left to conclude that the Japanese problem would disappear if only they would mingle and intermarry with Peruvians. However, this view, in turn, won the criticism of those who insisted that miscegenation involving the Japanese would inevitably lead to the deterioration of the Peruvian nation. For the Japanese there was neither social pattern nor economic role that pleased these Peruvians.

Although the Lima area contained the overwhelming majority of the Japanese and the major organs that attacked them, Japanese activity in other regions of Peru also provoked hostility. Another *La Prensa* reader, Pedro Gonzáles M., insisted that Japanese held 90 percent of the arable acreage in the Huaral Valley and that during the last decade all commecial activity in both that valley and that of Chancay had been "Japanized"—the bazaars, barber shops, carpenter shops, photographic shops, restaurants, theaters, buses, coming under Japanese ownership. In the Chancay Valley, José Manuel Ramírez y González declared "no Peruvian can prosper as artisan, as merchant, as professional. . . . The Japanese reserve everything for their fellow nationals; the Peruvian is systematically excluded." Peruvians who projected nation-wide these reports from Huaral and Chancay, readily accepted Dr. G. Salinas Cossío's thought, "After the merchant generally comes the soldier."[21]

In the mid-1930s, when Japanese trade with South America increased approximately 200 percent within twelve months, fear-ridden Peruvians associated military and political power with Japanese economic activity. Feeding those fears were rumors of proposed Japanese factories on the Río de la Plata and an exclusively Japanese city of two hundred thousand on the Amazon. José Manuel Ramírez y González, coupling the economic aims of

The Peru Colonization Association with the military activities of the Japanese in China, concluded, "The present war . . . is an eloquent lesson concerning which all Peruvians should reflect."²²

Among the statistics that evoked fears and hostility was one insisting that the Japanese in Huánuco Department held a veritable empire of more than two million hectares of land along the route toward tributaries of the Amazon. Countless residents of Lima and other cities of western Peru who had never visited the rugged slopes and steaming jungles to the east unhesitatingly accepted the propagandist's cry, "The montaña is full of Japanese."²³

In October 1937, Dr. Carlos Enrique Paz Soldán, asserting that the birth rate among the Japanese of Lima resulted in a 4 percent annual increase (a figure which a newspaper quickly raised to 5 percent), more than hinted that the Japanese would crowd all Peru. In the same season Manuel González Tello lamented that Peruvians were second-class citizens in their own land, declaring, "Peru is not for Peruvians but for Japanese." He insisted that Japanese-Peruvian school children were taught that the Incas were Japanese, that native Peruvians and Japanese were sister peoples, all of which amounted to a usurpation of Peruvian history by the aggressive Orientals.²⁴

By late 1937 an admixture of truth, half-truth, and wild rumor had intensified Peruvian dislike of the Japanese. Truth attended the aggression in China and the preponderance of the Japanese in certain businesses in Lima; half-truth attended their position in Peruvian agriculture and the degree of quasi-official Japanese support accorded the immigrants; while wild rumor characterized the accounts of their numbers in the country and their intentions in the montaña. Unbridled imagination spawned a belief in Japanese control of incalculable wealth of all kinds in the Amazon basin, as did the arithmetic that foresaw the Japanese outnumbering the Peruvians in that South American country. Peruvians recalled that the penetration of Acre by Brazilians had prefaced the loss of that territory by Bolivia, and the northward penetration of Chileans had led to the embarrassment of both Bolivia and Peru, the implication being that the penetration of the headwaters of the Amazon by Japanese might result in loss of Peruvian territory.

In the spring of 1938 Mexico provided an example in the realm of international relations that appealed to some Japanese-hating Peruvians. If President Lázaro Cárdenas could decree, as he did on March 18, the expropriation of American, British, and other foreign-owned oil properties in Mexico, could not Peru take an equivalent move against the Japanese? Nothing came of one unofficial proposal calling for the expropriation of all Japanese-held property in the montaña.[25]

As previously, an occasional Japanese reply appeared in the Peruvian press, but two Spanish-language pamphlets issued in 1938 represented a more concerted effort to combat the Peruvian propaganda. *Los agricultores japoneses en el Perú* by Counselor H. Hayasaka of the Lima consulate apparently had two objects. One was to set the historical record straight. Therein he detailed and hailed the Japanese role in effecting the Peruvian shift to cotton, stressing their scientific practices and use of farm machinery. Hayasaka also suggested a complete agricultural survey of Peru as an aid to the avoidance of congestion and the expansion of production as new areas became open. Hayasaka asserted that Japanese farmers, armed with topographical and climatic information, would be interested in moving into previously unexploited valleys. He additionally suggested that any redistribution of agriculturists include an intermingling of Japanese and native Peruvians.

In that same year T. Kurotibi's *Frente a la prosperidad peruana* represented a more broadly based appraisal of the Japanese contribution to the Peruvian economy. Contradicting the usual native propaganda, he insisted "the intention of the Japanese is not to be the competitor of the Peruvian in any industry." As for the Japanese small businessmen, he added that most of the types of establishments opened by Japanese were previously in the hands of Chinese, Italians, Ecuadorians, and other foreigners, a thought few Peruvians accepted.[26] In the war of words, however, the pleas of such shocktroops as Hayasaka and Kurotibi for understanding and cooperation did little, if anything, to alter Peruvian attitudes. The Furuya episode, to which Hayasaka was a party, and the rioting of 1940, in which many Peruvians participated, continued to demonstrate the gulf between Peruvian and Japanese and the role played by the press in the generation of anti-Japanese sentiment.

The "un-Peruvian" Japanese-Peruvians

Initially the ways of the Japanese immigrants and the Peruvians stood worlds apart. Most Japanese were totally ignorant of the

Spanish language and the difference between the two languages represented a mammoth obstacle. However, the immigrants' change from a largely rural labor force to urban businessmen absolutely necessitated a working command of Spanish, and that part of the cultural chasm many Japanese soon bridged. Accommodations also were made in reference to diet and dress. Although many Japanese converted to Catholicism, Peruvians commonly viewed their conversion askance, believing that social and economic pressures rather than deep personal conviction had dictated that action. However, even as the Japanese made many efforts to adjust to Peruvian life, there was within them, individually and collectively, a quiet insistence upon retaining their Japanese nature.

As early as 1909, the founding of Nihonjin Dōshikai ("Japanese Brotherhood Association") reflected the traditional yearning of Japanese residents of Lima for group organization. Needless to say, this constituted but the first development in the formation of societies which multiplied in Lima, reached out to other communities, and eventually led to the formation of a nationwide network of Japanese societies.

The Lima area experienced a fantastic growth of Japanese organizations. There the Okinawans were not alone in organizing an association identified with a specific area of the homeland. Among the other Japanese prefectures whose migrants formed their own associations were Kumamoto, Fukuoka, Mie, Fukushima, Kagoshima, Hiroshima, Ehime, Yamagata, Saga, Shiga, Okayama, Yamanashi, and Miyagi. Such assertions of regional pride and local loyalty not only promoted divisiveness among the Japanese in Peru, but they also slowed their Peruvianization. In addition to associations tying them to their geographical origins, other groups formed on the basis of neighborhood unity in Peru. Such were the Victoria, Rimac, Miraflores, Chorillos, and Magdalena associations and the Jesús María Club. Still another kind of Japanese association in Lima formed, as previously mentioned, on the basis of economic unity, as did those of the hotel operators, the coffee shop owners, the bazaar owners, and others. Lima, alone, spawned dozens of formally organized groups of Japanese. Their purposes varied widely, ranging from athletic and social to business groups but one condition prevailed—their exclusively Japanese nature.

Nor was the formation of Japanese societies limited to Lima. Along the coast Japanese communities established associations in Pisco, Callao, Chancay, Supe, Chimbote, Trujillo, Pacasmayo, and

Chiclayo. Other communities formed associations in interior locations ranging from Tacna near the Chilean border northward to Iquitos in the remote northeast of Peru in the Amazon basin, with intervening settlements and associations in Arequipa, Oroya, Tarma, Jauja, and Huancayo.[27]

These organizations and their activities not only satisfied certain desires of the expatriate Japanese, they also served official Japanese purposes. The first Japanese-language publication, a mimeographed item named *Jiritsu ("Self Support")*, appeared shortly after the arrival of the first Japanese consul; the founding of Dōshikai (1909) and Nihonjin Kyōkai ("Japanese Association") (1913) derived partially from the active support Minister Hioki gave the formation of such groups.

The societies aroused Peruvian suspicions and fears. By reinforcing the Japanese nature of the members they lessened the prospect of their incorporation into Peruvian society. The groups prolonged the retention of the Japanese language by the immigrants, further defying their complete Peruvianization. Because the membership was totally Japanese, a blanket of ignorance covered suspicious Peruvians with wild imaginings of secret military drills and caches of arms, which converted the Japanese into a threat to Peruvian security. The societies assisted in "calling" more Japanese to Peru. They also pooled funds, on occasion, for the launching of business establishments. The Japanese had founded the associations to protect their interests and promote their personal safety in Peru, to mediate any disputes between Japanese there, to promote mutual aid programs among the Japanese, and, if possible, to promote trade between Japan and Peru. Peruvians, on the other hand, feared the societies for political, economic, social, and military reasons. All, however, was not as united and harmonious among the Japanese as Peruvians thought. Witness the competing nature of many associations on the basis of geographical origins, economic status, and other distinctions. The founding in 1917 of the Perū Chūō Nihonjinkai ("Central Japanese Association of Peru"), an effort to bury much of the intra-Japanese rivalry, intensified Peruvian concern.

Contributing to the unity sought by the associations was the Japanese-language press they helped to launch. Although *Jiritsu* attained wide distribution, it, like the earliest societies, invited competition. Within a month of the founding of Nihonjin Kyōkai, that body launched, in November 1913, the bi-weekly *Andesu Jihō* (*"Andes Times"*), the first Japanese-language newspaper in South America.

Early in the 1920s the *Andesu Jihō* was joined by a second Japanese-language paper, the tri-weekly *Nippi Shimpō* (*"The Japan-Peru News"*) which soon attained a circulation of approximately twelve hundred. The general economic conditions, plus the increased Japanese immigration and the apparent success of the two newspapers, contributed to the emergence of yet another, the short-lived weekly *Dai Nambei* (*"Greater South America"*) (1927). Optimism quickly yielded to harsh realities and the two surviving publications, the *Andesu Jihō* and the *Nippi Shimpō* merged, in mid-1929, to form the *Rima Nippō* (*"Lima Daily News"*) which continued its distribution throughout Peru until World War Two.[28] Naturally the Japanese-language press played no part in the immigrant response to Peruvian critics.

In addition to their coverage of local Peruvian news—and that coverage, plus their associations, facilitated joint action when faced by regulations and laws that promised to work to their disadvantage—these publications informed their readers concerning events in Japan and East Asia. Awareness of events in the Far East, plus loyalty to Japan, surely contributed, in 1938, to the willingness of the Japanese-Peruvian community to raise funds for the purchase of two military planes for the Japanese armed forces.[29]

Meanwhile the establishment of Japanese-language schools reinforced the separatism fostered by the associations and newspapers. Indeed the greater interest of the average Japanese in education immediately set him apart from most Peruvians. To the normal pursuit of literacy which they brought with them to Peru, the Japanese joined a special concern about schooling as a means whereby their children could more successfully adjust to Peruvian life. Because many Peruvian schools offered more limited opportunity and fewer years of study than Japanese parents desired for their children, and also because of their desire to instill an awareness of Japanese culture among the *nisei*, it followed that the Japanese must themselves somehow shoulder the burden of financing and operating schools. Illustrating the relationship between the founding of associations and the establishment of schools is the fact that prior to the first association only a single school had been launched, Santa Barbara School at Cañete, founded in May 1908.

Elementary schools mushroomed to meet the needs of the Japanese in Peru. They established fifty schools as follows: one prior to 1910, another one during the 1910s, nineteen during the 1920s, twenty-eight during the 1930s, and one in 1940. The growth of the school program paralleled—indeed was derived from—the growth of associations. Among the earliest projects of the Perū Chūō Nihonjinkai, that effort to coordinate and centralize the activities of the Japanese organizations, was the establishment of a primary school in Lima.[30]

The organization and curriculum of the Escuela Japonesa de Lima, founded in November 1920 by the Perū Chūō Nihonjinkai, served as model for many, if not most, of the other Japanese schools. Its student body included Japanese of both sexes and its teaching corps was composed of both Peruvian and Japanese instructors. Every ten hours of instruction was distributed as follows: six in Japanese, four in Spanish. After several years the instruction was equally divided between Spanish and Japanese. A third and concluding cycle found 70 percent of the instruction in Spanish. This pattern illustrated the bicultural ends the schooling aimed to serve—young children first had their command of Japanese formally strengthened and then as they prepared to emerge into the workday world their competence in Spanish was attained. While assuring retention of pride in Japanese culture, the schools recognized the truth that education constituted the touchstone to the acculturation that promised social harmony and economic progress.

That parallel growth of associations and schools in the Lima area repeated itself elsewhere. The following locales, among others, hosted both association and school: Ica, Jauja, Chiclayo, Chancay, Chincha, Chimbote, Trujillo, Huacho, Huancayo, Cañete, Arequipa, Ate Valley, Supe, and Maldonado. In moments of financial stringency, political pressures, and mounting anti-Japanese sentiment, when schools closed for a variety of reasons, those that survived generally were the ones reinforced by active Japanese associations.

Twenty-six of the fifty elementary schools operated until the outbreak of war between the United States and Japan. Widely dispersed, they commonly functioned in conjunction with strong Japanese associations, such being the case in Lima, Callao, Chancay, the Huacho Valley, Huancayo, Chincha, Jauja, Chimbote, Ate Valley, Chiclayo, and Pisco among others. Meanwhile, of the twenty-four schools that closed operations between 1924 and 1940, only five did so prior to 1935. The majority of closings closely paralleled such pressures as the 80 percent law, the immigration legislation, and other restrictions.[31]

In Lima, the rioting of May 1940 produced several effects. A teaching staff that had consisted of twenty-six Japanese and nineteen Peruvians in 1940 suddenly included sixteen Japanese and twenty-seven Peruvians. The influence on media of instruction in those years was likewise startling (see table 18).

TABLE 18

Language of Instruction—Hours Weekly[32]

		1st yr.	2nd yr.	3rd yr.	4th yr.	5th yr.	6th yr.	7th yr.
1940	Japanese	24	16	16	17	17	17	15
	Spanish	0	13	13	17	17	17	19
1941	Japanese	24	11	10	10	10	10	9
	Spanish	0	23	24	24	24	24	25

At all levels the Japanese schools in Peru were planned qualitatively to match those of Japan, a fact that facilitated and encouraged advanced schooling there. The growing number of young Japanese males moving back and forth across the Pacific not only demonstrated the affluence of Japanese-Peruvians but also convinced Peruvians of the questionable loyalty of those individuals. According to an American estimate, about thirty-five hundred children of Japanese-Peruvians were in Japan in 1941 for schooling.[33]

The schools, newspapers, and associations guaranteed the retention of Japanese culture in the communities spread throughout Peru. Their love of beauty led to Japanese gardens and to courses in Japanese flower-arranging *(ikebana)*. Their interest in physical fitness led to *kendō* (Japanese fencing) rather than Peruvian football. In countless ways, from youth to old age, a chasm of cultural separatism existed, and promoted distrust and resentment. Fortifying this Peruvian reaction was the Japanese concept of indelible citizenship.

The leaders promoting Japanese unity and extolling Japanese culture, the diplomatic and consular officials, and the directors of the Japanese associations readily understood the importance of gestures of friendship and cooperation that might allay Peruvian ill-will. Special diplomatic missions journeyed from Tokyo to Lima for presidential inaugurations. On those and other occasions training units of the Japanese navy made courtesy calls at Callao.[34] More successful and informal than such activities, the visit of one Japanese scientist prompted an outpouring of sincere humane concern.

One of Japan's preeminent contributions to the world of science, bacteriologist Dr. Hideyo Noguchi, in the employ of the Rockefeller Institute for Medical Research, had long dedicated his efforts toward the eradication of yellow fever. In 1919 his travels in Latin America included Peru. In the Department of Piura and in Lima he spent time studying two local infectious diseases, *verruga peruana* and Oroya fever, the latter named for the Andean community to the northeast of Lima. The higher priority of other research interests kept Noguchi from giving verruga peruana and Oroya fever the attention they deserved and that he wanted to give them, but his involvement in the health problems of Peru did prompt an invitation to remain there. "In Peru," he wrote his friend Kobayashi, "the President offered me [the] directorship of Peru Research Institute . . . pay me 40,000 yen . . . contract for five years and renewable." Like some other flattering offers in this period, Noguchi declined the Peruvian appointment but his brief identification with Peru did provide officials of that country with added positive awareness of Japanese culture.[35]

Early in the 1920s, during the centenary of Peruvian independence, the Japanese seized upon an opportunity to identify themselves with Peru. In 1920 the Perū Chūō Nihonjinkai, spearheading the Japanese identification with the Peruvian celebrations, canvassed ways and means of doing so. Suggestions included a Japanese-style tower, a public bath, a stadium, and a grove of trees along the banks of the Rimac River. Finally the Japanese determined to give a monument related to the Inca civilization. Lesser projects also materialized, as the *glorieta,* or traffic circle, in the *barrio* of Victoria in Lima, a playground in the city of Huacho, and a clock tower for Hacienda San Nicolás, the initial place of settlement for the largest number in the first group of Japanese immigrants in 1899. However, the major effort focused on the aforementioned monument to the Incas—a bronze statue of Manco Capac, founder of the Inca dynasty and the Peruvian nation.

At the cornerstone ceremonies on August 15, 1922, Minister Shimizu spoke of the mysterious relationship that bound two peoples whose traditions so involved the sun. A Peruvian investigator, Francisco A. Loayza, lent credence to the idea "that Manco Capac . . . was a Japanese." S.G. Kitsutani, President of the Central Japanese Association, heaped cordiality and affection upon Peru. Climaxing the Peruvian sentiments were warm words from President Leguía.[36]

The Manco Capac monument was completed several years later, by which time Leguía was extolling it in a message to Congress as a gesture of "the industrious Japanese colony"; the monument afforded the Japanese a significant identification with a Latin American people, an identification which admitted of varying interpretations.[37] The Japanese obviously hoped that a presumed cultural affinity in remote times might promote Japanese-Peruvian harmony in the present. At the opposite extreme, cultural chauvinists among the Peruvians insisted that the Japanese were trying to steal Peruvian history. A third position, injecting an interpretation from a third nation, involved an American diplomat's insistence that "It has apparently been the policy of the Japanese to ingratiate themselves with the Indians and promote racial feeling among them with which they may identify themselves as leaders. The tendencies of the lower-class Japanese are said to be toward radicalism."[38] While all of these American suppositions may be held suspect, they, like the other expectations, clearly indicated that a gesture of goodwill by the Japanese community admitted of conflicting interpretations. In the meantime, while Japanese named hotels and other business enterprises for famous Incas, some of whom had posed considerable embarrassment to colonial Spanish authority, the same Japanese diligently cultivated the goodwill of a despot of Spanish descent notorious for his slight concern about the plight of Indian Peru, Augusto B. Leguía.

However much the Japanese did to ingratiate themselves, the record of Japanese-Peruvian relations at the people-to-people level continued to deteriorate. The expanding urbanization of the Japanese, accompanied by their growing role in business, increased their visibility in the cities, where the newspapers could most readily arouse anti-Japanese sentiment. The social and cultural separatism of the Japanese invited suspicions regarding their loyalty to Peru, particularly in view of the fact that few of them became naturalized Peruvian citizens and even those who did continued to enjoy Japanese citizenship. To all else, the economic depression of the 1930s, accompanied by repeated Japanese aggression in the Far East, widened the chasm between the two peoples, first through discriminatory legislation and then in rioting. By the summer of 1940, as many Japanese businessmen hurried their wives and children to Japan[39] and they themselves considered liquidating their operations, numerous Peruvians and Japanese-Peruvians were writing off the effort at a harmonization of relations that just had not materialized.

5

The Turbulent Decade, 1941-51

The year 1941 opened as a Japanese commercial mission, headed by Ryōichi Mizutani, prepared to descend upon Lima and closed amid a record flow of commodities between the two countries. That year Japan, Peru's best customer for her cotton, took 16.4 percent of all Peruvian exports, a figure that ranked second to that of the United States. From ninth place (2.4 percent) in 1939 and fourth place (7.8 percent) in 1940 among Peru's foreign customers, Japan had surged to indisputable significance as a trading partner.

In this same period other Latin American trading partners of Japan also registered record volumes. Between 1939 and 1940 Japanese exports rose as follows: Mexico, 71 percent; Brazil, 47 percent; Chile, 65 percent; and Argentina, 185 percent. From three of those countries the commodities imported by Japan mounted even more sharply: Mexico, 966 percent; Chile, 360 percent; and Argentina 255 percent. Brazil registered a modest decline of 9 percent. During 1941 Japanese inability to satisfy consumer demand abroad resulted in lower sales to all of them. However, the wartime economy that reduced Japanese export capacity increased her demand for foodstuffs, cotton, minerals, and scrap metal. Accordingly, in 1941, Japanese imports from Mexico, Brazil, Chile, and Argentina, as well as Peru, reached all-time highs.[1]

Peruvian willingness "to suspend during the present year the voluntary limitation agreement for the importation of certain Japanese goods made of cotton" contributed to that record trade volume.[2] The same months witnessed streams of invective in the Peruvian press, and the mounting exodus of Japanese.

In March 1941, Tokyo authorities hoped that the dispatch of Minister Ryūki Sakamoto to Peru would improve relations with Lima. In fact Latin America in general was receiving increased Japanese diplomatic attention. Until the mid-1930s Latin America had suffered a three-way downgrading by the Japanese Foreign Office. In the first place the missions were few in number and the appointments often concurrent in nature, matters in Uruguay and Paraguay, for example, being handled from Buenos Aires. Secondly, charges d'affaires *ad interim* commonly headed most of the missions. Lastly, Latin America was sufficiently a tertiary area of Japanese diplomatic consideration that it received few of the ablest and most mature members of the diplomatic corps. However, as the 1940s dawned, increased trade with numerous sectors of Latin America, mounting international tensions punctuated by considerable anti-Japanese sentiment, and the problems attendant upon protecting overseas Japanese and their interests prompted closer attention to Latin America. In 1940-41 new appointments affected every diplomatic mission. In February 1940 and April 1941, respectively, Ambassadors Ishii and Tomii went to Brazil and Argentina, the sites of the only Japanese embassies in Latin America. Among the new ministers, Miura went to Mexico in November 1940 and in March of the following year Yanai went to Colombia; Akiyama went to Panama in August and Yamagata to Chile in October. Every appointment anticipated improved relations. Working with Consul Masaki Yodogawa in Lima, who had assumed his post in November 1940, Sakamoto, experienced in immigrant matters, was expected to repair the badly deteriorated relations.

In mid-1941, friction between Peru and Ecuador included an unexpected Japanese factor. For years the boundary claims of the two governments had differed so greatly that their resort to arms surprised few, if any, observers. In July fighting erupted near Chacras. Other outbreaks occurred and as refugees fled from El Oro province, Ecuadorians "claimed that 3,000 Japanese troops were fighting for Peru." Without stating the obvious, namely that distrust of the Japanese in their country precluded their being armed, Peruvian officials termed the Ecuadorian charges preposterous and demanded an apology. Behind the Ecuadorian claim, in addition to her need for aid in an unequal struggle with larger and more powerful Peru, and the knowledge that an anti-Japanese stance could curry favor in Washington and give the Quito authorities a stronger position in their negotiations regarding the use of the Galápagos Islands by American armed forces, rested the basic truth that Japanese-Ecuadorian relations were sufficiently minor that the Japanese could play propaganda pawn.[3]

In late September 1941, Peru undertook a temporary and partial solution of the financial aspect of the Japanese-Peruvian riot claims of 1940. The Peruvian Minister of Finance urged a congressional appropriation in the amount of 1,424,506 soles to indemnify Japanese and Peruvian nationals for damages suffered. In the final settlement only 350,000 soles were paid in cash, an additional reimbursement of 1,050,000 soles being made in wool, salt, and sugar.[4] Neither the amount nor the form of the settlement contributed to any significant renewal of confidence within the Japanese-Peruvian community.

In October Minister Sakamoto, failing to obtain the information he desired from busy officials in Tokyo, set out for Washington to consult with Ambassadors Nomura and Kurusu, the latter a veteran of tempestuous times in Peru. The initiation of hostilities between Japan and the United States prevented Sakamoto's return to Peru.[5]

Immediately after the Japanese attack on Pearl Harbor, American Ambassador R. Henry Norweb met with Foreign Minister Alfredo Solf y Muro. The Peruvian official, who earlier had said, "if the United States and Japan became engaged in war, the situation for Peru would be delicate, since the local Japanese colony is so prominent," assured the American diplomat that should Peru remain neutral her neutrality measures would not apply to the United States. Following the meeting of the foreign ministers of the American states in Rio de Janeiro, at which the United States hoped to win unanimous support for a resolution binding all the Latin-American governments to sever relations with the Axis, Peru did so, on January 24, 1942.[6]

In the development of a political stance regarding the war in the Pacific, Peru stood neither first nor last in Latin America. To the north, in the Caribbean area, receipt of word of the widening war sparked immediate declarations of war by nine countries: Cuba, Haiti, the Dominican Republic, Guatemala, El Salvador, Honduras, Nicaragua, Costa Rica, and Panama. Later, but prior to the conference in Rio, several other states, among them Mexico, Colombia, and Venezuela, severed diplomatic ties with the Axis powers. At Rio the geographical focus rested on countries south of the equator and, before the end of January, Brazil, Bolivia, Paraguay, and Uruguay joined Peru in breaking with the Axis diplomatically.

Additional declarations of war, however, came more slowly. The Mexican declaration of June 1942 stemmed most directly from Nazi submarine activity, but Mexican participation later in the Pacific war represented the only military contribution of Latin America to the struggle against Japan. Some countries, among them Peru, Argentina, Chile, Ecuador, Venezuela, Paraguay, and Uruguay, tardily declared war against Japan, doing so in 1945 only when it became a prerequisite to charter membership in the United Nations.

Meanwhile, in Peru, in the wake of the severed relations, certain developments quickly ensued. Switzerland assumed protection of Peruvian interests in the Axis countries while Spain took charge of Axis interests in Peru. Their functions suspended and their offices closed, Consul Yodogawa and other Japanese officials and their dependents were detained, initially at the Hotel Balneario de Chosica in suburban Lima. Early in the spring of 1942, however, they were transferred to the United States to await repatriation.[7]

Economically the war dealt Peru a one-two punch, losing first the European—British, German and French—and then the Japanese trade. One United States businessman with interests in Peru declared that there the Japanese "are so closely integrated in the national economy that they couldn't possibly be shunted into an alien area."[8] Peruvian and American officials thought otherwise.

Several Peruvian writers fed American fears about the Japanese presence in Peru. Ciro Alegría, whose recent prize-winning novel, *El mundo es ancho y ajeno ("Broad and Alien Is The World")*, had deservedly won many readers in the United States, saw sinister implications in the fact that a majority of the Japanese males ranged from eighteen to forty-five years of age. The idea that the Inca Manco Capac was of Japanese origin Alegría considered a sinister cultural penetration. In a land in which high walls surrounded many structures, he judged it ominous that Japanese schools were set apart. Alegría penned an undocumented version of the Furuya episode according to which Furuya's love of his Peruvian wife had led to his refusal to help organize a fifth column in Peru, hence his seizure by Japanese authorities. Fernando de los Ríos authored another suspicion-tinged statement regarding the Japanese in Peru, especially those in the interior near the headwaters of the Amazon, whose activities he cloaked in vague and sinister terms.⁹ To any assessment of the justifiable fears entertained by Peruvians must be added the fact that their awareness of the recent Spanish Civil War had intensified their concern about fifth column activities.

The resultant effort to avert subversion—the roundup and expulsion early in 1942 of many Peruvian Japanese—reflected careful planning and international cooperation as well as Peruvian fears and prejudice. In June 1940, the United States congress authorized the Federal Bureau of Investigation to undertake nonmilitary intelligence operations throughout the Western Hemisphere and in 1941 agents were posted at embassies and consulates in Latin America. In Peru, as elsewhere below the Rio Grande, the Japanese had drawn the attention of FBI personnel for months. On occasion, attached to embassy and legation staffs, the FBI men cooperated with the host government at any desired level—from local police to national security agencies, including the military. Some FBI agents, assigned to embassies, became legal attachés; others, assigned to consulates, bore the title of assistant to the consul while still others, posing as salesmen, freely roamed the countryside. In such manner they identified individuals—Japanese, German, and Italian—who, in the event of war, would be classified as potentially dangerous enemy aliens.

Inasmuch as Peruvian and United States officials cooperated in the compilation of lists of undesirable enemy aliens, some confusion and mixed motives surely resulted. The confusion derived from a number of circumstances. In the first place, Peru never revealed the criteria it employed for designating individuals as potentially dangerous. Given the emotionalism, irrationality, prejudice, envy, and other subjective factors nurturing anti-Japanese sentiment in Peru, the whim of enforcing officials played a major part in the designation of the undesirables. From the American standpoint some of the hysteria that led to the relocation of Japanese-Americans surely led FBI agents to maximize their suspicions in Peru where two languages, Spanish and Japanese, hampered their efficiency. Accordingly the Japanese-Peruvians listed by Peruvian and United States investigators as potentially dangerous enemy aliens and persons to be deported, included individuals, chiefly men, whose roles in associations, schools, and businesses established them as leaders among the Japanese and/or as individual objects of Peruvian hostility. The planned removal of designated Japanese from Peru served two purposes: internal security for Peru and an added sense of security felt by United States officials regarding the western coast of the hemisphere.[10]

On March 31, 1942, the Spanish embassy in Lima, which had unsuccessfully protested the expulsion of Japanese subjects, announced that within the next fortnight two American ships would transport Axis nationals from Bolivia, Peru, Ecuador, and Colombia to the United States on the first leg of their repatriation. Occasionally Spanish diplomats aided Peruvian and American officials as Japanese-Peruvians voluntarily surrendered themselves through the embassy which was protecting Japanese interests. Most of the deportees resided in Lima, but they also came from Callao, Chimbote, Trujillo, Huacho, Palpa, Cañete, and elsewhere. The deportees included school administrators, teachers, barbers, bakers, bookkeepers, carpenters, clerks, salesmen, merchants, managers, laborers, importers, watch repairmen, laundrymen, farmers, and others—an occupational cross-section of the Japanese community.[11]

In many instances the officials deported entire families. A Lima dry goods merchant, resident in Peru since 1928, left with his Japanese wife and their three Peruvian-born children. From Palpa they expelled an operator of a cotton business who had lived in Peru since 1923. Accompanying him were his wife and their five Peruvian-born children. A Trujillo businessman, resident in Peru for twenty-eight years, had to depart. The deportees even included parents with infants in arms.[12]

Some of the deportees, in the wake of the 1940 rioting, had shipped their familes to Japan. A thirty-one-year-old teacher at the Escuela Japonesa de Lima fell into this category. A Lima barber, twelve years a Peruvian resident and one who had suffered the destruction of his shop in the 1940 rioting and awaited compensation, had sent his wife and their four Peruvian-born children to Japan.[13]

On many occasions Peru abused concepts of nationality, citizenship, and elementary human rights in the abrupt expulsion of those designated for internment in the United States.[14] Consider the case of the twenty-one-year-old bakery salesman of Callao who had been born on the Hacienda Esquival in Chancay. A nisei who had never seen Japan, did not understand the Japanese language, and whose parents, brothers, and sisters all lived in Peru, he insisted, "My home is at no other place but in Peru."[15] But Peruvian authorities could point to their action of July 31, 1940, whereby native-born Peruvians whose parents came from countries which recognized the *jus sanguinis* principle of dual nationality were stripped of their Peruvian citizenship. Patently absurd were such wartime statements as "Unfortunately these new laws do not affect the Japanese who became Peruvian citizens" (Kurt Severin) and "The Peruvian Japanese are now secure" (Manuel Seoane).[16]

Between April 1942 and June 1943 numerous American ships transported Japanese-Peruvians, among others, to the United States. The *Etolin* docked in San Francisco on April 20, 1942, disembarking seventy-seven Japanese among the Axis nationals it had picked up from several Latin American countries. On June 23, 1942, the *Shawnee* landed more internees, among them a contingent of diplomats, at New Orleans. Occasionally one of the deportees received additional scrutiny after arriving in the United States. Giving credence to a Peruvian rumor that he might have been manufacturing Japanese uniforms, Ambassador Norweb urged his Washington superiors to learn if Masami Uesugi, a passenger aboard the *Shawnee,* had a uniform in his baggage. Still other ships with Japanese-Peruvians traveled from Peru to the United States, the *Puebla* landing internees at San Pedro on February 6, 1943, and the *Monterey* doing likewise at San Francisco on June 15, 1943.[17]

Although it was only one of the twelve Latin American countries that cooperated with the United States, Peru, by deporting 1,771 Japanese, contributed more than 83 percent of the total of 2,118 deportees. Brazil, the Latin American country with the largest number of Japanese immigrants, did not send any north. Brazilians were more culturally tolerant concerning the Japanese than were Peruvians and despite growing suspicions and vitriolic outbursts by the press they took no equivalent actions against the Japanese. In addition, Brazil's location on the Atlantic removed it from the hysteria indulged by states bordering on the Pacific. The policies and controls established by Mexico, among which was a more humane program of removal from west coast zones than that practiced in the United States, meant that Mexico, like Brazil, kept her Japanese at home. Naturally neutral Argentina and Chile moved no Japanese to the United States for internment. The non-Peruvian Japanese of Latin America sent to the United States came from Bolivia, Ecuador, Colombia, Panama, Costa Rica, Nicaragua, Honduras, El Salvador, Guatemala, Haiti, and the Dominican Republic.

With the exception of Panama these countries contributed few deportees. Colombia, appreciating the law-abiding nature and agricultural role of the few hundred Japanese concentrated in the Cauca Valley, removed very few. Panamá, possessed of peculiar significance because of the canal and subject to unusual pressure from Washington, willingly shipped out a sizable percentage of its approximately 350 Japanese. Remote Bolivia sent 29 Japanese to the United States and Ecuador, so President Carlos Arroyo del Río reported, committed all 20 of her resident Japanese to American internment. The paucity of Japanese in Central America was clearly evident: Nicaragua sent 1 of her 2, El Salvador deported Benjamin Tanabe, and Honduras could find no Japanese in her roundup of Axis nationals.[18]

Interned in a number of camps administered by the Immigration and Naturalization Service, such as the one at Kenedy, Texas, the Japanese-Peruvians had a variety of experiences.[19] Hundreds sailed for Japan in September 1943. At the time of the second sailing of the *Gripsholm* in repatriation service, the United States government realized that the wide-ranging Japanese conquests in East Asia had resulted in the detention of many Americans; the United States, therefore, needed Japanese to exchange for those Americans. Accordingly, interned Latin-American Japanese were encouraged to petition repatriation, thereby supplying American officials with "bodies" for exchange. Naturally, many men seized the opportunity—merchants who had shipped their families to Japan after the rioting of 1940, and men who had concluded that regardless of the outcome of the war their future in Peru would be bleak. Others willing to accept repatriation included single young men whose roots, economically, socially, and otherwise, were not deep in Peru. Some of the Japanese who refused repatriation did accept opportunities to leave camp to work on road construction projects in the United States. After the war still other changes would come their way.

Meanwhile the governments of both the United States and Peru said little about the deportation-internment program, and that little frequently smacked of generalization removed from truth. In his message of 1942 to the Peruvian congress, President Manuel Prado declared, "As a measure of elementary precaution the Government invited a certain number of subjects of the Axis Powers to leave the country." He offered the public no details concerning the nature of that "invitation." President Prado, during an official visit to the

United States and his first press conference ever, minimized the Japanese danger in his country.[20]

The sense of security implied by the Peruvian president derived from many circumstances, of which the deportation program was but one. The various Japanese associations, which had long served as unifying factors, had been ordered to dissolve. In addition the closure of thirty-two Japanese schools, the prohibition of the right of assembly of more than five persons, the institution of economic restrictions, the cancellation of land leases, and the registration of all alien residents above the age of ten buttressed President Prado's belief that the situation was under control.[21]

Many of the Japanese-Peruvians who remained in Peru during the war also had the tenor of their lives disrupted. Successful cotton growers in the Chancay, Lurín, Pachacamac, and Rimac Valleys, all near Lima, were dislodged when the government confiscated their properties. Almost invariably, of necessity, those driven from rural Peru gravitated upon Lima and Callao and entered business, thereby multiplying Peruvian complaints about their tendencies to concentrate in the cities and compete with Peruvian enterprises. Kame Kina was luckier than many, his prior transfer of his agricultural holding to his nisei son enabled his family to escape the confiscation of their Rimac Valley property. Meanwhile, in Lima, Ryōshin Onaga's profitable bazaar drew official attention and he was compelled to pay a native Peruvian *interventor,* an appointee of the government, to supervise his business. After doing so throughout 1942, 1943, and 1944, he was notified, in June 1945, of the seizure of his establishment by the Peruvian government. For it, he received a sum which he considered less than 15 percent of its real value. Another Lima businessman, Sobuku Yamekawa, owner of a soy sauce factory, received no compensation when the government confiscated that establishment.[22]

To the early wave of restrictions and liabilities were added others. Early in 1943 Peru terminated all insurance contracts held by Japanese and Germans. The cancellation of their fire insurance proceeded from a belief that "should Hirohito send word to his subjects to set fire to their establishments at a certain time and date they would undoubtedly obey, and most of Lima would possibly be destroyed." It followed that they should also cancel the life insurance "since such a conflagration likely would produce a riot in which Japanese lives covered by insurance would be lost."[23]

Peruvians believed that many, if not most, of the Japanese were super-patriots, capable of fanatical actions because of their devotion to the emperor of Japan. After all, very few had obtained Peruvian citizenship, many clung to Japanese and learned little Spanish, most refused to intermarry with Peruvians, few engaged in Peruvian social and intellectual activities, and their special schools and newspapers reinforced the Japanese nature of their offspring at the expense of Peruvianization. Even when Japanese embraced Catholicism, and many did, they were not thought to be serious practitioners of Christianity. In sum, every circumstance that set the Japanese apart sparked dark suspicions in the tense wartime atmosphere.

In the spring of 1943 a series of Peruvian laws further affected the 90 percent of the Japanese population that remained in Peru. One cancelled the naturalization of former Axis subjects who had engaged in subversive activities or anti-democratic propaganda; a Ministry of Hacienda resolution authorized state control of farms belonging to Japanese nationals; and a decree ordered the expropriation of all goods and properties of any kind belonging to Axis nationals. However, words on paper were one thing, enforcement another, and much confusion and inconsistency attended the application of Peruvian regulations.

Of all the Japanese nationals remaining in Latin America, those in Peru were considered the most needy by the Japanese Red Cross. When it forwarded ¥150,000 to the International Red Cross at Geneva and indicated the desired distribution, Peru, one of eight countries to share the funds, received 42 percent of the total amount.[24] In the meantime, minimum friction occurred between Peruvians and Japanese as the latter quietly went about keeping body and soul together during the turbulent times that had dissolved so much of their social unity and economic well-being.

While many of these proceedings involving Japanese-Peruvians were unknown to, some even concealed from, the American public, American journalism did join the Peruvian press in creating a frenzy of anti-Japanese sentiment. Insistent that Japan had trained a large army of reservists in Peru, *Herald Tribune* correspondent John W. White declared, "On June 26, 1939, the Peruvian minister of war wrote to the chief of police at Arequipa informing him that the government was aware that all able-bodied Japanese residents had been enlisted in a secret military organization. It is a matter of public knowledge in Peru that these reserves have been trained by army officers sent out from Japan. The Japanese Minister's offer to President Benavides of 4,000 armed Japanese to help put down a threatened revolution shortly before the Lima Conference [December 1938] has been given widespread publicity and confirmed in diplomatic quarters in Lima."[25] Such undocumented statements derived largely from nationalistic Peruvians.

Limited significance attached to the announcement, in February 1945, that Peru considered herself in an "actual state of belligerency with Germany and Japan." That summer, a few weeks before the end of hostilities in the Pacific, the Department of State sought a reduction of the number of Japanese names on its Proclaimed List, a euphemism for "blacklist." At its wartime peak it had included, for Peru, 134 Japanese firms and 610 individual Japanese, both numbers being the largest for any Latin American country. However, authorities in Washington concurred when Chargé d'affaires Trueblood in Lima demurred, terming it "psychologically unsound to delete when pronounced anti-Japanese feeling exists among Peruvian public."[26]

In the early postwar months, when questionable and illegal procedures yielded to the rule of law, the interned Japanese-Peruvians, among other such internees, became a focus of attention, negotiation, and litigation. Wartime expediency had produced an internment program without any understanding concerning the ultimate disposition of the internees. Peru never said it had completely turned them over to the United States. On the other hand, the United States had never promised to return them. Nevertheless the authorities in Washington did not contradict Peruvian insistence upon having a voice in the matter.

Late in 1945, with the Truman administration desirous of sending the internees to Japan, Lima insistent upon exercising jurisdiction, internees agitating for release, the MacArthur occupation forces reluctant to receive them in devastated Japan, and *habeas corpus* cases in prospect, the time for action had come. At the end of hostilities, the United States shipped additional Japanese, some against their will, to Japan. In November 1945, 138 sailed aboard the *General Randall,* as did 677 in December aboard the *Matsonia,* and several score more in February 1946.

In the spring of 1946 the Department of State announced that the interned Japanese, cleared individually by FBI investigation, were no longer classified as enemy aliens. Shifting its position regarding the final disposition of the internees, the United States next urged

Peru to accept them. However, that government proved so reluctant that, in 1946, it permitted only seventy-nine Japanese-Peruvians to return there. Peruvian officials buttressed their adamant refusal to readmit the internees by citing laws dating from July and September 1940.

In the same period the Department of Justice, having closed twenty-six of its twenty-seven detention facilities for enemy aliens—and eager to conclude the entire matter—was losing court cases to internees. While pursuing fruitless negotiations with Peru and awaiting court decisions, United States authorities released internees under conditions variously termed "relaxed internment" and "restricted parole." Many went to Bridgeton, New Jersey as employees of the Seabrook Farms, a frozen food operation. Peruvian refusal to receive them continued unyielding, even in the face of American efforts to win support from the United Nations. In the meantime American law rendered them acceptable and several hundred of the Japanese whose wartime entry into the United States had been illegal elected, in peacetime, to remain there.[27]

In Peru, as in Brazil—where the difficulty assumed greater proportions—the early postwar years witnessed a peculiar fanaticism among those Japanese who refused to believe that Japan had suffered defeat. In both Latin American countries an underground movement, the Shindō Renmei ("The League of the New Way"), featured a number of unscrupulous and greedy individuals who exploited the fanaticism and ignorance of many of their countrymen. In Peru, by means of fake photographs, doctored news reports, and subtle psychological and patriotic appeals, they led hundreds to believe that the victorious homeland would soon send shipping for them and, upon their expense-free return to Japan, each person would receive the equivalent of $3,200 (U.S.) Meanwhile, all were urged to identify themselves with this victorious "back-to-Japan" movement by subscribing $500.00, plus monthly dues while awaiting transportation. Numerous Japanese-Peruvians succumbed to the blandishments of these swindlers, demonstrating their gullibility, their undiminished loyalty to Japan, and their realization that the postwar period in Peru, whether in victory or defeat, meant beginning anew. Although most of the Peruvian activity of the Shindō Renmei centered in the Lima-Callao area, it did extend beyond that region. Eventually truth punctured these dreams but that day was slow in coming, hostility even greeting the arrival in 1952 of the earliest postwar Japanese officials in Peru. In the meantime Shindō Renmei had promoted postwar divisions within the Japanese community along some of the prewar lines, the Okinawans constituting an overwhelming majority of these fanatics.[28]

Habituated to organization, to compete with the other Japanese in Peru, as well as to facilitate the channeling of remittances to Okinawa and the "calling" of relatives and friends to Peru, the Okinawans reestablished their Okinawa Association in 1948. Its members, most numerous in the Lima-Callao area, were hostile toward Shindō Renmei, a fact which introduced additional divisions among the Japanese-Peruvians. In the late 1940s and the 1950s no other Japanese-Peruvians made equivalent moves to reorganize their prewar associations. This stemmed not so much from a distaste for organization as from the fact that their prewar organizations, inspired and often guided by Japanese officials, had reinforced the nonassimilable nature which not only provoked Peruvian hostility in earlier years but also promised to hamper Japanese emigration there in the postwar years.

While many Japanese in Peru, for one reason or another, sensed that the postwar period would be different, some nonetheless plugged away optimistically and persistently at schemes which had failed to materialize in prewar times, as in the montaña. There the Hoshi Pharmaceutical Company's holding in the Tulumayo area, northeast of Huánuco, was considered one of the most promising agricultural zones of the entire region. A collateral assumption anticipated another exodus of farmers from Japan. For a combination of reasons, in both countries, that emigration never materialized.

In the meantime, while Peruvian animosity blocked the return of those expelled during the war, while fanaticism divided many of the Japanese-Peruvians regarding the outcome of the war, while optimism heralded the possible utilization of the montaña and pessimism attended the prospects of significant postwar emigration, the appearance in 1950 of a Japanese-language newspaper, *Perū Shimpō ("The Peru News")* in Lima marked another beginning. A daily publication with nationwide circulation, it promised to be a significant force within the Japanese-Peruvian community. Only time could tell whether it would contribute to the unity of that community and to understanding between Peru and Japan.[29]

6

Diplomatic, Social, and Cultural Affairs, 1945-68

Both Japan and Peru at the end of World War Two, however much they desired to return to prewar conditions, faced changing prospects and uncertain futures. Peru, like many other areas in Latin America and elsewhere, entered the postwar era on a surge of liberal sentiments born of wartime idealism. When the electorate freely expressed itself in 1945, it appeared that Aprista elements, once anti-capitalist and anti-imperialist—especially anti-American—could have their way at last. Despite the fact that the war years had mellowed both the leader of APRA (Alianza Popular Revolucionaria Americana), Víctor Raúl Haya de la Torre, and Aprista philosophy, President José Luis Bustamante refused to support their demands for agrarian reform, the construction of irrigation systems and schools, and the institution of various social welfare measures. When factionalism added violence to the disintegrating political scene, conservative military leaders asserted themselves, ousted Bustamante and installed tough-minded General Manuel Odría who, through a manipulated plebiscite, maintained his control of the country from 1948 to 1956. During those years he and the elite he represented concluded that the country should emulate Leguía's Peru of the 1920s and seek foreign capital and technical assistance. That outlook naturally guaranteed a continuing role for the United States, its capital and traders, as well as any other country that could serve the conservative leaders of Peru.

Meanwhile Japan, completely prostrate, belonged sufficiently to the victor for a half dozen years so that her political and economic affairs were totally controlled by General MacArthur's occupation forces. Consequently, until the Japanese regained their sovereignty, diplomatic ties between Tokyo and Lima remained broken. The same month, September 1951, that the United States appealed to the United Nations to help effect the return of Japanese-Peruvian deportees to that country, Peru signed the general peace treaty with Japan at San Francisco. The Peruvian ratification which made the treaty effective occurred on June 17, 1952, and it was followed by an exchange of diplomats. The initial appointments, Miguel Grau as the Peruvian Chargé d'affaires *ad interim* and Takeo Ozawa as the Japanese Chargé d'affaires *ad interim,* suggested modest beginings.[1] For a time those diplomatic relations, like the slowly reviving Japanese economy and the underdeveloped economy of Peru, limped along.

In October 1954, Foreign Minister Katsuo Okazaki included Peru on the Latin American trip during which he also completed a cultural pact with Mexico. Prominent in his thinking, at a moment when massive unemployment plagued Japan, was Japanese emigration, an idea which Peruvians did not entertain. As a by-product of Okazaki's visit, the two governments upgraded their respective diplomatic missions; Julio Fernández Dávila proceeded to Japan as minister and Kōhei Teraoka going to Peru in the same capacity. Early pronouncements by both men emphasized trade relations. As the two diplomatic missions were attaining their prewar ministerial levels and searching for binding economic ties, former Foreign Minister Rafael Larco Herrera, at the advanced age of eighty-three, made a goodwill visit to Japan.[2]

During the presidency of Manuel Prado (1956-62), Japanese-Peruvian relations improved at an accelerated tempo. At the elementary human level the easing of restrictions that previously had blocked foreign travel by members of the Japanese-Peruvian community proved helpful. In the late 1950s Prado's moderate program appeared to emphasize education, public works, and the nurturing of a middle class. Peruvian identification with changing economic and social conditions readily appealed to the Japanese who were undergoing related adjustments. Parliamentary Vice Minister for Foreign Affairs Kunio Morishita, who as special ambassador had attended Prado's inauguration, reported that Peruvian feeling toward Japan had improved and that Peru would welcome Japanese industrial experts.[3]

In the same period Japan was actively seeking admission to the United Nations. However, the bitterness of U.S.-U.S.S.R. "cold war" politics had repeatedly sidetracked the Japanese application. In 1956, while Victor A. Belaúnde of Peru was presiding, the application came before the Security Council. Addressing that body, Belaúnde reminded the delegates that three years earlier the Peruvian delegation had "laid particular stress on the admission of Japan." Elaborating, he said, "a close relationship has always existed between the Government of Peru and the Government of Japan, and . . . there have been and are many Japanese settlers living in Peru, contributing to its economic development, obeying Peruvian laws and adapting themselves to the outlook, ideals and customs of our nation." The Council unanimously supported the enabling resolution. Six days later, on December 18, 1956, fifty-one states, including Peru, sponsored and won unanimous support for the admission of Japan. Congratulations were the order of the day when Henry Cabot Lodge declared, "Let me in particular pay a tribute to the untiring efforts of the representative of Peru, Mr. Belaúnde."[4]

A half year later the two countries elevated their diplomatic missions to embassies. Kōhei Teraoka presented his credentials to President Prado as the first Japanese ambassador to Peru and Julio Fernández Dávila presented to Emperor Hirohito his credentials as the first Peruvian ambassador to Japan.[5] In a sense this action was double-barreled: it expressed the optimism attending their developing relations and it also found the two governments adopting a common practice in the postwar world. Prior to this time, May 15, 1957, Japan had established embassies in Latin America in Argentina, Brazil, and Mexico, all in April 1952. Simultaneous with the elevation of her mission in Peru, Japan in 1957 also authorized embassies in Chile, Colombia, Venezuela, Cuba, and the Dominican Republic.

Personal diplomacy, which already had counted a foreign minister among the prominent Japanese visitors to Peru, gained added emphasis when Prince Mikasa, a younger brother of Emperor Hirohito, journeyed to the land of the Incas and quickly proved to be a diplomatic asset. The interest in history that had led him to study and teach it and to publish several historical volumes prompted his sincere interest in the Peruvian past. His visits to Cuzco and to various museums and churches counted for more than did the speeches and commemorative tree planting. A year later Prime Minister Nobusuke Kishi traveled to Peru, dealing more directly than could a prince with economic issues. Also, as head of the Japanese government, he invited President Prado to visit Japan.[6]

In 1961 President Prado received permission from his congress to go to Japan. Preceding him there, Víctor Raúl Haya de la Torre, the veteran Aprista leader and one-time vigorous critic of the Japanese presence in Peru, publicly voiced the hope that financial and technical aid would soon flow from Japan to Peru. Prado became the first chief executive of the Western Hemisphere to visit Japan where, in addition to Tokyo, he visited Kyoto, Osaka, and Nara, gaining first-hand impressions of cultural antiquity and economic modernity. In Tokyo Sophia University conferred an honorary degree upon him and he, in turn, in a radio message to the Japanese people, acknowledged that Japanese know-how and investment were making major contributions to the Peruvian economy. Looking to the future, he urged stronger cultural relations and the early conclusion of a trade treaty. On his return home President Prado told his own people that Japan would soon send missions to Peru to study the financing and construction of the following: 1) port expansion in southern Peru, 2) a fertilizer plant at Chimbote, 3) an irrigation and electrification project in the Department of Tacna, 4) a paper factory, and 5) a factory to manufacture low-cost motor vehicles.[7]

The shift that brought architect Fernando Belaúnde Terry to the presidency as Prado's successor briefly threatened Peruvian calm but it did not ruffle Peruvian-Japanese relations. His advocacy of political stability, social reform, educational advance, and economic growth convinced Japan and other foreign countries that Belaúnde Terry would adhere to his predecessor's policies. Meanwhile economic prosperity and continuity of policy attended the Liberal Democratic Party's uninterrupted control of the Japanese government.

With growing frequency Peruvian diplomats lauded the economic ties between the two countries. In 1962, Ambassador Aníbal Ponce declared, "The main fact . . . that has contributed to a smooth economical relationship between Peru and Japan is the contribution of Japan to the construction of Peruvian public works such as railways, power lines and irrigation projects. This is, no doubt, the beginning of a new type of cooperation between the two countries that has won the goodwill of the people of my country." Ponce's successor, Ambassador José Carlos Ferreyros, said, "For many years Japan has been participating in the Peruvian government's development program through heavy investments and technical assistance." In 1966, he declared, "Peru is in constant need of Japan's technical know-how and capital. . . . Japan has become our No. 1 purchaser of iron ore, the second largest buyer of zinc and lead, third largest in silver, fourth largest of fish meal and seventh largest purchaser of cotton." Twelve months later the same Peruvian spokesman said, "I hope that our mutual economical relations will continue still closer."[8] Quite obviously economic matters crowded, even dominated, diplomatic agendas.

Occasionally naval power was used by both countries in the service of international understanding. Early in 1966 the Peruvian training ship *Independencia,* carrying 147 naval cadets and a 42-man band that performed on Japanese television, called at a number of Japanese ports. Two years later, on the anniversary of Peruvian independence, four Japanese destroyers dropped their anchors at Callao.[9]

Visits by prominent public figures also enhanced the routine efforts of the resident diplomats. In the spring of 1967 Vice President Mario Polar Ugarteche's visit to Japan had barely cleared the newspaper columns when Crown Prince Akihito's trip to Peru dominated public attention. The royal visitor, whose interest in Indian cultures had led him three years earlier to pyramids in Mexico, included the ruins of Pachacamac on his Peruvian itinerary. Reportedly twenty-five thousand nisei and Japanese greeted the imperial heir and Princess Michiko in Lima.[10]

In an effort to understand Peru and to be understood by Peruvians, first the Japanese legation and then later the embassy developed and probuced a series of publications. In midsummer 1951, even prior to the formal resumption of diplomatic ties, the bimonthly cultural review *Sakura* emerged. Three years later, at about the time the first postwar Japanese resident minister reached Peru, the legation launched several more publications. *Nikkō* appeared monthly in somewhat irregular fashion. *Japón al día,* distributed free of charge, was also a monthly. On a semi-monthly basis, and destined to long life, was the *Boletín Informativo,* another freely distributed item of the Japanese diplomatic mission. In 1957, still another publication, *Noticias sobre Japón,* appeared under embassy auspices. In the early 1960s *Fuji* became a means of recording the role of the Japanese in the Peruvian economy. In all of this publishing program the Japanese mission simply emulated practices already in vogue in Lima among the Swiss, United States, British, Argentine, Spanish, and other missions.[11] In one respect, however, the Japanese-sponsored publications differed from most of the others because they sought to heal old wounds, to placate hostile public opinion, and to launch a new beginning. This resulted in a low-profile stance by the Japanese government and no overt identification of the diplomatic mission with the resident Japanese-Peruvian community.

Between 1951 and 1968 the Japanese not only mended their diplomatic ties with Peru, they established them on a firmer, franker, and more friendly basis than ever before. Some of this happier state of international relations derived from the complementary nature of the Japanese and Peruvian economies. Some of it also followed from the fact that Japanese officials stationed in Peru did not cultivate and seek to direct the affairs of Japanese-Peruvians as in prewar years. Some of this latter development represented a lesson learned, some of it possibly was a by-product of the reduced role of Japanese emigrants in the relations between the two countries.

Japanese Emigrants

Neither mutual enthusiasms nor agreement attended the issue of postwar emigration. For at least two reasons Japanese authorities looked favorably upon the emigration of more of their nationals to Peru. The emigration that began in 1899 had constituted a cornerstone of early Japanese-Peruvian relations, and as Japan hoped to reestablish those relations she easily fell into a "let's-do-it-the-same-way" frame of mind. If the historical record suggested another wave of Japanese emigrants surging toward Peru, so did contemporary facts of Japanese life. Staggering unemployment in the early 1950s, as the Japanese wrestled with the reestablishment of a viable economy, prompted consideration of a sizable emigration as a socioeconomic safety valve for the struggling homeland.[12]

In August 1954, two visiting members of the Japanese Diet looked upon Peru in terms of such prospects. Uppermost in Foreign Minister Okazaki's mind later that year was Japanese emigration. While Japanese officials looked favorably upon its resumption, the official Peruvian view, compounded of hostilities dating from the 1930s and 1940s, remained unpromising, even hostile. The National Council for Immigration and Alien Affairs reported that "it is possible to consider immigration only on a limited scale, and of skilled and specialised workers only." To this they added the recommendation that "preference should be given to those belonging to comparable social groups and nationalities, which can easily be assimilated."[13] Japanese in general, not simply the overly abundant farmers, fell outside the scope of Peruvian preferences.

While one government favored and the other frowned upon their emigration, the Japanese people themselves were seemingly of one mind, namely that Peru constituted no favorite objective of would-be emigrants. This negative outlook on the part of rank-and-file Japanese was compounded of many distasteful ingredients: the discriminatory policies of the 1930s, the rioting of 1940, the U.S.-Peruvian internment program, the harassment as enemy aliens of Japanese-Peruvians, and Peruvian refusal to readmit the wartime deportees.

The movement of Japanese settlers to Peru during the two decades following the end of the war reflects the fact that it received scant attention from emigrating Japanese (see table 19).

TABLE 19
Emigration of Japanese to Peru, 1951-70

Year	Number	Year	Number
1951	5	1961	65
1952	7	1962	161
1953	1	1963	69
1954	0	1964	72
1955	0	1965	8
1956	7	1966	7
1957	114	1967	12
1958	58	1968	2
1959	46	1969	0
1960	115	1970	16

The total number of Japanese immigrants to Peru in 1951-70 totaled 763. During this same period, Japanese also emigrated to other

Latin American countries as follows: 56,341 to Brazil; 7,754 to Paraguay; 2,141 to Argentina; 1,971 to Bolivia; and 1,330 to the Dominican Republic. Those entering Peru represented less than 2 percent of the total for Latin America. As early as 1956 one knowledgeable student of Japanese emigration, Fr. John Sasaki, declared, "In Peru the Japanese meet all the obstacles to immigration." In this same twenty-year interval 84,738 Japanese emigrated to the United States and 4,938 entered Canada.[14]

The Kaigai Ijū Jigyōdan ("Japan Emigration Service," commonly termed JEMIS), an operational agency created by the Japanese government in mid-1963, faced harsh reality when it did not locate any of its twelve overseas branches—ten of which it placed in Latin America—in Peru. Between 1953 and 1973 the Japanese established a total of forty-eight new settlements in Latin America, as follows: twenty-five in Brazil, ten in Argentina, six in Paraguay, four in Bolivia, and three in the Dominican Republic.[15]

Postwar Japan negotiated immigration treaties with four Latin American countries which not only facilitated the movement of Japanese into them but also helped to guarantee conditions conducive to their success as settlers. Those agreements bore the following dates: Bolivia—August 2, 1956, Paraguay—July 22, 1959, Brazil—November 14, 1960, and Argentina—December 20, 1961.[16] If Peru had held forth the prospect of such a bilateral agreement, it might logically have followed the visit there, in October 1959, of a five-man Japanese mission that was surveying immigration possibilities throughout Latin America for Japanese farmers.[17] No attempt was made, however, even in this manner, to promote the emigration of Japanese to Peru.

Obviously since Peru was not one of the countries with which Japan signed immigration agreements and it was excluded from the survey, the indication was that both Japanese and Peruvian authorities were unenthusiastic regarding Japanese immigration. Significant also was the fact that the majority of those emigrating to other areas of Latin America were agriculturists, a category of foreign worker not welcomed by Peru.

While economic prosperity increasingly kept all but a few Japanese at home, Peruvian economic needs stimulated a willingness to receive limited numbers of Japanese technicians for short periods of time rather than as permanent residents. Meanwhile the long-term Japanese residents of Peru, those who had weathered the wartime years there and had increased in number, faced many problems as they adjusted to postwar Peru.

The Japanese-Peruvian Community

For a number of reasons the size of the resident Japanese-Peruvian community has defied precise statistical analysis in the postwar years. Confusion attended events during the long interval, between the 1940 census and that of 1961: the exodus of 1940-41 following the rioting of May 1940, the deportation program of the wartime years, and the birthrate among those who remained in Peru. Another, and possibly more subtle, factor was the Peruvianization of nisei and *sansei* (third generation of Japanese descent) by virtue of marriage, loss of contact with Japan, change of life style, and all else that tended to alienate Japanese descendants from the Japanese-Peruvian community. Compounding the uncertainties inherent in the above circumstances were actions taken by the two governments. In 1961 and 1972 Peruvian census takers accentuated statistical uncertainty by combining the Japanese with other aliens in a general category of "foreigners." At the same time the Japanese government, intent upon maintaining a lower profile in certain areas of postwar Peruvian-Japanese relations, never renewed its prewar tendency to maintain a strict accounting of the Japanese nationals and their descendants in Peru. One estimate of the Japanese in Peru suggested that in 1956, they numbered thirty-eight thousand.[18]

In mid-1952, by which time the agriculturally inclined had returned to farming, and the Japanese community in general had resumed normal living patterns, a revealing survey was made of the Okinawans who constituted approximately one-half of the total number of Japanese descent. To the south of Lima, in the Ica-Cañete region, where 46 percent of the Japanese-Peruvian population was rural, they also operated bakeries, bazaars, hotels, hardware stores, cafes, and taxis. To the east of Lima, in the Huancayo-Jauja zone, where 90 percent were urban, they operated bakeries, bazaars, cafes, barber shops and taxis. Close to Lima, in the Chancay Valley, where 64 percent were rural, the nonfarmers again were operating bazaars, cafes, barber shops, and taxis. In the Trujillo area, far to the northwest of Lima, where 36 percent were rural, the others counted auto mechanics, taxi drivers, and carpenters as well as operators of bazaars, hotels, cafes, pastry shops, and fruit juice stores. In the metropolitan area embracing Lima and Callao, where 87 per cent of the Okinawans lived, they worked as commission merchants, operators of fruit juice shops, poultrymen, barbers, bakers, salesmen, bazaar operators, hardware store owners, shirt makers, car painters, photographers, importers, distillers, and printers. In sum, two prewar circumstances persisted: though widely dispersed, a majority of the Japanese-Peruvians lived in urban settings and their contributions to the economic life of the nation embraced a wide array of occupations.

If economic endeavors remained relatively unchanged, not so the Japanese-Peruvian families. The 19,401 individuals surveyed, representing 3,932 households, were divided as follows: the immigrant generation numbered 5,963 (30.7 percent); the second generation—the nisei—came to 10,805 (55.7 percent); and the third generation—the sansei—totaled 2,633 (13.6 percent). Inasmuch as almost 70 percent of this sampling of the Japanese-Peruvian community was more Peruvian than Japanese by virtue of birthplace, time alone had done much to Peruvianize them. Additionally advancing that acculturation were the number of cases of intermarriage, there being sixty-six Peruvian women married to Okinawans and twenty-three Peruvian men married to Okinawans. Among the second and third generation descendants of the Japanese more and more practiced Catholicism and fewer and fewer understood Japanese. Affluence and urban opportunities also found the Okinawans increasingly furthering the education of their children, more than one thousand of whom were enrolled in secondary schools while approximately seventy-five attended universities.[19]

In 1952, an episode which dramatically illustrated the continuing hostility of Peruvian officials shattered the developing calm. That spring some of the Japanese-Peruvians of Lima and Callao "called" a number of their nisei children from Japan to Bolivia, assuming that they could then bring them into Peru on a permanent basis. When a dozen of the nisei overstayed in Lima the authorized two-week period, Peruvian officials arrested and imprisoned them and three of the parents. Although the latter won quick release, the children were deported to Bolivia. This Japanese effort to circumvent the immigration regulations of Peru led President Manuel Odría to decree that in the future any Japanese-Peruvian who left the country would forfeit his right to return. At the same time more of the first-generation Japanese in Peru, realizing that their destinies lay there, began to apply for naturalization, only to have their applications returned with the notation "not assimilable." Three years passed before Peru lifted the prohibition on the exit and reentry privileges of the Japanese community.[20]

In the meantime, during and immediately following World War Two, confusion attended the schooling of Japanese-Peruvian children. The parents, most of whom had always endorsed their Japanese educational program, possibly felt, under wartime restrictions, an intensified desire to continue it. However, the deportation of many school administrators and teachers, coupled with the closing of most of the schools, multiplied the problems. On the other hand, at least two circumstances contributed to the survival of schools: 1) the rapid Peruvianization (i.e., shift in curriculum, language of instruction, and nationality of teaching staff and administrators) of some institutions; and 2) the availability of some Japanese-Peruvians—teachers, and ex-journalists among them—who were determined to conduct schools.

Consider the case of Gino Igei, a former teacher turned plantation manager, who moved into Lima during the war and started a private Japanese-language school. Eventually his operation ran six days a week fourteen hours a day, from 8 A.M. to 10 P.M., on seven different class levels, each of which met two hours daily at the home of one of the students. Undisturbed by Peruvian authorities, this undertaking continued into the postwar years.

Among the Japanese-Peruvian schools operating in Callao in the confused interval between 1941 and 1951 were the Minato School, the Kairin School, the Shimazaki School, the Miyahara School, and the José de Gálvez School (formerly the Callao Japanese Primary School). The Minato School, founded during the war and later directed by former principal Yasuhiro Uchima of the defunct Callao Japanese Primary School, merged in 1948 with the José de Gálvez School. However, Uchima continued his efforts to educate the Japanese-Peruvian community by publishing the Spanish-language magazine *Nikkō* which proved to be a continuing influence. The Kairin School, founded in 1943, conducted classes in both Spanish and Japanese until it merged a decade later into the José de Gálvez School. The Miyahara School, headed by another prewar schoolteacher, operated from 1944 to 1952. The Shimazaki School, established in February 1945 and named for its founder, who had previously taught at one of the schools closed by the Peruvian government, continued its operations, in Spanish and Japanese, until 1953.

In the Lima-Callao area approximately a score of Japanese schools, rising to the wartime and early postwar emergency, helped to meet the educational needs of the Japanese-Peruvian community between 1941 and 1951. Later many of the teachers and administrators of those schools continued in educational service in the less confused years following the resumption of diplomatic ties between the two governments.[21]

Meanwhile, the wartime years, in many ways reinforcing old outlooks for some and engendering new ones for others, attested to the determination of educators. The Hoshi School was an especially good example of this. After the Pacific War enveloped the United States, Yoshino Hoshi, founder of the school, and her staff were expelled from Peru. Nevertheless the school survived and offered, under Peruvian administration, the national curriculum. During the war years Mrs. Hoshi's son Akio, a graduate of San Marcos University of Lima, became associated with the school. While still interned in the United States, she accepted the offer of repatriation which sent her to Japan in 1943. More than a decade later she reentered Peru, warmly welcomed by family and former students.

The replacement of the Callao Japanese Primary School by the José de Gálvez School additionally illustrated the changing educational scene. The removal of all of its Japanese staff, some of whom became deportees, and their replacement by Peruvians and a Spanish-language curriculum led to the name change and the survival of the school. Its prewar enrollment of over 300 dipped to about 250, but after the war the merging of the Minato and Kairin Schools into it expanded the operation. By the mid-1960s half of its students were native Peruvians. A similar pattern befell the Jishuryō School: first some of the staff were deported, next Peruvian replacements altered the operation sufficiently so that it escaped confiscation, and finally its expanded enrollment included both native Peruvian and Japanese-Peruvian students.

One of the new schools, Escuela Victoria, which the Victoria Japanese Education Association of Lima opened in 1948, mirrored the melding of the old and the new. The prospectus of the association basically appealed to the pride and tradition of the

Japanese community. Aiming as it did at a program that combined Spanish and Japanese instruction, the school won official accreditation as a private primary school. The school also added basic English courses to the Japanese curriculum offered during the morning hours and the compulsory Peruvian curriculum of the afternoons.

Numerous Japanese-Peruvian schools emerged in the postwar years but within that community they no longer monopolized, as had their prewar predecessors, the interests of the parents and the children. Many sansei attended Peruvian public primary schools and some turned to certain prestigious private schools. Some of the private ones were Peruvian while others, as the Abraham Lincoln School, the Roosevelt School, and the British primary school, smacked of their foreign orientation in their emphasis on English-language instruction.

Shifting patterns in higher education also accompanied this rupture in the primary and secondary school programs. No longer did either parents or students think automatically of Japan for advanced training. For many their limited command of Japanese precluded any consideration of transpacific study. Instead sansei by the thousands entered Peruvian universities in Lima, Trujillo, Arequipa, and elsewhere. In addition, Peruvian technical schools, agricultural colleges, and other specialized institutions attracted the increasingly acculturated Japanese-Peruvians. Some of the latter, however, reflected, as did other Peruvian students, the affluence of their families by going abroad for their collegiate study.[22]

Rooted in Peru and either denied or not interested in formally learning Japanese, postwar Japanese-Peruvians became ill at ease with that language. By the late 1960s one estimate insisted that 90 percent of the Japanese-Peruvians lacked a conversational command of Japanese. At successive conventions of the overseas Japanese the subject of Japanese-language instruction, termed "a very important problem," has led to the following: 1) financial assistance from Japan; 2) dispatch of teachers from Japan; 3) training in Japan of local teachers; and 4) the distribution of textbooks and teaching materials.[23] All of these efforts, however, represent losing battles because the rising Peruvianization of the Japanese-Peruvian community has diminished its basically Japanese nature.

Meanwhile in Peru and Japan a number of organizations, ofttimes revivals of prewar bodies, appeared. They ranged from the cultural provincialism of the prefectural society and the unity of economic outlook of the specialized business group to those binational associations concerned with promoting international understanding. When, for example, a mass was conducted at a Roman Catholic church in Tokyo in memory of Carlos Larco Herrera, a long-time protector of Japanese immigrants in Peru, the Japan-Peru Society sponsored the service. The publication, in Spanish, of the statutes of the Peru-Japan Cultural Association encouraged binational cooperation and allayed the kinds of Peruvian suspicions and fears that had poisoned relations in the 1930s. In Lima another effort to develop rapport between the two peoples saw the Japanese-Peruvian community erect and give to the city Union Stadium, the very name of which embodied a continuing hope. There, in 1959, visiting prime minister Kishi publicly invited President Prado to visit Japan. In April 1959, when the Japanese-Peruvian community celebrated the sixtieth anniversary of the arrival of the first of their countrymen, the 10 survivors of the original group of 790 still living in Peru were hailed by both peoples.[24]

By the early 1960s the smooth progression of Peruvian-Japanese relations included statements of public appreciation of the Japanese community by prominent Peruvians. Haya de la Torre, burying the bitter enmity he once had directed at the Japanese colony, termed it "a very welcome one." Ambassador Aníbal Ponce went further, saying, "The improvement in these relations is due to a great extent to the large well-liked Japanese colony in Peru."[25]

In 1965 construction of the Peru-Japan Cultural Center in downtown Lima began. When building costs soared beyond the financial capacity of the Japanese-Peruvian community, an appeal to Tokyo led Prime Minister Eisaku Satō's government to give some financial support to the project. In the same period, in Trujillo, a number of publications appeared which could assist any Peruvian or Japanese-Peruvian desirous of studying the Japanese language. A language study program in Lima was aimed at many adult Japanese-Peruvians on the basis of the report that 90 percent of the nisei and sansei there could not speak Japanese. Their ignorance of the language indicated the extent of Peruvianization; their wish to study it indicated a continuing regard for cultural ties with Japan. Meanwhile the translation and publication of Japanese poetry in Spanish in Lima suggested both their cultural interest and their language preference.[26]

Although the August 1966 survey of Japanese-Peruvian occupations may not be definitive, its statistics attested to the completeness of their identification with the Peruvian economy. First the survey revealed the following totals by category: agricultural (580), ranching and stock breeding (469), commercial and professional (4,042), foreign trade (76), manufacturing (266), and miscellaneous professions (635). Three of the categories deserve more detailed consideration.

Within the commercial and professional group of 4,042, the eating and drinking establishments (1,047) and the general merchandise operations (1,192) each represented more than 25 percent of the total. Among the 36 other occupations in this category were: 149 bakery shops, 216 clothing shops, 101 hardware stores, 115 watchmakers and jewelers, 151 barber shops, 16 laundries, 91 photographers, 62 hotel and rooming house operators, 14 transportation services, 6 motion picture theaters, 16 booksellers, 19 doctors' offices, 11 dental offices, 33 accountants, 4 lawyers, 15 medical suppliers, 21 tinsmiths, 20 pharmacies, 9 printers, 2 scrap-iron dealers, and 201 poultry and egg stores.

Among the 266 manufacturing establishments could be counted 47 clothing, 6 cloth, 49 hardware and machinery, 30 lumber and furniture, 31 tire repair, 10 beverages, 15 food processing, and 44 civil engineering and construction.

The 635 listed among miscellaneous professions included 50 public officials, 3 members of municipal councils, 190 company and bank employees, 66 engineers, 25 gardeners, 8 teachers of flower arranging, 5 religious leaders, 7 interpreters, and 13 fishermen.[27]

In terms of language, religion, schooling, occupations, life style—in sum, all the ingredients of day-by-day living—the Japanese-Peruvians who in 1959 celebrated the sixtieth anniversary of the initial Japanese immigration in Peru were much more Peruvian than Japanese, a fact that would become even more obvious before the arrival of that event's seventieth anniversary.

Visitors

In addition to decreased immigration and increased diplomatic and commercial activity, a variety of cultural activities should be noted, whose impact is difficult to assess. For instance, a company organized by Japanese residents of Lima planned a theater for the showing of Japanese films as well as venturing into film distribution throughout Latin America. More importantly, however, by 1957 Peru was attracting scholars whose work Peruvians admired, among them astronomer J. Ueda of the University of Kyoto and anthropologist Seiichi Izumi of the University of Tokyo. The former installed a coronograph at the Huancayo Observatory while the latter, working in the Huaral Valley, found additional evidence that associated ancient Peruvian culture with Asia. In 1960 the Japanese and Peruvian governments authorized an Izumi-led expedition which excavated ruins at several sites. Considerable success also attended his third expedition, that of 1966, into the central Andes in search of evidence of the origins of Andean culture.[28] Izumi's persistent identification with the Peruvian archaelogical scene and the resultant establishment of an Andean studies program at the University of Tokyo represented proof of Japanese fascination with the historical depth and the cultural riches of Inca Peru.

Unlike the Japanese-Mexican experience, athletics contributed little to relations between the two peoples. Baseball, a prewar outlet for Japanese-Peruvian energies, had won few adherents among native Peruvians. In early postwar years the Japanese-Peruvians showed little enthusiasm for reforming their one-time teams and leagues. Meanwhile soccer, the sports obsession of most Peruvians, counted few Japanese-Peruvian participants. When, however, postwar international relations did include touring teams, a Peruvian soccer team went to Tokyo and defeated an all-star Japanese team. When the Japanese love of mountain-climbing, fortified by growing personal affluence, brought the Andes within reach of energetic collegians on holiday, numerous peaks drew their attention. However, this determination to scale unconquered peaks, a lonely competition against the forces of nature, did little, if anything, to promote Japanese-Peruvian relations.

Few Peruvians crossed the Pacific to Japan but those who did so constituted a select and varied company. The famous multi-octave singer Yma Sumac created a sensation. Other Japanese responded to author Aurelio Miró Quesada during his one-month stay at the invitation of the Japanese Foreign Office and to the touring president of the Lima newspaper *El Comercio*. The activities of such individuals as Sumac and Miró Quesada along with the previously mentioned ones of Ueda and Izumi represented the dawning of cultural exchange programs. Meanwhile stay-at-home Peruvians gained another perspective on Japan when Ernesto Cáceres B. published an account of his personal experiences in Tokyo, Kyoto, Kamakura, Nikkō, Hakone, and elsewhere. Garnished with historical references, *La luz viene del oriente* was a rarity among travel accounts of Japan available to Peruvians.[29]

Unlike the Japanese exhibitions in Peru, which invariably promoted trade, Peruvian exhibits in Japan featured museum items. In 1958, shortly before his trip to Peru, Prince Mikasa formally opened a Tokyo showing of Inca artifacts which drew many visitors. Three years later the Inca Empire Gold Exhibition in the Japanese capital fascinated the emperor and empress, among many others.[30]

However slight the impact of travelers and traveling exhibits in this period of Peruvian-Japanese relations, they did represent promising beginnings, the kind of beginnings that had led to Japanese cultural agreements with Mexico (1954) and Brazil (1961),[31] increasing the visibility of each people and its culture in the eyes of the other. For both Japan and Peru, however, these stuttering cultural exchanges served primarily as handmaidens of the more basic ties, the economic ones, then developing between them.

7

Trade, Investment, and Technical Assistance, 1945-68

Prior to World War Two, Japanese-Peruvian relations had gravitated around two subjects—the emigration of Japanese and trade. Almost totally absent had been such postwar developments as cultural relations, technical assistance, and investment. Of the two, the emigration of Japanese to Peru had constituted the primary consideration, trade the secondary one. In the postwar years, for socioeconomic reasons to which both peoples contributed, these two themes were reversed. In all of the post-1945 years Peru, when not hostile, hesitated to receive Japanese settlers and with surprising speed after the war Japan's growing economy discouraged emigration. Workers had opportunities with Japanese industry which required the raw materials and produced the goods that constituted the growing trade between Japan and Peru.

Prior to the peace treaty of 1951 a quasi-diplomatic move by the American occupation forces in Japan had already renewed the more elementary bond between Japan and Peru. Lima became a major stop for the trade and financial mission of the Supreme Commander for the Allied Powers (SCAP) which General MacArthur dispatched to Latin America in 1949. On June 15, a signed agreement pledged the exchange of commodities between Japan and Peru at most-favored-nation price levels. Although the loosely stated agreement stipulated neither kinds nor quantities of commodities to be traded, the SCAP representatives did indicate that Japan might welcome sugar, cotton, antimony, lead, and anthracite while supplying Peru with cement and manufactured items, the latter

111

including electric goods and steel products. Like other SCAP-arranged agreements, this trade was conducted on a cash basis, in dollars. This arrangement of mid-1949 repaired the breach created by the abrogation in 1934 of the treaty of commerce between the two countries. Although intended only for a short time, this agreement, extended on occasion, served as the basis for Japanese-Peruvian trade for more than a decade, until the formulation of a trade treaty.[1]

There was one obstacle in the way of improved trade relations which the Japanese had to overcome. This was the prevailing estimate of Japanese goods. In prewar years Peruvians, like foreigners in general, had commonly considered Japanese products simple and shoddy, mere toys and exotic trivia. Enforcement of the quality control laws enacted in 1948 and 1957 regarding export products did much to reverse the old image of Japanese manufactured goods.[2] Early in the postwar era Japan offered Peru, and the rest of the world, the transistor radios and related products that catapulted her to leadership in the field of electronics, and the cameras that outsold famous German and American brands, not to mention bulldozers and countless other industrial products.

To assist the marketing of her products Japan quickly adopted a number of important measures. The Export-Import Bank of Japan was created in 1951 for the financing of exports by means of long-term loans. Seven years later the Ministry of International Trade and Industry (MITI) established the Japan External Trade Organization (JETRO), a semi-governmental market research agency. By 1970 JETRO's staff would exceed fifteen hundred, approximately 40 percent of whom manned seventy offices and fifteen trade centers—the latter with permanent exhibitions of Japanese products—throughout the world.[3]

In the spring of 1959 the voyage of the *Atlas Maru,* which included Peru on its itinerary, inaugurated an especially impressive aspect of JETRO-sponsored trade promotion. Fitted out as a "floating fair," the 10,747-ton vessel of the Osaka Steamship Company exhibited 9,856 different items, the products of some 820 Japanese companies. The "floating fair" had two objectives: to win customers by exhibiting convincing proofs of the Japanese economic recovery and to combat the prewar estimate of Japanese products. The voyage of the *Atlas Maru,* the first of many such projects in all quarters of the world, demonstrated the close cooperation between the private industrial sector and the government of Japan.⁴ Meanwhile a variety of trade missions had gone out from Japan, some representing specific industries, others more broadly offering the range of products of a major city or industrial zone.⁵

To such self-generated Japanese interest the Peruvians added their own. In December 1958, Minister Fernández Dávila, meeting with leaders of the Japan Chamber of Commerce and Industry, invited Japanese participation in an international sample fair in Lima. JETRO took charge of the Japanese preparations which included the erection of a pavilion for the display of approximately one thousand different commodities in fifty booths. Like other JETRO-sponsored operations elsewhere in Latin America at that time, the exhibited items ranged from small consumer products to large industrial machines. This represented the best opportunity, to date, to exhibit Japanese industrial products in Peru in a competitive setting. Japanese participation in this, the first such trade fair in Lima, naturally led to invitations to engage in the second (1961), third (1963), fourth (1965), and fifth (1967) trade fairs. As usual, JETRO managed the Japanese exhibits. By 1963, Japan, recognizing the Lima fair as the largest of its kind in Latin America, had decided to construct a permanent pavilion. The first Japanese undertaking of this kind at any international trade site, the pavilion also underscored the long-term attention Japanese manufacturers planned to direct to Peru. Seventy-one booths offering thirty-five hundred items stamped Japan as the second most active participant that year. In 1965, when JETRO's increased budget helped to sponsor sample fairs in fifty-four major cities of the world, the Lima fair was one of five held in Latin America.⁶

Meanwhile, and accelerated by the presence of President Prado, Japanese and Peruvian authorities signed, on May 15, 1961, a nine-article trade agreement, pledging each other most-favored-nation treatment in every matter concerning the importation and exportation of goods. Of particular interest to potential Japanese investors was the pledge, in the second article, of most-favored treatment for nationals and companies with respect to payments, remittances, and other financial arrangements. The third article, promising most-favored treatment for the citizens of both countries, their companies, access to courts, taxes levied, rights of property, and related economic interests, exceeded the limits desired by Peru. Accordingly a protocol of the same date indicated that

"Immigrants shall remain outside the scope of the provisions." Still another article placed limits on the exercise of expropriation. Beyond a stated life of three years this document, in the absence of written denunciation of it, would automatically continue in effect for similar periods.[7]

Supplementing the boosts given Japanese-Peruvian trade by the treaty and the fairs, each country also dispatched trade missions. Invariably the Japanese undertakings were more numerous, better organized, and demonstrative of greater long-range planning than were the Peruvian missions.[8] Some of this reflected the differing natures of Japanese and Peruvians but the Japanese efforts also sought to improve a distressing trade balance (see table 20).

TABLE 20
Japanese Trade with Peru in Relation to Japanese Trade with All of Latin America, 1947-68 (in U.S. $ thousands)[9]

	EXPORTS				IMPORTS			
Year	Latin America	Peru	%	Rank	Latin America	Peru	%	Rank
1947	$ 12	$ 0	0	—	$ 413	$ 0	0	—
1948	1,549	0	0	—	21,702	936	4.3	3
1949	6,305	131	1.6	8	9,915	13	.1	12
1950	45,923	485	1.6	14	68,712	576	.8	7
1951	92,119	1,073	1.1	8	276,005	6,956	2.5	6
1952	53,150	2,360	4.3	6	168,564	11,587	6.8	4
1953	106,352	2,797	2.5	8	264,997	15,248	5.7	5
1954	203,890	4,639	2.2	6	309,281	20,319	6.6	5
1955	183,494	4,989	2.7	7	242,979	10,777	4.4	6
1956	168,250	8,361	4.9	4	350,715	25,676	7.3	5
1957	154,046	11,882	7.7	4	269,792	39,225	14.5	4
1958	119,643	5,771	4.8	6	244,797	14,775	6.0	5
1959	231,927	7,569	3.2	8	300,562	20,310	6.7	5
1960	290,120	12,106	4.2	8	309,720	37,926	12.2	3
1961	331,717	17,494	5.2	8	479,767	67,179	14.0	2
1962	331,067	25,203	7.6	4	473,340	58,365	12.3	3
1963	330,780	27,535	8.3	4	556,916	68,957	12.4	2
1964	416,935	31,587	7.6	5	664,762	99,166	14.9	2
1965	424,845	47,575	11.2	3	691,445	111,066	16.0	3
1966	481,088	57,022	11.8	3	756,161	124,059	16.4	3
1967	519,809	50,628	9.3	5	828,392	154,567	18.6	3
1968	624,000	30,989	4.9	5	923,273	194,761	21.1	1

During this time Japanese trade experienced numerous and overlapping restrictions—first by the occupation forces and then by the Japanese government. Other impediments were: shortages of capital, raw materials, and shipping; enmity and reluctance on the part of many Peruvians; fierce competition from Europe and North America; and routinely adverse trade balances.

The early postwar state of Japanese shipping made more difficult the revitalization of Japanese-Peruvian trade. At the same time Peru, never recognized as a significant maritime power, could contribute little to resolve this dilemma. When the *Yavari* carried nine thousand tons of sugar to Japan in mid-1956, it was the first Peruvian vessel to dock in Japanese waters in almost twenty years and constituted a postwar rarity. Meanwhile Kawasaki Steamship Company (Kawasaki Kisen Kabushiki Kaisha, often termed the K.K.K.K. Line) and the Mitsui Products Company (Mitsui Bussan Kaisha), were teaming up to move Peruvian copper ore, the former to win cargo and the latter to acquire industrial raw materials. When increased trade prompted a wider interest in consular facilities, leading manufacturers, traders, and shippers in the Kobe-Osaka area urged the Japanese Foreign Ministry to request Peruvian authorities to open a consular office there.[10]

Although to a lesser extent than many countries with larger merchant marines, Peru joined the rest of the world in recognizing the genius which quickly elevated Japanese shipbuilders to the primary position. In the early 1960s Peru, through its state-owned agency, the Compañía Peruana de Vapores, ordered and then cancelled the construction of seven 8,500-ton freighters. The reason for the cancellation was a government regulation. When the shipbuilder won the contract by extending credit for seven years, the maximum then permitted by Japanese regulations, the failure of the bidder to comply with the ten-year installment conditions set down by the Peruvians led unsuccessful competitors to force the cancellation.[11] Never did Peruvian shipping compete with Japanese bottoms in the movement of cargoes between the two countries. Peru, however, did compete with other American customers and suppliers of the Japanese, as demonstrated in table 21.

Tables 21 and 22 gain added perspective when it is borne in mind that throughout this period: (a) the population of Peru approximated one and one-half times that of Chile, one-half that of Argentina, one-third that of Mexico, less than one-sixth that of Brazil and less than one-sixteenth that of the United States; and (b) Peruvian per capita income, never exceeding $250 in this period, ranked much below that of Argentina, Chile, and Mexico and scarcely amounted to one-tenth that of the United States. In all these years the United

TABLE 21

Japanese Exports to Peru and Selected Other American Trading Partners, 1947-68 (in U.S. $ thousands)[12]

Year	Peru	Argentina	Brazil	Chile	Mexico	U.S.A.
1947	$ 0	$ 12	$ 0	$ 0	$ 0	$ 35,403
1948	0	18	18	47	82	62,730
1949	131	2	615	49	660	81,992
1950	485	20,993	2,300	130	3,461	181,954
1951	1,073	47,360	21,642	641	3,349	204,907
1952	2,360	9,137	10,951	1,283	6,120	229,339
1953	2,797	15,622	21,733	3,156	12,012	261,549
1954	4,639	48,866	78,208	1,242	28,787	278,996
1955	4,989	79,124	33,422	3,892	7,377	431,960
1956	8,361	38,933	45,156	7,449	7,078	557,948
1957	11,882	8,259	24,989	11,853	7,553	600,510
1958	5,771	26,158	41,874	4,200	12,679	666,441
1959	7,569	19,809	37,352	6,962	15,982	1,028,696
1960	12,106	27,941	45,736	14,836	18,339	1,148,653
1961	17,494	41,312	86,029	19,324	21,124	1,054,695
1962	25,203	71,875	43,558	11,206	22,660	1,357,825
1963	27,535	24,779	56,275	11,887	24,505	1,498,086
1964	31,587	25,677	29,019	7,033	34,002	1,768,000
1965	47,575	44,231	26,556	25,797	40,649	2,414,000
1966	57,022	30,586	44,017	23,068	50,193	2,963,000
1967	50,628	39,263	54,556	11,865	91,752	2,999,000
1968	30,989	42,438	102,069	12,303	106,276	4,054,000

States was the principal trading partner of both Japan and Peru. The ominous 40 percent drop in Peruvian purchases from Japan in 1968 constituted but one of the many indicators of the economic stagnation which hurried President Belaúnde Terry out of office late that year.

While Peruvian capacity to absorb Japanese exports, like that of Argentina, Brazil and Chile, fluctuated widely in the 1960s, Peruvian ability to supply Japanese import needs showed more consistent growth than did that of either of the more populous Argentina and Brazil.

Japanese exports to Peru (table 23) graphically documented the Peruvian urge to industrialize while the imports from Peru (table 24) clearly indicated the great and growing appetite of Japanese industry for raw materials.

For centuries the Indian and European-descended inhabitants of the South American mainland had looked to the Pacific for part of their livelihood. At varying distances from the Peruvian coast, but undeniably related to it, arid islands hosted millions of sea birds

TABLE 22
Japanese Imports from Peru and Selected Other American Trading Partners 1947-68 (in U.S. $ thousands)[13]

Year	Peru	Argentina	Brazil	Chile	Mexico	U.S.A.
1947	$ 0	$ 27	$ 0	$ 0	$ 0	$ 60,075
1948	936	1,497	257	0	940	324,739
1949	13	1,251	2,467	662	174	467,521
1950	567	30,740	1,648	53	16,525	417,167
1951	6,956	49,660	32,304	1,356	111,404	597,680
1952	11,587	3,658	15,459	2,036	71,375	621,715
1953	15,248	51,604	39,115	4,136	84,167	670,563
1954	20,319	60,778	73,832	3,397	92,276	679,861
1955	10,777	22,240	59,278	773	83,972	643,101
1956	25,676	36,009	50,209	4,716	128,106	901,861
1957	39,225	18,870	4,658	8,495	82,741	1,233,971
1958	14,775	26,786	12,793	2,266	93,605	843,844
1959	20,310	32,193	9,366	8,950	123,108	935,221
1960	37,926	50,572	32,795	12,472	102,851	1,340,727
1961	67,179	65,057	61,269	46,295	134,990	1,739,342
1962	58,365	34,462	40,076	60,811	127,774	1,414,989
1963	68,957	42,014	38,387	62,466	134,152	1,697,486
1964	99,166	55,887	37,190	95,243	144,226	1,913,000
1965	111,066	47,939	49,573	131,596	144,784	2,058,000
1966	124,059	53,334	60,602	149,432	177,724	2,331,000
1967	154,567	52,256	85,633	166,911	171,796	2,666,000
1968	194,761	41,100	87,118	187,047	172,898	2,954,000

TABLE 23
Japanese Exports to Peru, 1961-68—Values and Major Categories

Year	Value ($ thousands)	% Machinery & Instruments	% Metal & Metal Products	% Light Industry Products	% Chemical Products
1961	17,494	38.5	24.7	n.a.	8.6
1962	25,203	34.1	20.2	n.a.	7.1
1963	27,535	34.9	27.6	n.a.	3.3
1964	31,587	42.2	29.2	23.8	3.8
1965	47,575	36.6	32.4	25.3	4.6
1966	57,022	42.3	26.5	23.5	5.4
1967	50,628	46.6	23.3	22.3	4.9
1968	30,989	33.0	34.6	21.4	8.1

which deposited the excrement known as guano whose valuable fertilizing qualities not only aided Peruvian agriculture but also attracted foreign attention. Bitter diplomatic battles, especially with Great Britain and the United States, had punctuated much of the nineteenth century, inducing special concern among Peruvian

TABLE 24
Japanese Imports from Peru, 1961-68—Values and Major Categories[14]

Year	Value ($ thousands)	% Raw Materials	% Metals & Alloys	% Foodstuffs
1961	67,179	84.9	10.1	4.2
1962	58,365	91.0	1.2	6.2
1963	68,957	82.0	2.0	13.8
1964	99,166	77.2	11.4	11.4
1965	111,066	86.3	6.3	7.4
1966	124,059	87.2	2.9	9.7
1967	154,567	91.6	4.7	3.7
1968	194,761	80.3	12.1	7.5

officials regarding those islands and the adjacent waters of the fish-rich Humboldt Current.

Peru was not far behind when Chile, the first Pacific coast state of Latin America to do so, proclaimed her sovereignty over two hundred miles of the continental shelf. The Chilean action of June 23, 1947, directly inspired the Peruvian decree of August 1, 1947. For several years, during which the United States and other governments protested and convened unproductive conferences, Japan remained a distant observer of this contest involving definitions of sovereignty over the high seas and territorial waters. By 1955 the United States had challenged the Peruvian position so insistently, in legislative acts and on the sea, that the Peruvian navy began to seize American tuna boats.

By the mid-1950s a number of developments further complicated this issue of fisheries and territorial waters. Advances in fishing technology, especially the rapid displacement of small "bait" boats by large purse-seiners, promised more profitable operations by vessels from distant ports. This, in turn, encouraged greater penetration of the Peruvian fishing zone by United States and Japanese vessels. Changed fishing technology also upset the arrangement that existed when bait fishing required direct contacts between foreign fishermen and Peruvians. While technology was changing and protests and seizures mounted, Peru and Chile were gaining adherents to their position, the two-hundred-mile limit also being claimed by Costa Rica (1948), El Salvador (1950), Honduras (1951), Ecuador (1952), Nicaragua (1965), Argentina (1966), Panama (1967), Uruguay (1969), and Brazil (1970).

Japan stubbornly resisted this changing concept of territorial waters. Tokyo authorities adhered so rigidly to the three-mile limit that they even ignored four conventions relative to jurisdiction over the seas adopted in 1958 by the United Nations' Conference on the Law of the Sea. Only in 1965 did Japan modify her position. By then a series of fishing agreements between Japan and the United States, Russia, and South Korea so established the twelve-mile limit that formal Japanese acceptance of it ensued. Needless to say, the difference between twelve- and two-hundred-mile zones of territorial waters promised trouble in Japanese-Peruvian relations.

Another factor, one with both trade and investment potential for the Japanese, sped their involvement in this maritime matter. The wide-ranging fishing industry of Japan entered the west coast South American fisheries just as Peru was expanding the fish meal industry which soon assumed such proportions that it earned more than 25 percent of Peru's foreign exchange while Peru was displacing Japan as the world's leading fishing nation.[15]

During the middle sixties much of what Japanese businessmen did in reference to Peru derived not only from changing conditions at home but also from Peruvian and more general Latin American circumstances. By 1963 the Japanese keenly appreciated the fact that regional economic planning in various parts of Latin America required intelligent responses from them. In Central America the treaty signed in 1958 by its five states demonstrated a desire to begin implementing steps toward the goal of regional economic unity as embodied in the Central American Common Market (CACM). Another hoped-for translation of ideals into realities accompanied the Latin American Free Trade Association (LAFTA) which was formulated in February 1960 in a treaty written in Montevideo. LAFTA membership, which counted Peru and all the other independent areas of South America, plus Mexico, potentially represented a Latin American counterpart of the European Economic Community and, as such, Japanese economic plans regarding Peru and other individual countries invited additional evaluation within regional contexts.[16] Needless to say, MITI, JETRO, the Federation of Economic Organizations (Keidanren), and other bodies, public and private, alertly observed these changing prospects.

Throughout these first two postwar decades trading considerations dominated Japanese-Peruvian economic ties which, in turn, were paramount. Emigration from Japan to Peru, a prime factor in the thinking of those who felt that the renewal of relations between the two nations had to repeat the earlier pattern, never competed with commerce in this period. On the other hand, Japanese investment in Peru rapidly complemented their commerical interests.

Investment

Japanese investment in Peru represented a postwar innovation. In prewar years numerous factors, among them the shortage of risk capital in Japan for overseas ventures, the limited stimulus afforded by the economic position of the Japanese-Peruvians, and the greater attraction of East Asia, had militated against such a development. In the postwar years, however, the changed nature and anti-Japanese outlook of East Asia and the greater productive capacity of newly built and efficient industrial plants demanded ever-increasing quantities of raw materials which, in turn, suggested overseas investments as a means of assuring a continuing supply. In addition to fulfilling real needs, Japan, as she boldly assumed the role of overseas investor, was again simply adopting a tactic already subscribed to by the United States, Great Britain, France, West Germany, and other advanced industrial nations.

From the very beginning, complexity and variety marked Japanese investment in Peru. Some of it went into enterprises calculated to meet the Japanese need for raw materials. Other investments improved Peruvian capacity to produce and transport products. Still other Japanese investment contributed to the unification and development of the Peruvian economy, increasing per capita income and capacity to consume. On occasion the investment was that of a single company. At the other extreme was the venture that embraced numerous businesses and banks in a single Japanese project. Some undertakings the Japanese financed completely, others took the form of joint Japanese-Peruvian ventures.

Reflecting the widening role of Peruvian minerals in Japan's industrial revival was the activity in the autumn of 1956. Two Japanese companies and a Peruvian company sought to establish a joint operation to develop an iron ore mine near the port of Chala in the Department of Arequipa. In addition to conducting surveys and providing capital, the two Japanese firms — the Mitsubishi Trading Company and the Mitsubishi Mining Company — needed their government's approval of the venture. By the following spring

Japanese mining interests were considering a Peruvian government bid for technical cooperation in the development of underground resources.[17] Changes characterized both of these moves — large-scale investment in Peru by Japan, and the reduction of Peruvian dependence on Western capital by drawing Japan into her program of economic development.

As the Japanese economy recovered and expanded, the need for copper, lead, zinc, iron, and other metals encouraged the surveys which prefaced both investment and trade. In the autumn of 1958 a six-man survey mission representing the Overseas Mineral Resources Development Association went to Peru to investigate mineral resources. Such visitors the Peruvians warmly welcomed, perhaps all the more so because recent quotas were limiting Peruvian penetration of the United States market.[18]

Although minerals predominated, other opportunities also attracted Japanese capital. The Japan Plant Association became interested in a fertilizer plant proposal by the Guano Development Public Corporation, a Peruvian government agency. Since yield of the offshore guano islands no longer satisifed Peruvian demands for fertilizer, a Japanese firm negotiated to establish a fertilizer plant at Chimbote. On occasion, as in the proposal to establish railroad communications between Cuzco and the rich Quillabamba Valley, Japanese investment aimed at regional economic development at the elementary level. Another example of Japanese investment serving Peruvian regional development was a twelve-year program in the Department of Tacna. A multipurpose project, it called for Japanese capital and technical know-how in the development of agricultural resources. Basic to that end was a hydroelectric and irrigation scheme which in turn required Tokyo Shibaura Electric (Toshiba) to furnish turbines and generators for the power station. In all this, the liberal economic outlook of Peruvian authorities complemented Japanese investment interests.[19]

During the 1960s additional factors prompted Japanese investment in Peru. Along with the mounting industrial prosperity of Japan that produced investment capital for export, several underlying truths characterized Japanese-Peruvian trade. The Japanese appetite for Peruvian raw materials, growing much faster than Peruvian capacity to consume Japanese goods, promised a mounting trade imbalance unless some other factor entered the picture. Profitable investment within Peru could counteract some of the imbalance. Increased investment possessed even more appeal because of Peruvian emphasis upon industrialization, the Japanese realizing that goods produced within the country would not generate as much opposition and restrictive legislation from economic nationalists as would foreign-produced commodities. For example, the proposed stiffening of the Peruvian tariff on ceramic ware, while routinely encouraging protest in 1963 from the Japan Porcelain and Ceramic Ware Export Association, also led the Japanese to consider investment within Peru preferable to endless efforts to hurdle higher and higher tariff schedules. Consequently the combination of available capital, a desire to improve their balance of payments with Peru, and Peruvian economic nationalism that increasingly emphasized industrialization sped Japanese investment there.

Promulgated on November 22, 1963, Supreme Decree No. 80 opened a tax-exempt door for the inauguration of new motor vehicle assembly operations in Peru. Accompanied by tighter restrictions on the importation of assembled cars, this sparked the interest of North American and European as well as Japanese auto manufacturers as all eyed the market that previously had welcomed approximately twenty thousand vehicles annually. Nissan Motor, Toyota Motor, and Mitsubishi Heavy Industries promptly planned to produce cars in Peru. By mid-1964 Nissan had plans for a Lima-based plant capable of producing two thousand cars yearly. While Nissan was financing its Peruvian operation 100 percent, Toyota projected a smaller one, a joint Japanese-Peruvian undertaking. The less elaborate plans of Mitsubishi Heavy Industries anticipated the production of two of its passenger car models in Peru. Before the end of 1964 a fourth Japanese manufacturer, Isuzu Motors Ltd., formed a joint venture for the marketing of its cars in Peru but made no move to manufacture them there.[20]

Japanese investment in Peruvian oil was designed to produce petroleum products for Peru, not Japan. Whereas need and geography had long since wedded the domestic oil requirements of Japan to Middle East sources, the Japanese contribution, via Nissan, Toyota, and other automotive manufacturers, toward Peru's entering more fully into the automotive age, suggested lively concern about the fuel supply that Peru did and would need. In mid-1965 the Peruvian state oil enterprise granted to a Japanese consortium consisting of Marubeni-Iida and Japan Gasoline Company the contract to construct the $18 million oil refinery "La Pampilla" near Ventamilla, a small coastal community north of Callao. Late in

1967 President Belaúnde Terry dedicated the completed twenty-thousand-barrel-per-day facility. Three years later this refinery, the second largest in Peru, would be scheduled for 50 percent expansion.[21]

The major magnet, however, for Japanese investors proved to be Peruvian mining. Generally a big project precipitated long study and a complex consortium arrangement. The Chapi copper mine development in southern Peru illustrated this. Numerous technicians and technical studies preceded the proposed investment of $200 million by a Peruvian-Japanese consortium. Needless to say, every project did not succeed and some that collapsed provided unpleasant memories. For example, the Mitsui Mining & Smelting Company's failure to complete a transaction involving a zinc and lead mine near Pallasca resulted in a fine being assessed against that company. Nevertheless Japanese mineral interests persistently focused on Peru, that country constituting the principal supplier of zinc and the fourth largest supplier of lead and copper to Japan. The head of a twelve-man mining mission, S. Yamagata, voiced optimism when he foresaw an 80 percent increase in Japanese mineral needs in 1967-72.[22]

Marine products also attracted Japanese capital to Peru, in spite of the fisheries dispute that was causing friction between the two nations. As early as mid-1963 Mitsui and Company, Ltd. contributed to the rapid expansion of the fish meal industry when it advanced 65 percent of the capital needed to launch Industrias Marítimas de Supe, S.A. in conjunction with a Peruvian operator. Inasmuch as Peru lagged behind advanced nations in the utilization of fish products as food supplies, it was not unexpected when Lima also looked to Tokyo for expert assistance. The request sponsored by both the Peruvian and Ecuadorian governments that brought a semi-official Japanese mission to help develop the fishing industries fitted into the plans whereby Peru projected fishing fleets and canneries—both of which might call for Japanese financing—at Paita or Bayovar in the north, Callao in central Peru, and Mollendo in the south.[23]

Some moves by Japanese industrialists and investors reflected not only responses to Japanese economic needs and Peruvian economic nationalism but also an awareness of the structure of regional economic integration in Latin America. Action in 1965 by Sanyō Electric Company of Osaka illustrated this. A manufacturer of electric appliances, Sanyō Electric noted the tightening of import controls by numerous Latin American governments, controls intended to protect infant domestic industries. Accordingly the company moved to become one of those "domestic" industries by manufacturing washing machines and refrigerators in two Latin American settings, in Costa Rica, by virtue of which it gained entry into the CACM, and in Peru, which afforded it access to the far-flung LAFTA market.[24]

In a few years, in the 1950s and 1960s, Japanese investment in Peru moved from small, tentative beginnings to large, long-range commitments. Enthusiasm and optimism from both sides accompanied the moves. The Japanese saw fewer obstacles to their access to needed raw materials and a bigger market for their products. The Peruvians welcomed aid that advanced their economy in general and their industrialization program in particular while diminishing their dependence upon the Western powers that had long contributed to the inferiority complex of many Peruvians.

Technical Assistance

Both Japan and Peru quickly recognized the desirability of combining technical assistance with investment. Some of that assistance was short-term, preliminary, and related to individual enterprises, but on other occasions it was of long duration, touching multi-faceted regional undertakings. Like trade and investment, Japanese technical assistance in Peru started from scratch and attained significant proportions in a few years.

The early postwar Peruvian attitude concerning immigration, that of welcoming "skilled and specialized workers only" hinted both at the emphasis to be given her economic development and at an important role that foreigners might play in it. A decade later in mid-1956, Kunio Morishita, back home from Peru, reiterated Peruvian interest in industrial experts. Early in 1957 Peru applied to the Japanese government for technical cooperation in the development of her underground resources. The Japan Mining Industry Association concluded that this request was prompted by the recent visit to Lima of seven mining experts en route to Bolivia. In 1958 the Japan Plant Association ordered its fertilizer plant mission, then in Brazil, to Peru in response to another request from Lima authorities. In this manner a pattern of Japanese activities that embraced much of Latin America and other areas of the developing world came to Peru. When César F.F. Libao arrived in Tokyo in October 1958 for six months' training, he represented the first technical trainee from Peru to go to Japan.[25]

Needless to say, the language barrier constituted a tremendous obstacle to any technical assistance program of the Japanese. Spanish was not one of the freely available foreign languages in Japanese schools and Japanese remained completely outside the scope of any Peruvian student's education. This and other problems, however, did not diminish Japanese enthusiasm for initiating and pursuing technical cooperation programs. Between April 1954 and March 1968 a total of 12,754 trainees from developing countries went to Japan, 9,497 on a government basis, 3,257 privately. Very few Latin Americans joined Libao of Peru in the Japan-based training programs that overwhelmingly involved Asians. The government-financed programs included agriculture, forestry, fisheries, public administration, postal services, national health, and other fields. The privately financed training, on the other hand, concentrated on numerous areas of production related to light, heavy, and chemical industries.

In 1960 Japan established her first technical training center abroad, in Pakistan. By 1968 that number had risen to twenty-nine, one of which, a textile industry training center, was located in Brazil.

In 1968 Japan, through her Overseas Technical Cooperation Agency, had sent out 2,905 government-sponsored technical experts to various countries, chiefly in Southeast Asia. On a private basis, by 1968, the Economic Cooperation Center of the Japan Chamber of Commerce and Industry had dispatched 3,189 technical experts throughout the world. Their research and formulation of programs did much to expand investment and trade. The Latin American research projects of 1966, for example, included the following: surveys for electric power resources in the Patia River of Colombia and in Northeast Brazil; and surveys for electrification of Puno Department in Peru, and urban transportation in Chile.[26]

Against the backdrop of Japanese activity throughout the world, the technical assistance rendered Peru might appear statistically insignificant but even a cursory survey of some of it points up its contribution to the changing Peruvian economic scene. In 1960 the Japanese government's training ship *Umitaka Maru,* a "fishing university," spent time at Chimbote, discussing problems with Peruvian fisheries experts. Later that same year a private economic mission dispatched by the Japanese Overseas Electrical Industry Survey Institute of Tokyo studied the prospects for generating electric power in various parts of Peru. A technical assistance agreement that resulted from President Prado's long-range plan for the general development of the Tacna region called for Japanese financing. The construction of a new wide-gauge railroad near Lima included in the contract a stipulation for technical assistance. Following the sale of four YS-11 planes to Lansa Air Line of Peru, Japan, for the first time since World War Two, sent technical aircraft instructors abroad as part of the technical assistance rendered the airline. Early in 1968 Mitsui Consultants Company Ltd. won a consulting contract relative to the overall development of Callao, the leading commercial port of Peru.[27]

The Peruvians frequently expressed this desire for Japanese technical assistance, which was reflected in numerous contracts. Víctor Raúl Haya de la Torre, visiting Japan, hoped his country would receive technical assistance. Four years later in 1965, Peruvian Ambassador José Carlos Ferreyros declared, "For many years Japan has been participating in the Peruvian government's development program through heavy investments and technical assistance." A year later he said, "Peru is in constant need of Japan's technical know-how and capital."[28]

****

Between the peace treaty that reestablished Japanese sovereignty and the Peruvian revolution of 1968, trade, investment, and technical assistance had assumed growing importance in Peruvian-Japanese relations. Trade, nonexistent in 1947, had reached the level of $225 million by 1968. Japanese investment, unknown in Peru prior to the 1950s, reached significant levels a decade later. In technical assistance, Japan, employing both government and privately sponsored programs, advanced rapidly. Japanese loans, initially small and short-term, gradually became more competitive, involving larger sums of money and longer periods of time. The Japanese shared the sentiment expressed in mid-1967 by Ambassador Ferreyros in Tokyo when he said, "I hope that our mutual economic relations will continue still closer."[29]

8

In a Revolutionary Era, 1968-73

A Time of Transition

Hailing the 151st anniversary of Peruvian independence, Ambassador José Carlos Mariátegui declared in Tokyo, "the world has realized that, starting October 3, 1968, Peru experienced and is experiencing many a transformation." The calm assurance of the Peruvian diplomat in 1972 regarding the revolutionary changes undergone by his country differed considerably from certain sentiments widely held at the time of that seizure of power. The bloodless coup which sent President Fernando Belaúnde Terry into exile and catapulted General Juan Velasco Alvarado to power gave pause to every foreigner and foreign power, including Japan, with interests in Peru.[1] However, in view of Japan's *de facto* recognition policy, the revolution scarcely disturbed Japanese-Peruvian relations politically. Its economic implications, on the other hand, proved quite significant. Although the Japanese exhibited no critical dependence upon Peruvian commodities, they did covet that ever-increasing trade as well as the survival of their investments.

Because much of the inspiration and rhetoric of the coup struck at the United States and an American corporation, a series of unsettling questions emerged. Were the United States and the International Petroleum Company, which had been nationalized during the first week of the new government, the only foreign "whipping boys," or was the attack on the American role in the economy simply the first barrage in a continuing anti-foreign campaign? Also, the Japanese and others were troubled by questions about the underlying philosophy, which for months remained unclear, of Velasco and his fellow-generals. Was it simply pro-Peruvian and blatantly nationalistic in a capitalistic context, or was it the exponent of "leftist" policies that would produce expropriations and expulsion of the foreign investments and investors? Awaiting answers, the Japanese conducted business as usual, consoled by the fact that their relations with Peru were solely economic, unfettered by strategic considerations and differences over the social, economic, and political reform programs and ideas that complicated United States-Peruvian relations.

Early in 1969, while uncertainty cloaked the Peruvian future and stability and prosperity marked the half-decade-old leadership of Japan by Prime Minister Eisaku Satō, overtures by both countries hinted at a mutual desire to strengthen the friendly ties between them. Peruvian authorities indicated their country would participate in EXPO '70 in Osaka, and the Japanese sponsors of the famed "floating fair" announced that the *Sakura Maru* would visit Peru first on its South American tour. For days the ship drew crowds that included President Velasco, industrialists and merchants, and the general public. Thoughtful sponsors, visiting Peru just a few months after revolution had changed the politico-economic scene there, might have recalled that exactly ten years earlier the same kind of trade exhibition had anchored at Havana in the wake of Fidel Castro's assumption of power. Following a Trade Center exhibit in Lima and the call of the *Sakura Maru* at Callao, the annual meeting of JETRO's Latin American representatives to discuss plans for increasing trade took place in the Peruvian capital.[2]

As months passed, Japan, like other major economic powers with Peruvian interests, riveted attention not only on the military junta in Lima but also on the emerging Andean Common Market. Born of dissatisfaction with LAFTA, wherein they felt individually unable to compete with such giants as Brazil, Mexico, and Argentina, and encouraged by a sense of geographic unity on the Pacific side of South America, the five governments of Colombia, Ecuador, Peru, Bolivia, and Chile took their first step toward economic unification by signing, on February 7, 1968, the Andean Development Corporation Treaty. That agreement aimed at the allocation of investment, financial aid, and technical assistance on a regional basis in much the same manner as national development corporations within individual countries. The agreement of 1968 crystallized a common outlook, but a more basic contribution to the launching of the Andean Common Market (ACM) came in the Cartagena Agreement of May 26, 1969, by which, as one writer expressed it, the big step was taken toward "making the integration idea over into developmental nationalism as a strategy of international cooperation."[3] The common denominators of rising expectations and economic nationalism might unite the five states, but their internal political and economic conditions differed considerably — increasingly so after the presidential victory of Dr. Salvador Allende in Chile. Consequently, in light of realities presented by the Andean states themselves, plus awareness of limitations suffered by both LAFTA and CACM, foreign observers of this latest regional Latin American effort at economic integration entertained a healthy skepticism.

During the second half of 1969 the commission representing the ACM member states met repeatedly and formulated policy decisions which required ratification by the individual governments. One policy decision, bearing the title "Common Policy for the Treatment of Foreign Capital, Trade Marks, Patents, Licenses and Royalties," drew more foreign attention than had any of its predecessors.[4]

With the passage of time and the promulgation of additional decisions by the Commission, the Japanese and others realized that this regional pursuit of greater economic independence discouraged certain activities by foreigners while encouraging others. The endorsement of mixed ventures, as well as the restrictions on stated activities, among them banking and insurance, proved less disconcerting to recently arrived Japanese capital than to the Americans and Europeans whose identification with Peru was longer in time and broader and deeper in scope. The need for capital and trade to implement policy statements encouraged the Andean states to promote understanding abroad. In one instance of this, in October 1971, a mission was sent to Japan which included representatives of all five Andean states. There its pronouncements emphasized the treatment of foreign capital. From the Peruvian standpoint this visit also reciprocated one to Lima earlier that year by Japanese businessmen.[5] Regulations and visits notwithstanding, the real tests of the Andean Common Market and the Japanese relationship to it lay ahead.

Eighteen months after General Velasco's assumption of power, by which time most Peruvians apparently endorsed the changes effected in landholding, mineral exploitation, business organization, municipal government, and university administration—along with a strong reassertion of Peru's claim to two hundred miles of the Pacific Ocean—calamity hit the country. A severe earthquake which centered in the coastal department of Ancash devastated large areas. The Japanese joined other foreigners in hurrying aid to the survivors of the rock slides, floods, and tidal waves that reportedly killed between thirty-five thousand and fifty thousand people. Yokohama sent a gift of funds, from Nagoya the Japanese Red Cross shipped sixteen hundred tons of rice and the appeals to visitors of EXPO '70 produced more than four times the targeted sum for relief aid. Scientific investigators from the University of Tokyo and observers from the Japanese Diet visited the stricken area.[6]

In addition to the physical and human problems, the earthquake accentuated the international fiscal problems that had been partly responsible for the ouster of President Belaúnde Terry. The junta now renewed the appeals for postponement of debt payments that had been typical of previous administrations. Four Japanese companies, Mitsui and Company, Marubeni-Iida, Nippon Electric, and Mitsubishi Shōji, agreed that debts totaling $8,700,000 and due in 1970 and 1971 could be paid between 1972 and 1976.[7]

In 1969 General Francisco Morales Bermúdez, Minister of Economy and Finance, had included the Japanese among the principal creditors with whom refinancing of the national debt must be sought. Given the size of the short-term indebtedness, the stagnant state of the Peruvian economy, and the programs of the revolutionary regime, in which, for example, the emphasis on nationalization of industry promised to curtail future revenues, Minister Morales discussed with Finance Minister Takeo Fukuda an extension of the repayment period for the approximately $50 million owed Japan, a figure which represented less than 5 percent of the Peruvian foreign debt due in the period 1970-72. When Japan extended the repayment schedule approximately a half decade, she not only accepted the inevitable but also followed the line adhered to by such bigger creditors as the United States, West Germany, Italy, and France. Cushioning somewhat the uncertainty attending this extension of credit, Peru indicated she would welcome additional Japanese investment. Although many Japanese were gingerly assessing the situation, the belief grew that Peru would not become another Cuba. Although the autumn of 1969 tidied up certain aspects of Peru's international relations, the earthquake of 1970 had speedily brought new ones.[8] However, that calamity of 1970 generated people-to-people concerns whereas the fiscal pinch of the previous year had involved only bankers and bureaucrats. Nonetheless and despite all—political revolution, nationalistic planning of the regional economy, fiscal distress, and natural calamity—a note of optimism permeated Japanese-Peruvian relations as the 1970s dawned.

The Japanese-Peruvian Colony

The assimilation of the resident Japanese-Peruvians into national life had been quietly and persistently pursued in all the postwar years, and it continued in this most recent period. The schooling received by Japanese-Peruvians, even in institutions they had established, Peruvianized them even as it contributed to their lingering Japanese ethnicity. Consider, for example, the operation of Escuela Victoria which in its early compliance with Peruvian law served somewhat as a model for other Japanese-Peruvian elementary schools of the postwar era. Its curriculum consisted of language, history, science, citizenship, mathematics, geography, catechism and sewing, plus the elective subjects painting and music. Most of these subjects clearly reinforced the Peruvianization of the student, as did the media of instruction and the teaching staff.[9]

Some of the uses to which Japanese-Peruvians did and did not put their money also indicated their reduced ties with the ancestral homeland. In 1967, the average remittance sent to Japan by a Japanese-Peruvian amounted to $3.51, a sum that indicated the paucity of financial commitment to relatives across the Pacific (see table 25).

Expenditures covering the so-called pickled radish *(takuan)* trade—those dozens of specialty imports styled for Japanese tastes—also afforded keys to ethnicity among the Japanese-Peruvian population. In 1967 that trade included dozens of items, the total value of which amounted to $143,664. Among the most popular ones were: magazines and other periodic publications ($30,139), mushrooms ($26,625), books ($11,483), cooking utensils ($9,880), sake ($6,792), toilet articles ($5,625), straw mats ($5,442), and Japanese clothes ($4,739). Reading habits, diet, dress—indeed many

TABLE 25
Overseas Japanese Remittances to Japan, 1967 (in U.S. $)[10]

Country	Number of Japanese (March 1966)	Total Remittance	Average Remittance
Argentina	19,200	102,000	5.31
Brazil	595,053	489,000	.82
Canada	29,157	759,000	25.69
Chile	365	35,000	95.89
Mexico	6,500	141,000	21.69
Peru	60,000	211,000	3.51
United States	464,332	25,941,000	55.87

sectors of everyday life—suggested that for some Japanese-Peruvians the ethnicity factor persisted.[11] However, any distribution of the total value of the specialty items among all sixty thousand Japanese-Peruvians clearly indicated the minor role played in the life of the total community by these continuing identifications with Japanese living. Even concerning those who imported the rice wine (sake), the straw mats, and the Japanese clothing (kimonos), for example, one must wonder how much of this represented refreshment and dress for special festival days only, along with the novelty of one Japanese room or alcove in an otherwise Western-style house.

To the social and economic activities which identified the Japanese-Peruvian with the broader Peruvian spectrum must be added still other factors. Metropolitan Lima-Callao, as always their primary locale, had so increased in population—the census of 1972 reported 3,485,411—that its sprawling mass of humanity made easier the incorporation of ethnic groups which in earlier times had been conspicuous. The pattern of Peruvian census-taking in 1972, like that of 1961, so lumped together all foreigners that it was no longer possible for the census reports to pinpoint specific foreigners and contribute to nativistic campaigns against them.

For a long time in the postwar era, Japanese-Peruvian population estimates remained. couched in rapid-growing round figures that challenged credulity. The estimated total of thirty-eight thousand in 1956, sixteen years after the last previous census, jumped to fifty thousand in Haya de la Torre's offhand 1961 comment, to sixty thousand in 1966, and to seventy thousand in 1971.[12]

Meanwhile the most complete, and possibly most accurate, recent study of the Japanese abroad—that by the Japan Emigration Service—had revealed the following population statistics for Peru and other leading Western Hemisphere nations. (See table 26).

TABLE 26
Western Hemisphere Japanese Communities, 1970

Country	Number
Brazil	657,250
United States	491,193
Peru	51,484
Canada	32,692
Argentina	18,790
Bolivia	11,267
Mexico	9,366
Paraguay	5,367
Chile	1,098
Colombia	1,021

No other country in the Western Hemisphere had, in 1970, as many as 1,000 Japanese residents.[13] In August 1971 the registration of resident aliens revealed that the 11,958 Japanese in Peru constituted the largest group of foreign nationals in the country.[14]

Occasionally, activity that joined representatives of the new breed of Japanese traders and investors with Peru and the Japanese-Peruvians additionally diluted and diminished the focus that otherwise might have singled out the resident colony. When the Japanese Chamber of Commerce in Peru was officially installed in September 1969, the assemblage included the Peruvian Ministers of Economy and Finance, Industry and Commerce, and Energy and Mines as well as Japanese Ambassador Yoshio Kasuya. The dominant role of Japanese nationals in this body so liberally approved by Peruvian officialdom was reflected in its Board of Directors, among whose members were representatives of Marubeni, Mitsubishi, Nissan, Mitsui, Toyota, the Bank of Tokyo, Ajinomoto, and other powerful interests.[15]

Some publications, among them the cultural and economic ones which the Japanese embassy continued to sponsor, served dual purposes: they informed interested Peruvians and identified the Japanese-Peruvian colony with their transpacific antecedents. In them what might be termed the "soft sell" handling of Japanese interests avoided any semblance of cultural arrogance or superiority.

Other publications, likewise in Spanish, were brought out by the nisei community. Apparently at least two motives inspired these efforts at communication—the community's unwillingness to be totally identified, indeed swamped, by the new presence from Japan and, secondly, a sincere desire to be understood and accepted as essentially Peruvian. As the number of Japanese visitors to Peru increased and their interests took them to all regions, the need for a Japanese-language guidebook arose. Sponsored by the Kinjyō Travel Service of Lima, and published by the two-decade-old *Perū Shimpō*, which continued its role as a culturally unifying factor, the illustrated 48-page *Perū Kankō ("Peru Sight-seeing")* conveyed much helpful information. Quite possibly the liberally distributed ten thousand copies of the guidebook encouraged even more Japanese to travel in a country whose historical antiquity and modern economic development intrigued them.[16]

While the Peru-Japan Cultural Center promoted understanding between the two nations in Lima, and the Central Japanese Association of Peru promoted numerous programs which identified Japanese-Peruvians with Peru, some prominent Japanese visitors exhibited a particularism that savored of continuing provincialism. For example, prefectural interests led the governor of Hiroshima to include Peru on his tour of "overseas Japanese colonies", and a delegation of Okinawan businessmen and journalists visited Peru hoping to develop cultural relations, among others.[17]

One fine gesture appreciated by both Japanese and Peruvian intellectuals involved a monument dedicated to the late Dr. Seiichi Izumi. In the city of Huánuco in the central Andes, close to the pre-Inca ruins of Kotosh and Shillacoto associated with his scientific achievements, there was a permanent reminder honoring the man who helped to establish the Andean Institute of the University of Tokyo.[18]

Although nisei of means continued to visit Japan, this was done without the sense of undying loyalty that motivated many such travelers in prewar years. As Peruvian universitites increased in number and the Peruvian nature of the Japanese-Peruvians prevailed, fewer children went to Japan for schooling. Such changes, part of their studied lower profile, also attested to the Peruvianization of the second largest Japanese community in Latin America. However, occasional activities still indicated that Japanese-Peruvians and other expatriate Japanese, despite the roots that identified them with Latin

America, still proudly relate to a distant and former mother country. One such episode, in April 1973, brought about two hundred Japanese-Latin Americans from Brazil, Argentina, Paraguay, and Bolivia to Lima to join local Japanese-Peruvians in an athletic tournament. In twenty-year-old Union Stadium they gathered to celebrate Emperor Hirohito's birthday. Other assertions of unity occur annually with an element of inspiration and support from Japanese officials. Regular meetings of the Kaigai Nikkeijin Kyōkai ("The Overseas Japanese Association"), usually held in Tokyo, draw representatives from Peru and all the other lands in which Japanese immigrants have settled.[19] Even as Tokyo authorities cultivate continuing ties with the overseas Japanese, it is realized that all of them—and especially the Japanese-Peruvians—have severed most of the bonds that once stamped them as Japanese.

Diplomats and Visitors

The Peruvian embassy in Tokyo and the Japanese embassy in Lima, primary and continuing conduits for bilateral relations of many kinds, have been, in these latest years, in the hands of dynamic and capable ambassadors. Career diplomats of broad experience have headed the Japanese mission in Peru, among them Yoshio Kasuga, Tetsuo Ban, Hiroshi Nagasaki, and Shigeto Nikai. Simultaneously José Carlos Ferreyros, René Hooper López, and José Carlos Mariátegui represented Peru in Tokyo. Perhaps, for a number of reasons, no Japanese ambassador has received the credit due him for the smooth progress of Japanese-Peruvian relations. They have always shared credit with high-level missions that visited Peru for specific purposes, just as they have with those officials in their own Foreign Ministry with whom numerous visiting Peruvian dignitaries reached understandings and concluded agreements.

On the other hand, in part because very few economic missions representing the private sector of the Peruvian economy journeyed to Japan, the Peruvian ambassadors conspicuously asserted themselves, implementing Foreign Minister Edgardo Mercado Jarrín's announced policy of stronger economic links with Japan. In mid-1970 Ambassador René Hooper López declared, "Japan . . . now holds second place as a buyer of Peruvian products. . . . In exports to Peru, Japan holds fourth place." Two years later the next Peruvian ambassador, José Carlos Mariátegui, listed some of the Japanese contributions to the recent transformation of Peru: loans supporting communications, fertilizer, and power projects; feasibility studies and other technical assistance; and various missions and agreements.[20] Both the Japanese and Peruvian diplomatic arms facilitated such activities.

In June 1972, the Peruvian embassy in Tokyo initiated a publication that promised to increase Japanese awareness of Peru. *Perū Tayori (Peru News)* appeared monthly, featuring economic matters, covering such themes as foreign loans, minerals, technical cooperation, fisheries, electric power projects, and petroleum. Along with concise summaries it included tidbits of spot news, historical notes, and a hotel directory for the Lima area. Needless to say, this action by the Peruvians in Tokyo, the first such publication there by a Latin American mission, possibly found inspiration in the *Boletín Informativo,* a long-time product of the Japanese embassy in Lima. Yet another contribution to communication came when the two governments eliminated the need for visas for passport-carrying visitors whose stays did not exceed ninety days.[21]

Visits by prominent individuals in public and private life continued to supplement the labors of the diplomats in both countries. Because Peru encouraged investment and sought loans and technical assistance, her cabinet-level travelers outnumbered those of Japan. Sharply focused motives inspired the trips, as the following examples will demonstrate: Deputy Foreign Minister Pérez de Cuéllar to discuss Japanese fishing operations (February 1969); Minister of Economy and Finance Morales Bermúdez to confer concerning the refinancing of debts (July 1969); Minister of Energy and Mines Fernández Maldonado to solicit joint venture production of minerals and to promote their export (August 1970); Minister of Fisheries Tantaleán Vanini to study the Japanese fishing industry, promote fish meal exports, and obtain financial and technical aid for Peruvian fishing projects (April 1971); and Minister of Industry and Commerce Jiménez de Lucio to bolster bilateral trade (April 1972).

While Peruvian officials elicited much Japanese interest in their economy and prompted the dispatch of many economic missions, surveys, and feasibility studies, the few official Japanese visitors seemingly gathered more generalized impressions of Peru. Consider the mid-1970 delegation from the Diet that talked broadly of trade and the mid-December 1972 government mission that explored possibilities of increasing and improving Japanese technical cooperation with Peru. EXPO '70, by the range of its offerings, was one magnet drawing Peruvians to Japan, and it did impress upon numerous influential visitors a richer appreciation of Japanese culture than their more specialized trips to Tokyo usually permitted.[22]

Emphasizing the rich Inca culture which had won the admiration of Prince Mikasa, Crown Prince Akihito, archaeologists, and many other Japanese, the Peruvian exhibit at EXPO '70 featured ancient artifacts of gold, wood, cloth, and ceramics. Ordinarily each foreign country, assigned a National Day, enjoyed a short-term focus of attention by EXPO visitors but for Peru the devastating earthquake of May provoked continuing concern on the part of the Japanese people. On August 28—Peru's assigned National Day—the speeches of Peruvians and Japanese widened both nationalities' awareness of each other.[23]

Private Japanese visitors to Peru, most of whom were businessmen, pursued their interests variously, in large groups concerned about trade and/or investment in general, in multicompany delegations representing a single industry, and as representatives of individual companies. In early 1973, for example, a thirty-eight-man delegation of bankers and industrialists went to Lima on a financing and investment mission. At mid-year an industrial mission arrived in the Peruvian capital to promote trade and other economic relations.[24]

Except for EXPO '70, most nonofficial and noncommerical contacts between Peruvians and Japanese took place in Peru. Professor Kazuo Terada, leading a survey team into the Tumbes Valley of northern Peru, continued the tradition of scholarly study pursued by Izumi. Another kind of publicity and challenge, that attending Peruvian peaks, combined happily with Japanese affluence to direct more and more Japanese climbers to the Andes. Meanwhile, in Japan, growing numbers of Peruvians fitted into training programs. "During 1971-1972," Ambassador Mariátegui reported, "the Government of Japan granted 129 technical scholarships to Peruvian specialists."[25]

Language, distance, expense—all limited the movement of private citizens between the two countries, but the number of transpacific travelers did increase friendlier sentiments and stronger ties characterized Peruvian-Japanese relations.

However, one kind of visitor, the Japanese fishing boat in Peruvian waters, continued to produce incidents that involved diplomats and other officials. Not long before the coup of October 1968, Peruvian authorities had detained at the northern port of Zorritos the *Hakuryū Maru* for fishing within the two-hundred-mile limit. Not long after the coup, Deputy Foreign Minister Javier Pérez de Cuéllar discussed with Fishery Agency officials some of the problems attending Japanese fishing activity off the Peruvian coast. Shortly thereafter Peruvian authorities seized more Japanese fishing units. Against the tuna boat *Zenkō Maru No. 30* they levied a fine of $11,432, plus licensing and registration fees of $3,716.[26] Lessening the prospect of a crisis, however, was the fact that even as the Japanese embassy entered into negotiations to win the release of the vessel, the new Peruvian administration was seeking an extension of the repayment schedule of certain Japanese loans. The resultant diplomatic flexibility and dispassionate consideration of problems proved important because some, among them Peruvian fiscal distress and Japanese violations of the two-hundred-mile zone, persisted.

In Tokyo, Ambassador René Hooper's words, "Foreign vessels coming to fish inside the Peruvian jurisdictional waters do not undergo any limitation other than the payment of the duties to obtain the corresponding permit" amiably prefaced the departure of a Japanese mission for conversations in Peru. Despite the best efforts of the diplomats, however, certain problems did not disappear. When the Peruvians seized the *Seishō Maru No. 5*, a tuna clipper, in the spring of 1970 and fined her operators $3,400, the case mirrored both past experience and future prospect.[27]

Trade

The revolutionary urge to create a new Peru, neither capitalist nor communist but nationalist, constituted an invitation, not a threat, to the postwar trade patterns that had developed with Japan. Her developing economy needed machinery, instruments, chemical products, and much more in pursuit of industrial advancement (see table 27). Peru had every old reason for trading with Japan, plus some new ones. It served Peruvian dignity to diminish her dependence upon some of her traditional trading partners by the diversification that directed more attention to Japan. And the Japanese economy, which by the early 1970s had become the second largest in the noncommunist world, required more and more raw materials that Peru could supply.

TABLE 27

Japanese Trade with Peru in Relation to Japanese Trade with All of Latin America, 1969-73 (in U.S. $ thousands)[28]

	EXPORTS				IMPORTS			
Year	Latin America	Peru	%	Rank	Latin America	Peru	%	Rank
1969	797,552	41,984	5.2	6	1,132,596	210,694	18.6	2
1970	992,323	52,934	5.3	7	1,342,351	210,429	15.7	3
1971	1,369,874	69,250	5.0	6	1,309,911	174,042	13.3	3
1972	1,742,423	70,840	4.1	7	1,385,638	185,464	13.4	3
1973	n.a.	140,554		6	n.a.	235,522		4

In 1969, for the first time, the total volume of trade between Japan and Peru exceeded $250 million. Monotonous regularity produced one unfavorable trade balance after another for Japan but the appetite of Japanese industry and the limited Peruvian capacity to consume necessarily kept it that way. Inasmuch as Japan's total trade with all of Latin America in the period 1969-72 produced a favorable balance, her unbalanced trade with Peru produced no serious concern in Japanese circles.

Meanwhile, in the period 1969-73, Peruvian exports to Japan increased more dramatically than did those of any other leading Latin American trading partner of Japan with the exception of the rapidly developing giant, Brazil (see tables 28 and 29).

Peruvian capacity to buy from Japan proved remarkably high when population size and per capita income level are considered. In 1970 the population ratios of 1950 and 1960 remained substantially unaltered, the population of Peru being one and one-half times that of Chile, one-half that of Argentina, one-third that of Mexico, less than one-sixth that of Brazil, and about one-sixteenth that of the United States. The per capita income of Peruvians, approximately $480 in 1971, ranked much below that of Argentina, Chile, and Mexico and did not equal one-tenth that of the United States. In this period, as previously, the United States continued to be the most important trading partner of both Japan and Peru.

Important to Peru's industrialization program were the mounting percentages of total imports represented by the machinery and instruments from Japan (see table 30). The fact that, on the average, more than 80 percent of Japanese imports from Peru continued to be

TABLE 28

Japanese Exports to Peru and Selected Other American Trading Partners, 1969-73 (in U.S. $ thousands)[29]

Year	Peru	Argentina	Brazil	Chile	Mexico	U.S.A.
1969	41,984	92,408	120,541	21,253	88,473	5,017,087
1970	52,934	95,801	166,731	31,441	93,949	6,015,462
1971	69,250	165,293	235,211	43,923	102,001	7,608,966
1972	70,840	125,797	395,337	32,454	150,663	8,970,202
1973	140,554	249,704	610,448	37,513	190,374	9,554,581

TABLE 29

Japanese Imports from Peru and Selected Other American Trading Partners 1969-73 (in U.S. $ thousands)[30]

Year	Peru	Argentina	Brazil	Chile	Mexico	U.S.A.
1969	210,694	96,415	148,283	196,756	215,553	4,094,100
1970	210,429	153,811	217,853	212,396	151,209	5,564,706
1971	174,042	119,709	223,063	241,121	170,502	4,991,937
1972	185,464	78,208	249,403	179,965	201,821	5,856,608
1973	235,522	168,459	450,851	269,209	275,542	9,279,783

TABLE 30

Japanese Exports to Peru, 1969-72—Values and Major Categories[31]

Year	Value ($ thousands)	% Machinery & Instruments	% Metal & Metal Products	% Light industry Products	% Chemical Products
1969	41,984	34.8	32.9	21.2	8.5
1970	52,934	28.1	42.9	17.2	8.7
1971	69,250	40.0	33.4	16.7	8.2
1972	70,840	47.0	26.4	11.9	8.2

TABLE 31

Japanese Imports from Peru, 1969-72—Values and Major Categories[32]

Year	Value ($ thousands)	% Raw Materials	% Metals & Alloys	% Foodstuffs
1969	210,694	77.0	16.3	5.9
1970	210,429	80.4	11.4	8.1
1971	174,042	87.6	9.1	3.0
1972	185,464	80.2	16.0	3.7

in the raw materials category reaffirmed the complementary nature of the two economies (see table 31).

Critical to soaring trade statistics were the hard-working trade missions which increasingly sought new markets and expanded established ones. In February 1972, a group of two dozen Japanese businessmen on a tour of South American coffee-producing areas, met with the Peruvian Minister of Agriculture. Simultaneously another Japanese mission met with iron, oil, and fishing interests in Peru, discussing proposals for mixed enterprises and the financial and technical assistance that could be tendered a prospective research center for Peru, Chile, and Ecuador.[34] The coffee mission reflected a growing appetite of affluent and Western-oriented Japanese, while the proposal to aid an economy-oriented research center attested to Japanese awareness of the potential of the Andean Common Market. In matters of trade, therefore, the Japanese were deeply involved, whether pursuing the possibly transitory taste of a Japanese elite or the long-term aspirations of entire South American nations (see table 32).

TABLE 32

Levels Attained
in
Japanese Trade with Leading Latin American Trading Partners[33]

$100 million-plus
    Mexico (1951)   Venezuela (1968)
    Brazil (1954)   Panama (1969)
    Argentina (1954)   Cuba (1970)
    Peru (1964)   Ecuador (1970)
    Chile (1964)   Colombia (1972)

$200 million-plus
    Mexico (1966)   Argentina (1970)
    Peru (1967)   Panama (1971)
    Brazil (1969)   Venezuela (1972)
    Chile (1969)   Cuba (1973)

$300 million-plus
    Mexico (1969)   Peru (1973)
    Brazil (1970)   Chile (1973)

$400 million-plus
    Brazil (1971)   Mexico (1973)
    Panama (1972)   Argentina (1973)

$600 million-plus
        Brazil (1972)
        Panama (1973)

$1 billion-plus
        Brazil (1973)

Investments, Loans and Technical Assistance

The Japanese role in the Peruvian economy has assumed a variety of forms, including both government and private loans, private investment, materials and technical assistance in joint ventures, and occasional direct private cash investment. The Japanese have minimized efforts at outright control in order to reduce risks and also to avoid criticism by economic nationalists. Lengthy studies by company officers, by experts producing feasibility studies, and others who contribute to the Japanese practice of decision-making by consensus have preceded most investments. Often the consensus sought involved several companies. On other occasions it included a highly complex set of decisions, as when a large trading firm or a number of Japanese companies wishing to join Peruvian interests in a joint venture needed the support of some semigovernmental development agency, the Japanese Foreign Office, the Japan Export-Import Bank or a number of private banks. In the 1970s, Japanese loans and lines of credit, virtually nonexistent in the 1950s and very limited during the 1960s, assumed proportions that made the Japanese genuinely competitive. Besides the prosperous conditions which made Japanese funds available as risk capital, the urge to invest them included a desire to expand the Peruvian market for Japanese exports, a desire to adapt to the demands of Peruvian economic nationalism, and a desire to compensate, through profitable investment, for unavoidably adverse trade balances.[35]

Feasibility studies continued to be the touchstone to all other areas of Japanese involvement with the Peruvian economy. One feasibility study illustrative of the magnitude and widening range of Japanese interest in Peru concerned a proposed hydroelectric plant at the Pongo de Manseriche, a major series of rapids on the Marañón River where it finally breaks through the Andes into the Amazon basin. A complementary phase of the study included the possibility of irrigation projects and the promotion of agriculture. In another feasibility study of mammoth proportions the Japan Gasoline Company considered a petrochemical plant which would supply products to all five member states of the Andean Common Market.

Feasibility studies not only prefaced the availability of Japanese capital, they also reflected the intensity and breadth of Japanese interest in the Peruvian economy. In October 1970, representatives of seven companies journeyed to southernmost Peru to take a close look at the Cuajone project, then the largest mining project in the country. Two months later, in northernmost Peru, a Japanese mission studied the prospects for a fertilizer plant at Talara. Early in 1971 a projected four-hundred-kilometer power transmission line between Lima and Chimbote prompted another feasibility study. Before mid-year the pipeline needed by oil fields in the jungles of northern Peru induced a feasibility study. Time and again metals drew Japanese attention. On one such occasion a Japanese mission conducted, at the request of Mineroperu and the Ministry of Energy and Mines, a detailed survey of the feasibility of developing the Michiquillay copper deposit in the Department of Cajamarca. On occasion, too, foodstuffs inspired feasibility studies, as when a mission pursued the interest of the Nippon Green Coffee Association.[36] Willingness to conduct feasibility studies led often, but not always, to additional involvment of Japanese know-how and capital. The sector-by-sector consideration of the Peruvian economy which follows illustrates this interlocking identification of Japanese feasibility studies, investment, loans, and technical assistance in contemporary Peru.

Communications

Communications, an area of modernization and national unification drawing attention in many developing countries, found Japan cooperating in the development of the Peruvian microwave system. When Entelperu, the state telecommunications agency, sought bids for such a system, Nippon Electric Company, the builder of the earth satellite receiving station which had been operational in Peru since mid-1969, won the right to supply the equipment and technology for the 960-channel microwave network scheduled to carry television, telephone, and radio service to a major portion of Peru. A loan of $13 million at 5½ percent interest which Peru would repay over the period 1977-91 backed the construction program. Authorized by the Japan Export-Import Bank, that loan also involved the cooperation of several private Japanese banks.[37] In this instance, as in others, a combination of public and private agencies in Japan assisted a state-owned operation in Peru whose services improved the quality of life for numerous private citizens.

Power Transmission

Long after the Peruvian government had contracted in 1962 with Japanese interests concerning a hydroelectric power development program in Tacna, Japanese technical missions, feasibility studies, and loans figured in the Velasco administration's power transmission program. In January 1971, a group of technicians sent by the Electric Power Development Company assessed the proposed project to install hundreds of miles of power transmission lines between Lima and Chimbote. Their favorable report won an approval of credit from the Japanese Foreign Office. The formal notes signed by the two governments embraced a package arrangement whereby the Japanese provided so much that local Peruvian companies, wanting at least to share in the processing of raw materials, complained. However, in this program, like some others, the desire of the Peruvian administration to develop higher levels of self-sufficiency lost out momentarily to the insistent demand for rapid industrialization. The Japanese government loan financing the project called for repayment over a twenty-five-year period, the first seven constituting a grace period, at an annual interest rate of 3½ percent.[38]

Oil

The emotion-laden case of the International Petroleum Company, having contributed to the 1968 coup, guaranteed a special focus on petroleum by the revolutionary regime. Yet even as the generally anti-imperialist and specifically anti-American Peruvians reveled in the seizure of the IPC holdings and their ambassador in Tokyo honored the anniversary of that event as the "Day of National Dignity",[39] it was evident that a financially pinched government with industrialization schemes needed not only additional oil supplies but also the credits and know-how that must come from abroad. Their earlier identification with the Peruvian oil industry, plus the anti-American sentiment, redounded to the advantage of the Japanese.

In March 1970, Petroperu, the state oil agency, awarded the contract for the expansion of La Pampilla Refinery to the Marubeni-Iida Company and the Japan Gasoline Company, the builders of the original twenty-thousand-barrel-per-day facility. In mid-1971, when the 50 percent expansion of the refinery was inaugurated, the two Japanese companies declared, "we repeat our desire to collaborate with the growing Peruvian industry," a desire that was speedily fulfilled.[40]

While two Japanese companies thus expanded the second largest refinery in the country, seven major Japanese oil companies and the Japan Petroleum Development Corporation were developing a large-scale project to exploit oil resources in northeastern Peru along the Amazon's tributaries. Feasibility studies included a five-hundred kilometer pipeline through the mountains that lay between the jungle and the coast. The physical and financial demands, the latter alone approaching $500 million, proved momentarily discouraging but Japanese interest revived when two test wells proved successful. In April 1973, Petroperu and Japanese interests signed a basic agreement whereby a loan of approximately $350 million for the trans-Andean pipeline will commit Peru to supply the Japanese with 375 million barrels of oil over a twelve-year period beginning in 1976.[41] This Amazon oil venture will demand Herculean labors from all concerned during the 1970s.

In 1972, the semi-governmental Japan Petroleum Development Corporation established a prospecting operation which drew five, then even more, Japanese oil companies into the Andes Petroleum Company, a joint venture related to southernmost Peru. There, in the Madre de Dios region, the new company, operating in a ten-thousand-square-meter concession from Petroperu, promised at least four test borings within the next four years. The service contract behind this venture distributes 54 percent of the prospective profits to Peru and 46 percent to the Japanese. If the test drillings bring in oil of low sulfur content, the next stage of development will include Japanese offers of additional capital and technical assistance.[42]

While Japanese oil interests were aligning themselves with future prospects in difficult interior zones, they also increased their identification with facilities already in production. In 1972, the Japan Gasoline Company contracted with Petroperu to install a catalytic cracking plant capable of producing sixteen thousand barrels of high octane gasoline daily at the state-owned refinery near Talara.[43]

Fertilizer

In the early 1970s Japanese participation in the production of commercial fertilizer in Peru resulted from a sequence of interlocking circumstances. The steady increase in population which for years had exceeded 3 percent annually was imposing heavier demands for food production from the limited arable acreage. Simultaneously the rapid expansion of the fish meal industry, based as it is on the anchovy catch, had reduced the food supply of the marine birds whose excrement had produced guano, the traditional fertilizer. The rising demand for food production and the declining supply of natural fertilizer logically encouraged the production of commercial fertilizer. In November 1970, the Tōyō Engineering Company discussed with Peruvian officials the possibility of building a plant on the north coast which would produce ammonia and urea. A Japanese technical mission directed attention to the Talara area and before year's end General Fernández Maldonado, Minister of Energy and Mines, was inspecting fertilizer plants in Japan.

In competition with a score of companies from the United States, Europe, and Latin America, Tōyō's proposal won. Backed by a government-to-government loan in the amount of $44,200,000, to be repaid between 1977 and 1991 at 5½ percent interest, Tōyō Engineering began construction of the facility. Located close to Petroperu's oil refinery at Talara in order to utilize the available natural gas, the new complex was scheduled to produce ammonia for conversion to urea at the rate of 510 tons daily, all of which was earmarked for domestic Peruvian consumption.[44]

Minerals

Encouraged by both countries, mining continues at the heart of Peruvian-Japanese economic relations. Early in 1969 Hidemasa Kubo of the Nippon Mining Company headed a mission that studied the possibilities of increased Japanese investment in the mining industry, especially in copper, lead, and zinc. A year later another mission, composed of top officials of more than a half dozen major Japanese mining companies, reiterated Japanese interest in expanding their investments if adequate safeguards existed. When

Minister of Energy and Mines Fernández Maldonado visited Japan in mid-1970, he hoped to allay fears as he explained recent mining legislation and invited Japanese participation in joint operations. Whereas Law No. 17792 of 1969 had ordered companies holding concessions granted prior to June 18, 1965, to present five-year development programs to bring the concessions to full production, the new legislation, Law No. 18368 of August 19, 1970, called for readjustment of the development schedules in order to bring about production in the shortest time possible.[45]

Early in 1969 the recently increased capacity of the concentrator at the Japanese-owned Minas de Chapi near Arequipa promised to yield two thousand tons of zinc concentrates monthly for shipment to Japan. At the same time another all-Japanese mining venture, the zinc-lead-copper Huanzala mine, deep in the interior in Huánuco Department, was shipping five thousand tons of concentrate monthly to Japan from the port of Supe. Other mines in which the Japanese held majority interest included the Condestable copper mines and the manganese and zinc-producing Gran Bretaña mines.[46]

Peru, as of 1972, was supplying Japan with 30.5 percent of her zinc imports, 13.1 percent of her lead, 7.6 percent of her iron ore, and 7.1 percent of her copper imports, the tonnage totals of which greatly exceeded that available from the Japanese-owned mines alone in Peru. Nippon Steel Corporation, for example, contracted in 1970 for the importation of 10 million tons of iron ore from the Marcona Corporation of Peru at an annual rate of 1 million tons. At the beginning of the decade six major Japanese steel firms contracted for 11,300,000 tons of iron ore to be delivered from the Santa Barbara mine over an eight-year period. Two Japanese companies also contracted for copper, lead, and zinc ores from the Madrigal mine in Arequipa Department.[47]

Some plans to have Peru serve Japanese mineral needs have been projected almost indefinitely into the future. Such is the case with the Cuajone copper project in southern Peru. Mineroperu and two Japanese companies completed negotiations which promised a refinery to produce electrolytic copper early in 1975. Behind this facility at the port of Ilo is a Japanese loan in the amount of $13,230,000 which Peru is to repay over a ten-year period at 6.75 percent interest. Another operation emphasizing the future concerns the Michiquillay copper mine near Cajamarca. Until October 1970 this concession belonged to the American Smelting and Refining

Company but failure to comply with the law of 1969 regarding financial commitment and scheduled development caused it to revert to the Peruvian government. Still another indication of Japanese interest in Peruvian minerals, this time the iron deposits in the Apurimac region of south-central Peru, found C. Itoh and Company exploring the possibilities of a joint venture with an estimated annual output of 10 million tons of good quality iron ore. The seemingly unlimited Japanese appetite for Peruvian minerals has encountered ever-expanding resources in that country, prompting greater identification with Peruvian mining.[48]

Although the extraction of ores has received their heaviest emphasis, the transportation and processing of those ores have also involved the Japanese. The *San Juan Vanguard,* a 129,000-ton ore-carrier launched by the Kawasaki Dockyard Company for the Marcona Corporation became one of forty vessels in a fleet carrying iron ore and iron pellets from the Marcona mines in Peru to the industrialized countries of America, Europe, and Asia. In Asia the cargoes commonly went to the Kawasaki and Nisshin Steel companies. In 1971, at the request of the Peruvian government, a Japanese delegation studied the possibility of establishing a new iron and steel plant in Peru whereby that country's steel production could rise from 350,000 tons yearly to 1,500,000 tons.[49]

Motor Vehicles

The Velasco government and the 1970s are revolutionizing the motor vehicle industry in Peru. Stiff regulations imposed in 1970 eliminated eight of the thirteen manufacturers. Aiming at standardization and other economies that would move Peru more rapidly into the automotive age, the government stipulated certain requirements, including prior approval of production plans. The relation of all this to emerging manufacturers of automotive parts in Peru was apparent in the requirement that the vehicle makers increase their use of Peruvian-made parts to 70 percent by February 1, 1973, and that they stop importing motors entirely by January 1, 1974. The government also dictated the production of only two models in four different categories. Nissan (Datsun) and Toyota survived the competition which forced General Motors and Ford, among others, out of Peru. Toyota gained an especially favorable position, winning the competition to produce the smallest and cheapest car, the so-called "people's car." Meanwhile the production figures for 1970, the last before the new regulations, indicated that Nissan had 5.46 percent and Toyota 10.3 percent of the market.

Toyota's "people's car," the Daihatsu, a two-cylinder, two-door sedan, soon passed a series of grueling road tests. Using a mixture of oil and gasoline for its fuel, it attained a top speed of 140 kilometers per hour. Its price approximated $1300. Despite sincere efforts, none of the five companies had complied, as of April 1, 1971, with the requirements that at least 35 percent of their automotive parts be of Peruvian origin. Although related Peruvian industry developed slowly, Toyota del Perú S.A., announcing the export of floor mats for its Land Cruiser to Bolivia, quickly exploited the advantage of working within the general framework of the Andean Common Market by establishing Peru as its distribution center. However, unyielding regulations and unrealized Peruvian industry soon stymied production of the Daihatsu. The great leap forward planned by Peruvian bureaucrats was proving exceedingly difficult of accomplishment.

Nonetheless the Japanese manufacturers viewed their Peruvian prospects optimistically. The Ministry of Interior's purchase of sixty four-wheel drive trucks for use by police patrols inspired some of Toyota's confidence. As Nissan enlarged its production capacity and investment by buying the old General Motors facility, it aimed at an output of nineteen thousand units in 1975. Helping both companies was the move whereby Nippon Densō, a major manufacturer of automobile electrical parts, established itself in Peru. In the constantly shifting automotive scene Toyota scored its greatest success when it won the competition to build and operate the only Peruvian assembly plant for auto motors and gear boxes, a triumph that dimmed its competitors' prospects (see table 33).[50]

TABLE 33
Vehicle Production, 1971-73[51]

Manufacturer	1971	1972	1973	% of 1973
Chrysler	8,212	9,530	9,897	31.18
Motor Perú (Volkswagen)	3,740	5,421	8,867	27.94
Nissan Motor	1,806	3,711	6,025	18,98
Toyota del Perú	2,584	4,501	6,096	19.20
Volvo (trucks & buses)	297	633	856	2.70
	16,639	23,796	31,741	100.00

Fishing

The persistence characteristic of Japanese land-based activities also marked their interest in Peruvian fishing projects. The week that witnessed the fall of the Belaúnde Terry administration also saw Taiyō Fishery Company, a Japanese leader in that field, move toward 100 percent control of Industrias del Mar, a fish meal firm in which it had bought a 50 percent interest in 1966. Anticipating good hauls of anchovies and stable prices for the resulting fish meal, Taiyō planned to launch thirty fishing boats, to set up plants at Chimbote, Callao, and Pisco, and to produce one-hundred-thousand tons of fish meal annually, a figure representing a 300 percent increase. Some of this optimism derived from recent experience and some, quite probably, related to the survey of the ocean currents and varieties of fish off Peru conducted by the *Kaiyō Maru,* a research facility of the Fisheries Agency of the Japanese Ministry of Agriculture and Forestry.[52]

While Taiyō Fishery, basing its operation at Atico, was becoming one of the top fish meal producers (30,746 metric tons in 1970) and while Momoi Fishing Net Manufacturing Company and Teijin Limited were successfully marketing their nets in Peru, the export of Peruvian fish meal to Japan fluctuated widely (see table 34).

TABLE 34
Japanese Purchases of Peruvian Fish Meal, 1965-72

Year	Metric tons
1965	53,529
1966	67,937
1967	45,939
1968	97,578
1969	54,242
1970	65,372
1971	n.a.
1972	22,000

A periodic shift of the Niño Current so reduced the anchovy catch that Peruvian authorities, on June 28, 1972, suspended all anchovy fishing in their territorial waters for an indefinite period. Fish meal exports, a perennial earner of foreign exchange for Peru, dropped 18.8 percent that year.[53]

While Taiyō Fishery was having its problems with anchovies, Compañía Ballenera del Kinkai S.A., the Peruvian-based whaling operation of Nihon Kinkai Hogei Company, was looking for the whales whose meat formed a basic ingredient in a Japanese sausage. In time the success of the only whaling station in the country drew the attention of Peruvian officials, including Minister of Agriculture José Benavides. [54]

Early in 1971, in response to official Peruvian invitations, two groups of Japanese experts went to Peru, one to assist the expansion of the edible fisheries program of that government, the second, a group of marine engineers, to assist in the construction of small fishing vessels. Both were technical assistance programs of considerable duration, the fisheries consultants going on one-year assignments and the boat-builders for at least six months.

In the same period Minister of Fisheries Javier Tantaleán Vanini visited Japan at the invitation of the Mitsui Company to study fishery practices and to obtain financial and technical aid. Simultaneously, under terms of an agreement signed in mid-January 1971, steps were taken to implement the intended six-months experimental fishing operations which, if successful, anticipated a joint fishery venture between the Peruvian government and two Japanese companies, Nihon Hogei and Mitsubishi. Early in 1973 the Peruvian government ordered the construction in Japan of a seven-hundred-ton fishing boat and before mid-year a joint fishery venture, Challwa del Perú S.A., with authorized capital of $325 million, of which Peru would supply 34 percent, was established by the Peruvian government and the two Japanese companies.[55]

In the early 1970s the fish resources of the Pacific portended that those waters, in addition to moving commerce between the two countries, would in the future provide episodes of friction as well as instances of cooperation between Japan and Peru.

Shipping

Transpacific shipping lines, long monopolized by Japan in Peruvian-Japanese traffic, also reflected the changing economic outlook of Peru. While Ishikawajima-Harima Heavy Industries agreed to provide technological and management assistance to Metal Empresa S.A., a Peruvian shipbuilding company whose prior experience had been limited to very small vessels, Compañia Peruana de Vapores, a state agency, charted plans for regular service to Japan. By 1972, Ishikawajima-Harima had designed a large drydock for the Peruvian naval shipyard at Sima and had delivered giant cranes to facilitate the program by which Peru hoped to build supertankers. That year Japanese attention also included the prospective operation of a mercantile fleet under the combined auspices of the Andean Common Market countries. However, while plans for national and regional merchant marines occupied Peruvians and other South Americans, Kawasaki Kisen Kabushiki Kaisha, (K.K.K.K.) Ltd., Mitsui (O.S.K.) Line Ltd., and other Japanese shippers continued to serve the transpacific maritime needs of Peru.[56]

****

In view of the economic outlook and the policies of the post-1968 administration in Peru, technical assistance, a minor factor in earlier years, has assumed major proportions in Japanese-Peruvian relations. In this matter Japan naturally was but one of many countries to which Peru turned. For the development of the petroleum industry, for example, the Ministry of Energy and Mines received and welcomed offers of assistance from France, Italy, Mexico, and Rumania as well as Japan. Helping to coordinate the Japanese assistance, public and private, was the Japan Consulting Institute, a semi-official technical consulting organization with offices in Peru. The resulting technical assistance varied greatly, involving the relatively simple and the obviously complex, the short-term and the long-term, specific instances of which have been discussed.[57] On occasion the circumstances inviting Japanese technical assistance derived from the revolutionary outlook of contemporary Peru. In other instances longer-range continuity of Peruvian policy was discernible. Meanwhile the Japanese have shown continued willingness to cooperate.

Increasingly the long-term economic identification of Japan with Peru—in terms of surveys, feasibility studies, trade, investment, loans, and technical assistance—has been through joint ventures. Because joint operations afford Peru greater control over her total economic development, the Velasco administration has repeatedly insisted upon them. Numerous statements by Minister of Economy and Finance Morales Bermúdez and Minister of Energy and Mines Fernández Maldonado, among others, have attested to this. The resultant mixed companies call for a minimum 25 percent holding by the Peruvian government. In terms of taxes, financing, and political influence, the advantages accruing to mixed companies make competiton by purely private foreign companies almost unthinkable.[58] However, as the Peruvian government becomes a party to economic enterprises, workers in these joint operations appear increasingly inclined to engage in strikes, trusting that their government will support their demands in the eventual settlements.

Any strictly statistical account of Japanese and American aid and investment in Peru, while overwhelmingly favorable to the United States, would ignore so many diverse realities and trends as to prove deceptive. In terms of individuals involved in technical assistance programs, for example, the number of American Peace Corpsmen, alone, would dwarf the total number of Japanese technicians in Peru. However, the Japanese presence, employing a single-focus economic emphasis, does not fragment its identification with Peru as have those members of the Peace Corps.

In similar fashion Japanese and American investments there have not meant the same thing. Whereas Japanese investment and loans, whether public or private, have related almost 100 percent to economic matters, those of the United States have fallen into a number of categories, many of them economically unproductive (see table 35).

TABLE 35
U.S. Foreign Aid to Peru, 1948-72[59]

Period	Total	Loans
Marshall Plan (1948-52)	$ 1,800,000	$ 0
Mutual Security Act (1953-61)	56,000,000	32,500,000
Agency for Int'l Development (1962-72)	173,000,000	111,300,000

In the 1948-52 interval, during which Japan lacked the capacity to give or lend any funds to Peru, the United States was also disinclined to do so. In the second period, 1953-61, when Japanese economic aid to Peru began, much of the United States aid, related to security issues born of the Cold War, had little or nothing to do with the economic development of the country. In the third interval, 1962-72, during which Japanese aid, rapidly advancing, stayed closely allied to economic considerations, the larger American sums again represented such a maze of military, political, and social considerations—as well as economic ones—that meaningful comparison with the Japanese is impossible.

Meanwhile direct investment by Japanese and Americans has registered trends that are more significant than precise annual statistics (see table 36).

TABLE 36
U.S. Direct Investment in Peru, 1955-71[60]

Year	Value (Millions of $)
1955	305
1960	496
1965	565
1968	692
1969	721
1970	688
1971	688

In all these years American direct investment greatly exceeded that of the Japanese, but in the post-1968 years Japanese investment has grown rapidly while American investment has become relatively static, in some instances reduced.

Significant in any statistical view of the two countries' relations with Peru are several underlying truths: (1) Japanese relations have been single-focus, totally economic, while those of the United States, born of military, social, and political considerations as well as economic ones, have been widely dispersed and even contradictory; and (2) the present revolutionary regime in Peru is synonymous with an anti-imperialist outlook that darkens the prospects of enterprises owned outright by Americans while the joint venture concept which makes the Japanese partners of the Peruvian government affords them continuing optimism.

The Centenary of 1973

As the day approached, both countries scheduled numerous activities to honor the century of diplomatic relations that dated from August 21, 1873.

In Japan, coinciding with the hundredth anniversary of Captain Aurelio García y García's presentation of his diplomatic credentials, the Peruvian training ship *Independencia* paid a seven-day visit.

There, too, hundreds of items reflective of Peru and Peruvian life went on exhibition, sponsored jointly by the Peruvian government and JETRO.

In Peru the Japanese training ship *Katori* and the destroyer *Kikuzuki* made goodwill calls at Callao and some forty-five stars of the Japanese stage, screen, and television presented, as a contribution to the centennial ceremonies, a charity performance at the Peru-Japan Cultural Center in Lima.

On the exact anniversary a more formal ceremony in the Peruvian capital brought Foreign Minister Miguel Ángel de la Flor Valle and Ambassador Shigeto Nikai together with other dignitaries in Torre Tagle Palace.

On both sides of the Pacific expressions of friendship and optimism were exchanged. In Tokyo the dedication of a new Peruvian embassy building signified the solid basis on which the Lima authorities approached the second century of relations with Japan. In Peru tens of thousands of prosperous, law-abiding descendants of Japanese settlers, along with the investments, loans, and technicians from Japan, reflected both the achievements and the aspirations of the Japanese.[61]

9

Retrospect and Prospect

In 1873 a single, accidental issue—the movement of Chinese laborers from China to Peru—forced the opening of Japanese-Peruvian relations. In 1973, on the other hand, a multiplicity of planned interests guarantee continuing relations between the two nations.

Because their first contacts derived from accidental circumstances and enjoyed no mutual and continuing factors, the treaty of 1873 ushered in a sterile quarter of a century in the history of Japanese-Peruvian relations. In the absence of meaningful contacts, the tie between the two governments lapsed and none developed between the peoples. In the 1890s, however, the changing nature of Japan—increasingly world-oriented, overcrowded, and emigration-minded—sufficiently coincided with a Peruvian need for agricultural laborers, and the movement of Japanese there represented the initial element serving the ends of both peoples.

However, between 1899 and World War Two, in the era marked by significant Japanese emigration to Peru and insignificant trade between the two, many social and economic factors created friction between host and immigrant. Japanese ethnicity contributed greatly to the rise of Peruvian ill-will. The unflagging loyalty to Japan that included failure to become naturalized Peruvians induced suspicions and hostility, as did the establishment of Japanese-language schools, the creation of numerous affiliated societies, the sending of children to Japan for advanced schooling, and the looking to and taking of directions from official representatives of Japan in Peru. Quite simply, and for decades, the Japanese in Peru resisted, even defied, Peruvianization, aided and abetted by Japanese officialdom.

The first four decades of the twentieth century also witnessed bitter Peruvian reaction to the Japanese settlers on economic grounds. The Japanese tendency to follow and compete with one another in given occupations gave voice to Peruvian complaints of monopoly by the immigrants in numerous areas, but especially in metropolitan Lima-Callao. Indeed the measure of economic success enjoyed by the Japanese tended, in Peruvian minds, to magnify their numbers and to present a threat to the Hispanic nature of Peru. To every earlier economic reason for Peruvian hostility toward the Japanese, the Great Depression gave added emphasis which, in turn, rumor and emotion magnified unreasonably.

When World War Two became a concern of Peru, that government eagerly accepted the opportunity afforded by wartime suspicions, fears, and hatred to relieve itself of approximately 10 percent of its Japanese-Peruvian population. The wartime deportation policy, plus postwar refusal to readmit deportees, did much to blacken the name of Peru in the minds of would-be postwar Japanese emigrants.

The last quarter century, unlike earlier periods of Japanese-Peruvian relations that either lacked any foundation or had a weak one, has featured economic interests that are both mutually advantageous and economically complementary for Japan and Peru. Trade, significant for the first time in those relations, has emphasized Peruvian raw materials and Japanese manufactured goods. Expanding trade logically encouraged the Japanese to extend credits, make investments, advance loans, and send technicians. During the half decade synonymous with the advent of the Velasco regime and its revolutionary program, every economic tie between the two nations has intensified. Meanwhile the wartime break in the contacts between Japan and the Japanese-Peruvians, the almost total absence of recent immigrants from Japan, the marked Peruvianization of the second- and third-generation descendants of Japanese, and the failure of the postwar Japanese government to attempt to shepherd them as in prewar years—all have changed the human factor in present-day relations between Japan and Peru.

Although statistics and elusive plans, offered by diplomats, political administrators, and businessmen, have ushered in the 1970s, rapidly changing circumstances have raised numerous questions. Because the Japanese have gone to Peru with their needs and products and capital and technical assistance—and not the reverse—conditions in the Andean state are especially critical to their future relations.

In Peru President Velasco, in addition to his personal health problems, no longer enjoyed the united support he once commanded. Numerous cabinet changes injected elements of administrative discontinuity. Growing political and economic opposition surfaced—to agrarian reform, to the absence of elections, and to the closing of congress. Commonly the heavy-handed responses of the regime invited continuing opposition. Even proponents of the economic revolution engineered by Velasco suggested that insufficient time had elapsed to permit the nation to digest the measure of change thrust upon it. Natives and foreigners alike were confused by the mushrooming of new state agencies that includes Aeroperu, Electroperu, Entelperu, Fertiperu, Induperu, Mineroperu, Pescaperu, Petroperu, Siderperu, and EPCHAP (fish meal marketing). Once a kingpin of growth and prosperity, the fish meal industry tumbled in almost total collapse. The government halted the granting of additional oil concessions. Uncertainty stalked Peru long before the coup of August 1975 ousted Velasco from power.

Now increased uncertainty characterizes Japanese-Peruvian relations. More than anything else, inflation and the fuel crisis may threaten those primary economic ties between Japan and Peru in the immediate future. Fewer sales of her industrial products, at higher prices, may lessen need for Peruvian raw materials. Reduced Japanese profits, in turn, may curtail, even eliminate, further investment there. Inflation may dictate the modification or renegotiation of long-term purchase contracts and loan repayment schedules, to the accompaniment of mutual recriminations. In addition, higher and higher wages for Japanese workmen have removed much of the advantage Japanese industry once had on the score of low labor costs while striking Peruvian workers have endangered the fulfillment of contract commitments. Political instability in Peru, if prolonged, can compound these problems.

Distance has always rendered difficult the human contacts that might reinforce the admiration that elites in both countries have for the cultural antiquity of the other, but it scarcely disturbs the economic interests on which Japan and Peru have founded and will continue to base their friendly economic ties.

A Select Chronology of Japanese-Peruvian Relations

1868   19 September: The vessel *Cayaltí,* out of Callao and manned by mutinous Chinese coolies, entered the port of Hakodate
1870   15 March: The Peruvian Foreign Ministry requested the U.S. Department of State to authorize its minister to Japan to represent Peruvian interests there
      13 April: Secretary of State Hamilton Fish instructed Minister C.E. DeLong to represent Peruvian interests in Japan
1872   10 July: The Peruvian vessel *María Luz,* carrying Chinese coolies, entered the port of Kanagawa
      27 September: A Japanese court ruled against Captain Ricardo Herrera in the *María Luz* case
1873   3 March: Minister Aurelio García y García presented his credentials
      25 June: Protocol designating the czar of Russia as arbiter in the *María Luz* case executed in Tokyo
      21 August: Preliminary Treaty of Peace, Friendship, Commerce, and Navigation signed in Tokyo
1875   29 May: Arbitral award in the *María Luz* case handed down by Czar Alexander II of Russia
1895   20 March: Treaty of Commerce and Navigation signed in Washington
1897   17 May: Yoshibumi Murota, minister resident to Mexico, named concurrently to Peru
      August: Peruvian minister to Japan reportedly began duty
1898   27 December: Guillermo Espantoso named honorary Japanese consul in Lima
1899   3 April: First group of Japanese immigrants arrived in Peru
      17 July: Treaty of 1895 effective, invalidating that of 1873
1903   20 June: Second group of Japanese immigrants arrived in Peru
1906   21 November: Third group of Japanese immigrants arrived in Peru
1907   12 February: Fourth group of Japanese immigrants arrived in Peru
      4 April: Edward Clarence Davis named honorary Peruvian consul in Yokohama
1908   21 May: Fifth group of Japanese immigrants arrived in Peru
      5 November: Eki Hioki, minister plenipotentiary to Chile, named concurrently to Peru
      10 December: Sixth group of Japanese immigrants arrived in Peru
1909   22 January: Consulate established in Tokyo and Enrique A. Vigil named honorary consul
      16 December: Honorary Japanese consultate closed and imperial consulate general opened in Lima, Kōji Aiba being named vice consul
1910   21 June: Eduardo Muelle named consul in Yokohama
1913   27 October: Japanese Association (Nihonjin Kyōkai) founded in Lima
      30 November: *Andes Times (Andesu Jihō),* first Japanese-language newspaper in Latin America, published in Lima
1917   31 October: Central Japanese Association of Peru (Perū Chūō Nihonjinkai) founded in Lima
1919   Dr. Hideyo Noguchi visited Peru in the employ of the Rockefeller Institute
1921   12 December: Seizaburō Shimizu named minister plenipotentiary
      22 December: Legation established in Lima
1922   14 January: Minister Seizaburō Shimizu presented his credentials
      15 August: Cornerstone of the Manco Capac Monument laid in Lima, a gift of the Japanese colony on the occasion of the centenary of Peruvian independence,
      December: Peru denounced the treaty of 1895

1924	30 September: Treaty of Amity, Commerce, and Navigation signed in Lima
1925	30 October: Honorary consulate established at Trujillo and Carlos Larco Herrera named honorary consul
1926	5 April: Dedication of the completed Manco Capac Monument
	7 June: Minister plenipotentiary Manuel Elías Bonnemaison presented his credentials
1930	19 February: Treaty of 1924 effective, invalidating that of 1895
	August: Heavy damage suffered by Japanese properties during Sánchez Cerro-led revolt against President Leguía
1931	March: Minister Saburō Kurusu established the Peruvian Colonization Association (Perū Takushoku Kumiai) to promote settlement in the montaña
1932	May: Peruvian law requiring Peruvians constitute 80 per cent of every work force effective
1933	25 September: Honorary consulate established in Arequipa and Francisco Gómez de la Torre named honorary consul
1934	5 October: Peru denounced treaty of 1924 which had been in effect since February 19, 1930
1935	31 December: Peruvian decree established quotas for imported Japanese cotton products
1936	26 June: Peruvian decree regulated the immigration and activities of foreigners
	December: Piscina Nippon, a gift of the Japanese colony, commemorated the 400th anniversary of Lima and also honored deceased Japanese
1937	3 November: Japan-Peru Cultural Association established
1940	13 May: Anti-Japanese rioting in Lima began
1942	24 January: Peru severed relations
	14 April: Japanese legation and consulate general closed
1945	12 February: Peru declared war
1949	15 June: Commercial and financial agreement regarding renewal of trade signed in Lima by Peru and Ocupation authorities (SCAP)
1951	8 September: Peru signed peace treaty
1952	8 June: Takeo Ozawa named chargé d'affaires *ad interim*
	17 June: Peace treaty effective for Peru
	5 August: Minoru Takada named consul
1954	1 October: Honorary consulate at Trujillo reestablished and Carlos Larco Herrera renamed honorary consul
	October: Foreign Minister Katsuo Okazaki visited Peru
1955	14 February: Julio Fernández Dávila named minister plenipotentiary
	September: former Foreign Minister Rafael Herrera Larco visited Japan
1956	28 February: Kōhei Teraoka named minister plenipotentiary
1957	15 May: Reciprocal elevation of diplomatic missions to embassies
	15 May: Minister Kōhei Teraoka named ambassador extraordinary and plenipotentiary
	20 May: Minister Julio Fernández Dávila named ambassador extraordinary and plenipotentiary
	14 June: Kōhei Teraoka presented his credentials as ambassador
	26 June: Julio Fernández Dávila presented his credentials as ambassador
1958	June: Prince Mikasa visited Peru
	October: First technical trainee from Peru arrived in Japan
1959	Floating exhibition facility, the *Atlas Maru*, visited Callao
	March-April: Author Aurelio Miró Quesada visited Japan at the invitation of the Foreign Ministry
	August: Prime Minister Nobusuke Kishi visited Peru
	1-18 October: JETRO-sponsored exhibition of Japanese products in Lima
1960	1 October: Jaime Luis de Orbegoso Alvarado named honorary consul at Trujillo

A Select Chronology of Japanese-Peruvian Relations

1961 May: President Manuel Prado visited Japan
15 May: Commercial agreement signed in Tokyo (effective on 18 December)
1963 22 November: Supreme Decree 80 concerning tax exemption for motor vehicle assembly industry promulgated
1964 February: Peruvian government honored Professor Seiichi Izumi of the University of Tokyo for his scientific studies in Peru
1966 February: Peruvian training ship *Independencia* visited Japanese ports
1967 April: Vice President Mario Polar Ugarteche visited Japan
May: Crown Prince Akihito and Princess Michiko visited Peru
October: Minister of Labor Takashi Hayakawa visited Peru
1968 January: Vice President Edgardo Seoane Corrales visited Japan
July: Four Japanese destroyers made a four-day visit to Callao
1969 February: Deputy Foreign Minister Javier Pérez de Cuéllar visited Japan
March: Floating exhibition facility, the *Sakura Maru*, visited Callao
July: Minister of Economy and Finance General Francisco Morales Bermúdez visited Japan
1970 May: Premier Ernesto Montagne Sánchez visited EXPO '70
28 August: National Day for Peru at EXPO '70
August: Minister of Energy and Mines General Jorge Fernández Maldonado visited Japan
August-September: Six Japanese Deputies visited area of May earthquake in Peru
September: Director-General Ichirō Satō of the Japanese Economic Planning Agency visited Peru
1971 February: Kichihei Hara, President of JETRO, visited Peru
April: Minister of Fisheries General Javier Tantaleán Vanini visited Japan
14 August: Monument dedicated in the city of Huánuco to late Professor Izumi, renowned for discovery of pre-Inca ruins of Kotosh and Shillacoto
September: Parliamentary delegation, headed by Juko Nakamura, visited Peru
October: Mission from Andean Common Market countries visited Japan
November: Minister of Energy and Mines General Jorge Fernández Maldonado visited Japan
28 December: Bilateral elimination of visas for citizens of the other country
1972 April: Minister of Industry and Commerce Rear Admiral Alberto Jiménez de Lucio headed mission to Japan
April: Minister of Fisheries General Javier Tantaleán Vanini headed mission to Japan
June: Peruvian embassy inaugurated monthly information bulletin *Perū Tayori (Peru News)* in Tokyo
July: Peru contracted for construction of embassy building in Tokyo
1973 March: Training ship *Independencia* made seven-day visit to Japan in commemoration of 100th anniversary of conclusion of first Japanese-Peruvian treaty
March: Peru offered Japan oil in exchange for loan
21 August: One hundredth anniversary of 1873 treaty, the first agreement between Japan and a Latin American country

Abbreviations

Boletín RREE	*Boletín del Ministerio de Relaciones Exteriores*
CD-H (T-113)	U.S. Consular Dispatches: Hakodate
Colección	*Colección de los tratados, convenciones* . . .
DD-J (M-133)	U.S. Diplomatic Dispatches: Japan
DI (M-77)	U.S. Diplomatic Instructions
FRUS	*Foreign Relations of the United States*
Gaimushō mf	Nihon (Japan), Gaimushō (Foreign Office) microfilm, 1868-1945
HAHR	*The Hispanic American Historical Review*
HAR	*Hispanic American Report*
"Japanese Migration"	"History of Japanese Migration to Peru," *HAHR*
JEJ	*The Japan Economic Journal (Nihon Keizai Shimbun)*
JIA	U.S. Decimal File, 1910-29, Japan: Internal Affairs
JT	*The Japan Times*
María Luz Case	*Case of the Peruvian Barque María Luz*
Memoria RREE	*Memoria . . . Relaciones Exteriores* . . .
NT	*The Nippon Times*
NYT	*The New York Times*
"Okinawans"	"The Okinawans in Latin America"
Perū kiroku	*Nihonjin Perū ijū no kiroku (Record of Japanese Emigration to Peru)*
PIA (M-746)	U.S. Decimal File, 1910-29, Peru: Internal Affairs
PT	*Andean Air Mail & Peruvian Times*
RAJ	*Raten Amerika Jiten (Latin America Handbook)*
RSEJ	*Résumé Statistique de l'Empire du Japon*
Shokoku ijūshi	*Raten Amerika shokoku e no nihonjin ijūshi (History of Japanese Emigration to Various Countries of Latin America)*
Treaties and Conventions	*Treaties and Conventions . . . (Japan)*

Notes

Chapter 1

1. *RAJ 1968*, pp. 176-77.

2. Two spellings of the ship's name appear in the records, as *Cayaltí* in those written by men closest to the vessel—in Callao and Hakodate (then often spelled Hakodadi), and as *Cayalte* in items penned by men more removed, in Yokohama and Washington.

3. This summary of the transpacific voyage derives from "Testimony in the Case of the American bark *Cayaltí*," an enclosure in Consul E. E. Rice to Minister R.B. Van Valkenburgh, Hakodadi, November 20, 1868, which, in turn, became Enclosure No. 2 of Van Valkenburgh to Secretary of State W.H. Seward, Yokohama, December 5, 1868, DD-J (M-133), roll 11.

4. Rice to Van Valkenburgh, Hakodadi, August 20, 1868, CD-H (T-113), roll 1.

5. Through the eyes of foreign diplomats, the civil war is reported in Payson J. Treat, *Diplomatic Relations Between the United States and Japan 1853-1895*, 3 vols. (reprinted Gloucester, Mass., 1963), 1:306-35. A recent Japanese statement of the northernmost phase of that struggle is offered by Isamu Yonekura, "The Last Outpost of Resistance: Enomoto Takeaki and the Republic of Hokkaido," *The East* 8, No. 2 (February 1972): 48-56.

6. Frederick B. Pike, *The Modern History of Peru* (New York: Frederick A. Praeger, 1967), pp. 115-24 and Jorge Basadre, *Historia de la república del Perú* 5th ed., 8 vols. (Lima: Ediciones "Historia", 1961-63), 4:1664.

7. Van Valkenburgh to Seward, Yokohama, November 23, 1868, DD-J (M-133), roll 11.

8. Rice to Van Valkenburgh, Hakodadi, October 20, 1868, a copy of which is Enclosure No. 2 of Rice to Seward, Hakodadi, November 20, 1868, CD-H (T-113), roll 1.

9. Copies of the Survey are in Enclosure No. 2 of Rice to Seward, Hakodadi, November 20, 1868, CD-H (T-113), roll 1 and Enclosure No. 2 of Van Valkenburgh to Seward, Yokohama, December 5, 1868, DD-J (M-133), roll 11.

10. List of Officers and Crew of the *Cayaltí*, certified by Consul J.H. McColley, Callao, January 16, 1868 and [?] to Gregorio I. Riviero, Macao, September 19, 1868, Enclosure No. 2 of Van Valkenburgh to Seward, Yokohama, December 5, 1868, DD-J (M-133), roll 11.

11. "Testimony in the Case of the American bark *Cayaltí*," Enclosure No. 2, *ibid*. Romanized a variety of ways, the renderings of the Chinese names are, at best, approximations.

12. Rice to The Japanese Authorities, Hakodadi, November 9, 1868, Enclosure No. 2 of Rice to Seward, Hakodadi, November 20, 1868, CD-H (T-113), roll 1.

13. U.S. Congress, *Statutes at Large*, Vol. 12 (Boston, 1865), p. 1058.

14. Rice to British Consul R. Ensden, Hakodadi, November 9, 1868, Enclosure No. 2 of Rice to Seward, Hakodadi, November 20, 1868, CD-H (T-113), roll 1.

15. Van Valkenburgh to Seward, Yokohama, November 23, 1868 and Rear Admiral J.C. Rowan to Van Valkenburgh, Shanghai, December 3, 1868, which is Enclosure No. 1 of Van Valkenburgh to Seward, Yokohama, December 18, 1868, DD-J (M-133), roll 11.

16. Seward to Van Valkenburgh, Washington, January 12 and February 19, 1869, DI (M-77), roll 104.

17. The full decision is in Richard Peters (ed.), *Reports of Cases Argued and Adjudged in the Supreme Court of the United States*, Vol. 15 (Philadelphia, 1845), pp. 518-98. Seward quoted from p. 594.

18. Statement of Juan Cudina certified by Consul J.H. McColley, Callao, February 26, 1869, an enclosure of Consul William P. Mangum to Van Valkenburgh, Nagasaki, May 21, 1869 and subenclosure of Van Valkenburgh to Secretary of State Hamilton Fish, Yokohama, June 2, 1869, DD-J (M-133), roll 12.

19. Acting Secretary of State J.C.B. Davis to Minister C.E. Delong, Washington, August 27, 1869, DI (M-77), roll 104.

20. Consul A.C. Dunn to Secretary of State, Hakodadi, December 1, 1870, CD-H (T-113), roll 2.

21. Pike, *Peru,* pp. 120-25 and Watt Stewart, *Chinese Bondage in Peru: A History of the Chinese Coolie in Peru, 1849-1874* (Durham: Duke University Press, 1951), p. 160.

22. Fish to DeLong, Washington, April 13, 1870, DI (M-77), roll 104, a translation of which is in *Colección,* vol. 10, p. 9. Other items related to the *Cayaltí* are included, in translation, in this volume.

23. *Colección,* vol. 10, pp. 10-12, 29.

24. Published documents concerning the *María Luz* are in *María Luz Case, Colección,* vol. 10, *FRUS 1873,* Vol. 1 and Nihon (Japan) Gaimushō (Foreign Office), *Dai Nihon gaikō bunsho [Japanese diplomatic correspondence],* 10 vols. (Tokyo, 1936-40), vols. 8 and 9. Brief historical accounts are in Treat, *Diplomatic Relations,* I and Stewart, *Chinese Bondage.*

25. Chargé d'affaires C.O. Shepard to Captain Hereiro [sic], [Kanagawa], July 10, 1872, a copy of which is Enclosure No. 1 of Shepard to Fish, [Kanagawa], July 20, 1872, DD-J (M-133), roll 20.

26. *FRUS 1873,* vol. 1, p. 530.

27. *Memoria RREE 1874,* p. 106 and *FRUS 1873,* vol. 1, p. 594.

28. *Colección,* vol. 10, p. 24.

29. *FRUS 1873,* vol. 1, p. 594-95.

30. Ibid., pp. 532-33. Apparently DeLong contributed to the non-delivery of some of his Peruvian correspondence. Instead of sending those communications in the diplomatic pouch to Washington, from which point the Peruvian minister might forward them to Lima, DeLong resorted to what he considered a faster routing of them. By ordinary mail they went to a frequently absent Peruvian consul on the West Coast of the United States. At what stage their loss occurred is uncertain.

31. *María Luz Case,* p. 4.

32. *FRUS 1873,* vol. 1, p. 527.

33. Ibid., pp. 528-29.

34. Ibid., p. 533.

35. Ibid., p. 552.

36. Ibid., p. 531.

37. *María Luz Case,* p. 13.

38. *FRUS 1873,* vol 1, pp. 526-27.

39. Ibid., p. 558.

40. Minister Manuel Freyre to Secretary of State, Washington, November 7, 1872, U.S. National Archives, Department of State, Notes from Foreign Legations: Peru (T-802), roll 4.

41. *FRUS 1873,* vol. 1, pp. 580-81.

42. Ibid., pp. 558, 561-63.

43. Ibid., p. 581

44. *Memoria RREE 1874,* pp. 76-83.

45. *FRUS 1873,* vol. 1, pp. 563-64.

46. Ibid., pp. 568-70, 581-82.

47. *Memoria RREE 1874,* pp. 84-100 and *FRUS 1873,* vol. 1, pp. 572-80, 584-85.

48. Ibid., pp. 606-629 and *Memoria RREE 1874,* pp. 121-139. At this time, as well as both earlier and later, the Mexican peso was a standard currency in East Asian financial transactions.

49. *Colección*, vol. 10, 200-201.
50. *Treaties and Conventions* (1884), pp. 529-35 and *Colección*, vol. 10, pp. 201-206. The latter title also contains (pp. 188-89) García's detailed narrative of the treaty negotiation.
51. *Ibid.*, pp. 133-184H; John Bassett Moore (ed.), *History and Digest of International Arbitrations to Which the United States Has Been a Party*, vol. 5 (Washington, 1898), pp. 5034-5036; and Stewart, *Chinese Bondage*, pp. 158-59.
52. Related documents are in *Colección*, vol. 10, pp. 207-11 and *Treaties and Conventions* (1884), pp. 536-40.
53. Clarence F. Jones, *Commerce of South America* (Boston: Ginn and Company, 1928), pp. 197-98, 218; Basadre, *Historia*, vol. 6, pp. 2690-91, 2695-96, Hugh Borton, *Japan's Modern Century* (New York: Ronald Press Company, 1955), pp. 112-15; S. Uyehara, *The Industry and Trade of Japan*, rev. ed. (London: P.S. King & Son, Ltd., 1936), pp. 10-11; Alberto Ulloa, *Perú y Japón* (Lima: Impr. Torres Aguirre, 1943), pp. 4-7 and *Perū kiroku*, p. 224.
54. "Japanese Migration," pp. 438-40 and *Perū kiroku*, p. 224.
55. *Memoria RREE 1892*, pp. lxxxvii-lxxxix and *Memoria RREE 1896*, pp. 343-46, 349-50.
56. Basadre, *Historia*, vol. 6, pp. 2996-3003 and *Memoria RREE 1896*, pp. 353, 355, 357.
57. *Treaties and Conventions* (1899), pp. 173-81 and *Memoria RREE 1896*, pp. 358-76. Related official Peruvian correspondence is in *ibid.*, pp. xx-xxvii, 342-58, 376-92 and a Peruvian analysis is in Ulloa, *Perú y Japón*, pp. 8-11.

Chapter 2

1. Kaigai Nikkeijin Kyōkai ("The Overseas Japanese Association"), *Dai kyūka kaigai nikkeijin taikai, Hawai 1968 (9th convention of Japanese abroad, Hawaii 1968)* (Tokyo, 1968), pp. 21-24.
2. "Japanese Migration," pp. 440-45; *Perū kiroku*, pp. 14-18; *Shokoku ijūshi*, pp. 45-49; Perú, *Memoria de la Dirección de Fomento al Sr. Ministro del Ramo 1899* (Lima, 1899), p. 20 and Howard Laurence Karno, "Augusto B. Leguía: the Oligarchy and the Modernization of Peru, 1870-1930" (Ph. D. diss., UCLA, 1970), pp. 77-80.
3. "Japanese Migration," p. 445.
4. Ibid., pp. 445-48; *Perū kiroku*, pp. 15-18, 36 and *Shokoku ijūshi*, pp. 49-50.
5. "Japanese Migration," 448-52 and *Shokoku ijūshi*, pp. 50-51.
6. "Japanese Migration," pp. 648-52; *Perū kiroku*, pp. 18-19; *Shokoku ijūshi*, pp. 52-53 and J.M. Macedo, "Los japoneses como cultivadores de arroz en el Estado de Texas," *Boletín del Ministerio de Fomento* (Peru) 4, No. 1 (January 1906): 80-81.
7. *Perū kiroku*, p. 25 and *Boletín RREE*, vol. 7, pp. 124-25.
8. Ibid., vol. 2, No. 7, p. 124; vol. 2, No. 9, pp. 174-78; vol. 4, p. 108; vol. 9, pp. 174-78; *Perū kiroku*, pp. 16, 20; *Shokoku ijūshi*, p. 53 and "Japanese Migration," p. 651.
9. Ibid., pp. 654-58 and *Shokoku ijūshi*, pp. 53-54.
10. "Japanese Migration," pp. 651-54 and *Perū kiroku*, pp. 19-21.
11. E. Figueroa y Parra to Japanese Foreign Minister, Lima, January 25, 1908 and Director, Commercial Affairs, Japanese Foreign Office to Eusebio Figueroa y Parra, Tokyo, August 25, 1908, Gaimushō mf, roll 735, MT 3.8.2.205, frames 440-44.
12. *El Comercio* (Lima), June 16, 1908, a photographic copy of which is in Gaimushō mf, roll 735, MT 3.8.2.205, frames 420-21.
13. Consul E.C. Davis to Governor Sufu Kōhei (Kanagawa), Yokohama, February 20, 1908, Consul E.C. Davis to Foreign Minister Tadasu Hayashi, Yokohama, February 20,

1908, and idem to idem, Yokohama, February 28, 1908, Gaimushō mf, roll 734, MT 3.8.2.205, frames 248, 254.

14. Edward L. Houghton to Honorary Consul L.N. Bryce [sic], Lima, April 5, 1909; Hon. Consul L.N. Brayce to Foreign Minister Count Komura, Lima, April 30, 1909; Vice Minister of Foreign Affairs to Hon. Consul Brayce, Tokyo, July 8, 1909; Hon. Consul Brayce to Edward L. Houghton, Lima, September 6, 1909; and Edward L. Houghton to Hon. Consul Bryce [sic], Lima, September 7, 1909, Gaimushō mf, roll 735, MT 3.8.2.205, frames 549, 636-37, 639-43, 878-79.

15. George H. Kerr, *Okinawa: the History of an Island People* (Tokyo: Charles E. Tuttle Company, 1959), pp. 398-409, 437-39. A brief account of the Okinawans in Peru is in *Perū kiroku*, pp. 73-77.

16. Gaimushō mf, roll 735, MT 3.8.2.205, frames 846-53.

17. H.H. Henry to T. Ogawa, Santa Lucrecia, México, November 29, 1911 and Japanese Steerage Passengers from Callao to Salina Cruz per Tōyō Kisen Kaisha, Tokyo, March 18, 1912, Gaimushō mf, roll 735, MT 3.8.2.205, frames 1191, 1193 and "Japanese Migration," p. 654.

18. Ibid., pp. 659-60.

19. *Perū kiroku*, p. 21.

20. Ibid., p. 22; "Japanese Prosper Along West Coast," *The Americas 7*, No. 3 (December 1920): 18; and "Okinawans," pp. 600, 603-604.

21. *El Comercio* (Lima), January 16, 1916 and *La Prensa* (Lima), January 17, 1916, photographic copies of which are in Gaimushō mf, roll 735, MT 3.8.2.205, frames 1339-40.

22. Ambassador Charles MacVeagh to Secretary of State, Tokyo, September 16, 1926, 823.52J27/1, which enclosed article from *The Japan Advertiser,* September 13, 1926, and Ambassador Miles Poindexter to Secretary of State, Lima, November 24, 1926, which included report by Pierre de L. Boal, 823,52J27/2, PIA (M-746), roll 23.

23. "Japanese Migration," p. 73. For an illustration of statistical variation, compare the years 1924-27 in Mario E. del Río, *La inmigración y su desarrollo en el Perú* (Lima; Sanmartí y Cía., 1929), pp. 159, 161.

24. "Okinawans," pp. 585-86, 606-607.

25. Gaimushō mf, roll SP 44, SP 125, frame 34 and Chargé d'affaires *ad interim* Matthew E. Hanna to Secretary of State, Lima, October 29, 1928, 823.5593/7, PIA (M-746), roll 23.

26. T.B. Cavalcanti (ed.), *Las constituciones de los Estados Unidos del Brasil* (Madrid; Instituto de Estudios Políticos, 1958), p. 438; Rollie E. Poppino, *Brazil: the Land and the People* (New York, Oxford University Press, 1968), p. 193; Yukio Fujii and T. Lynn Smith, *The Acculturation of Japanese Immigrants in Brazil* (Gainesville; University of Florida Press Monograph No. 5, 1959), pp. 6-7, José Thiago Cintra, *La migración japonesa en Brasil (1908-1958)* (México, D.F.; El Colegio de México, 1971), pp. 65, 107; Hiroshi Saito, *O Japonês no Brasil; estudo de mobiladade fixação* (São Paulo: Editora "Sociologia e Política," 1961), p. 37; T. Lynn Smith, *Brazil: People and Institutions*, rev. ed., (Baton Rouge: Louisiana State University Press, 1954), p. 229; K. Inahara (ed.), *The Japan Year Book 1936* (Tokyo, [n.d.]), p. 77 and (Anon.), *The Japan Year Book 1939-40* (Tokyo, [n.d.]), p. 56.

27. Full texts of these decrees are in *Memoria RREE 1936,* pp. 142-46 and Gaimushō mf, roll S449, S 10.1.1.0-12, frames 766-76. See also Ulloa, *Perú y Japón,* pp. 21-24.

28. *Memoria RREE 1936,* pp. ci-cii and Ulloa, *Perú y Japón,* p. 24.

29. *El Comercio,* May 14, 1940, p. 2, and *Perū kiroku,* p. 44.

30. The statistics that follow are drawn from Perú, Ministerio de Hacienda y Comercio, Dirección Nacional de Estadística, *Censo nacional . . . 1940,* Vol. 1, (Lima, 1944), *pp. 498-532 passim*. For the range and interrelationship of Japanese-Peruvian organizations, see Mischa Titiev, "The Japanese Colony in Peru," *Far Eastern Quarterly 10*, No. 3 (May, 1951): 229-32.

Chapter 3

1. *Boletín RREE*, vol. 1, No. 23, pp. 237-40, vol. 32, 192-95 and *Perū kiroku*, pp. 36-37, 46. For a select chronology of Japanese-Peruvian relations, see pp. 159-61.
2. Minister Benton McMillin to Secretary of State, Lima, December 29, 1916, 894.20223/1 and Secretary of State Robert Lansing to American Embassy (Mexico), Washington, July 3, 1917, 894.20223/2a, JIA (M-422), roll 17.
3. Ulloa, *Perú y Japón*, pp. 16-18; *Memoria RREE 1917*, pp. 89-92 and *Memoria de labores de la Secretaría de Relaciones Exteriores de Agosto de 1926 a Julio de 1927 presentada al H. Congreso de la Unión* (México, 1927), pp. 15-17.
4. *Memoria RREE 1917*, p. 89 and *Memoria RREE 1918*, p. 48.
5. Lansing to American Legation (Lima), Washington, August 14, 1919, 894.20223/3a, JIA (M-422), roll 17.
6. Minister Shichita Tatsuke to Foreign Minister César A. Elguera, Santiago, October 22, 1918 and Elguera to Tatsuke, Lima, May 9, 1919, Gaimushō mf, roll 735, MT 3.8.2.205, frames 1497-98, 1506-1508.
7. Ulloa, *Perú y Japón*, p. 16; Minister William E. González to Secretary of State, Lima, January 27, 1921, 894.3323, JIA (M-422), roll 20; Chargé d'affaires *ad interim* William Walker Smith to Secretary of State, Lima, April 8, 1920, Enclosure, 823.00/356, PIA (M-746), roll 3; *Memoria RREE 1922*, p. 113 and *Perū kiroku*, pp. 37-38.
8. González to Secretary of State, Lima, February 10, 1921, 823.00/379, PIA (M-746), roll 3; Chargé d'affaires *ad interim* F.A. Sterling to Secretary of State, Lima, April 4, 1922, 823.00/419, *ibid.*, roll 4 and *Memoria RREE 1923*, p. 89.
9. Sterling to Secretary of State Charles E. Hughes, Lima, May 15, 1922, 823.00/421, PIA (M-746), roll 4 and *Memoria RREE 1923*, p. 90.
10. *Memoria RREE 1922*, p. 113; Sterling to Hughes, Lima, September 19, 1922, 823.00/425, PIA (M-746), roll 4 and *Perū kiroku*, p. 37.
11. Vice Consul James H. Roth to Secretary of State, Callao-Lima, October 22, 1919, 823.55/4, PIA (M-746), roll 23; *Memoria RREE 1922*, pp. 113-14; *Memoria RREE 1923*, pp. 88-89; Sterling to Hughes, Lima, June 24, 1922, 823.00/422 and idem to idem, Lima, August 8, 1922, 823.00/423, PIA (M-746), roll 4. The Peruvian constitution of 1920, however, reflected no anti-Japanese stance.
12. G. Fr. de Martens, *et al* (comps.), *Nouveau recueil général de traités*, 3rd series, vol. 17 (Leipzig: Libraire Dieterich, 1927), pp. 317-18, 626-35 and vol. 18 (Leipzig: Libraire Dieterich, 1928), pp. 899-901; *Perū kiroku*, p. 37; League of Nations, *Treaty Series*, vol. 102 (Geneva, 1930), pp. 33-47; Great Britain, Foreign Office, *British and Foreign State Papers 1927 Part 1* (London, 1932), pp. 932-39; and Martens, *Nouveau recueil*, 3rd series, vol. 22, pp. 360-68.
13. Consul E.A. Dickover to Secretary of State, Kobe, February 26, 1924, 823.5594/3; Wilbur J. Garr to Dickover, Washington, April 12, 1924, 823.4494/3; and Hughes to Poindexter, Washington, April 11, 1924, 823.5594/3, PIA (M-746), roll 23.
14. Chargé d'affaires *ad interim* Gustave Pabst, Jr. to Secretary of State, Lima, April 29, 1924, 823.5594/6 and Ambassador William Miller Collier to Secretary of State, Santiago, July 18, 1924, 823.5594/8, PIA (M-746), roll 23.
15. Pabst to Hughes, Lima, June 2, 1924, 823.00/456, PIA (M-746), roll 4 and Poindexter to Hughes, Lima, October 18, 1924, 823.5594/9, ibid., roll 23. See also Genaro Arbaiza, "Acute Japanese Problem in South America," *Current History* 21, No. 5 (February 1925): 735-40.
16. Poindexter to Secretary of State, Lima, June 2, 1925, 823.00/494, PIA (M-746), roll 5; *Memoria RREE 1927*, p. xcvii; and *Perū kiroku*, pp. 38, 231.
17. Poindexter to Secretary of State, Lima, July 27, 1925, 823.00/497 and idem to idem, Lima, October 6, 1925, 823.00/502, PIA (M-746), roll 5 and *Perū kiroku*, p. 38.

18. Ibid., pp. 37-40; Third Secretary Ellis O. Briggs to Secretary of State, Lima, June 4, 1929, 823.00 General Conditions/27, PIA (M-746), roll 7 and *Japan Biographical Encyclopedia & Who's Who* (Tokyo, [1958]), p. 753.

19. *Perū kiroku*, pp. 39-40.

20. *El Pueblo* (Lima), January 7, 10, 11, 1931, *El Comercio,* January 9, 1931 and *Libertad* (Lima), January 10, 1931, photographic copies of which are in Gaimushō mf, roll S449, S 10.1.1.0-12, frames 433-37.

21. *Perū kiroku,* p. 40 and "Okinawans," p. 595.

22. *Perū kiroku,* p. 234. For a comparison of the Peruvian constitutions of 1920 and 1933 in this regard, see José Pareja Paz-Soldan (ed. and comp.), *Las constituciones del Perú* (Madrid: Ediciones Cultura Hispánica, 1954), pp. 752, 783-84.

23. Minister Yoshiatsu Murakami to Foreign Minister Solón Polo, Lima March 5, 1934, and Solón Polo to Murakami, Lima, March 13, 1934, Gaimushō mf, roll S449, S 10.1.1.0-12, frames 318-20 and *Perū kiroku,* pp. 41-42, 234.

24. *Memoria RREE 1934-1936,* pp. lxxi-lxxiii, 99-102 and Ulloa, *Perú y Japón,* p. 19.

25. *Memoria RREE 1934-1936,* pp. lxxii-lxxiii.

26. *Memoria RREE 1936,* ci-civ.

27. *Perū kiroku,* pp. 42-43; 236-37; Ulloa, *Perú y Japón,* pp. 24-25; *Memoria RREE 1936-1937,* p. xxxix and *Memoria RREE 1937-1939,* pp. lxxxix-xc.

28. *Perū kiroku,* pp. 43-44.

29. Ibid., pp. 26-28. For one Peruvian version of the Furuya incident, see p. 84. Another Japanese statement of the episode is in "Okinawans," p. 622.

30. Chargé d'affaires *ad interim* Hitoshi Satō to Peruvian Foreign Office, Lima, May 13, 1940, Gaimushō mf, roll S450, S 10.1.1.0-13, frame 53; ibid., frames 69-70, 345; *El Comercio,* May 14, 1940, p. 2; May 16, 1940, p. 2; and *The Japan Advertiser* (Tokyo), May 16, 1940, p. 2; May 18, 1940, pp. 3, 6.

31. Peruvian Foreign Minister to Chargé Satō, Lima, [n.d.], Gaimushō mf, roll S450, S 10.1.1.0-13, frames 48-52.

32. Ibid. and "Reclamos de la colonia japonesa," *Boletín mensual de la Cámara de Comercio de Lima* 11, (May 1940): 227.

Extended coverage of the rioting, countermoves concerning Japanese damages, the sending of an inquiry, and the issue of an indemnity can be found in Perū hai-Nichi bōdō jiken [Peru: anti-Japanese riots] in Gaimushō mf, roll S450, S 10.1.1.0-13, frames 1-770. This file, the most extensive on any single episode in Japanese-Peruvian relations, includes official narrative and both Japanese and Peruvian newspaper accounts in addition to statements of damage and diplomatic correspondence.

33. *The Japan Advertiser,* May 18, 1940, pp. 3, 6; May 28, 1940, p. 8; and Announcement of the Foreign Office Information Bureau, Tokyo, May 30, 1940, Gaimushō mf, roll S450, S 10.1.1.0-13, frames 356-58.

34. Digest of proceedings of secret session of the Peruvian Senate, November 18, 1940, Gaimushō mf, roll S449, S 10.1.1.0-12, frames 599-609.

35. *Boletín RREE,* vol. 38, p. 157.

36. *RSEJ,* Yr. 16 pp. 34-35, Yr. 17 pp. 40-41, Yr. 18 pp. 42-43, Yr. 19 pp. 42-43, Yr. 20 pp. 42-43, Yr. 21 pp. 42-43, Yr. 22 pp. 44-45, Yr. 23 pp. 46-47, Yr. 24 pp. 46-47, Yr. 25 pp. 62-63, Yr. 26 pp. 56-57. The value of the yen approximated $.50 (U.S.). Prior to 1919, no annual averages for the yen in terms of the dollar are available. All that is available are the monthly high and low of the yen—twenty-four different figures for each year.

37. *Boletín RREE,* vol. 38, pp. 158-159, vol. 42, pp. 91-123.

38. Ibid., vol. 46, pp. 242-43 and *RSEJ,* Yr. 27 pp. 56-57.

39. Ibid., Yr. 27 pp. 56-57, Yr. 28 pp. 64-65, Yr. 29 pp. 46-47, Yr. 30 pp. 46-47, Yr. 31 pp. 44-45, Yr. 32 pp. 34-35, Yr. 34 pp. 34-35 and Henry Walsworth Kinney, "Japan's Problems in South American Trade," *The Trans-pacific* 3, No. 6 (December 1920): 70.

Notes 171

40. Y. Takenobu (ed.), *The Japan Year Book 1920-21* (Tokyo, [n.d.]), p. 523; *The Japan Year Book 1921-22* (Tokyo, [n.d.]), p. 399; *The Japan Year Book 1929* (Tokyo, [n.d.]), p. 638; K. Inahara (ed.), *The Japan Year Book 1934* (Tokyo, [n.d.]), p. 482 and *Memoria RREE 1929*, p. xlvi.

41. *Memoria RREE 1925*, p. 43 and *Memoria RREE 1928*, p. ccxxviii.

42. Inahara, *The Japan Year Book 1934*, pp. 404-405; idem, *The Japan Year Book 1936*, pp. 416-17; *The Japan Year Book 1943-44* (Tokyo, [n.d.]), pp. 463-64 and Japan, Bureau of Statistics, Office of the Prime Minister, *Japan Statistical Yearbook 1949* (Tokyo, [1950]), p. 482.

43. Carlos Uribe Gaviria, *La verdad sobre la guerra* 2 vols., (Bogotá: Editorial Cromos, 1936), 2: 144-47, 254 and C. Harvey Gardiner, "Los japoneses y Colombia," *Boletín de la Academia de Historia del Valle del Cauca* 40, Nos. 158-60 (August 1972): 225.

44. *Japan Statistical Yearbook 1949*, pp. 481-82 and *Japan Statistical Yearbook* (Tokyo, [1955]), p. 260.

Chapter 4

1. *The Times* (London), December 27, 1910, photographic copies of which are in Gaimushō mf, roll 735, MT 3.8.2.205, frame 1077 and in Consul General W. Henry Robertson to Asst. Secretary of State, Callao, March 14, 1911, 823.5594/1, PIA (M-746), roll 23; see also *Perū kiroku*, pp. 23-24.

2. Minister Eki Hioki to Foreign Minister Germán Leguía y Martínez, Lima, April 10, 1911, and Leguía y Martínez to Hioki, Lima, May 1, 1911, Gaimushō mf, roll 735, MT 3.8.2.205, frames 1092, 1096.

3. *Perū kiroku*, pp. 133, 135.

4. *NYT*, Jan. 7, 1919, p. 7; Jan. 14, 1919, p. 3; Jan. 16, 1919, p. 3; May 28, 1919, p. 17; May 29, 1919, p. 2; July 28, 1919, p. 1; *Memoria RREE 1920*, p. 53 and David Chaplin, *The Peruvian Industrial Labor Force* (Princeton: Princeton University Press, 1967), p. 251.

5. "Japanese Migration," p. 664.

6. *Ultima Hora* (Lima), May 7, 1932, photographic copy of which is in Gaimushō mf, roll S449, S 10.1.1.0-12, frame 304.

7. "Okinawans," p. 592.

8. Francisco García Calderón, *Latin America: Its Rise and Progress* (London, T.F. Unwin 1911), pp. 324, 329-30. Manuel Ugarte of Argentina and Augustín Edwards of Chile also shared this concern. See also G. Charles Hodges, "Japanese Ambitions and Latin America," *Sunset* 36, No. 4 (October 1916): 83-85.

9. Sterling to Hughes, Lima, June 24, 1922, 823.00/422, PIA (M-746), roll 4 and *Memoria RREE 1923*, p. 89.

10. *El Tiempo* (Lima), January 19, 22, 27, 1926, photographic copies of which are in Gaimushō mf, roll S449, S 10.1.1.0-12, frames 421-23 and "Okinawans," p. 621.

11. *La Tradición* (Lima), February 21, 1927, a photographic copy of which is in Gaimushō mf, roll S449, S 10.1.1.0-12, frame 22.

12. A photographic copy, from an unidentified Peruvian newspaper, is in ibid., frame 23.

13. Poindexter to Secretary of State, Lima, May 11, 1927, 894.20223/9, JIA (M-422), roll 17.

14. *El Tiempo* (Lima), June 29, 30, July 1, 1927, photographic copies of which are in Gaimushō mf, roll S449, S 10.1.1.0-12, frames 60-61(1).

15. Poindexter to Secretary of State, Lima, March 16, 1927, 823.00/532 and idem to idem, Lima, July 6, 1927, 823.00/537, PIA (M-746), roll 6.

16. For Japanese translations and commentary as well as photographic copies of articles from *La Prensa* (Lima) and *La República* (Lima) in the period August 27-September 19, 1930, see Gaimushō mf, roll S449, S 10.1.1.0-12, frames 113, 118, 120, 124, 127, 130, 133, 138, 144, 149, 152, 154, 171-77, 180-83, 185-88, 190-92.

17. *El Nacional* (Lima), September 12, 20, 1931, photographic copies of which are in Gaimushō mf, roll S449, S 10.1.1.0-12, frames 295-98.

18. *Perū kiroku*, p. 39 and a photographic copy, from an unidentified Peruvian newspaper, Gaimushō mf, roll S449, S 10.1.1.0-12, frames 99-100.

19. *NYT*, January 22, 1939, p. 30. Somewhat later an Aprista, in exile, remarked, "it was better to be a Japanese than Aprista in Peru;" see Manuel Seoane (Lloyd Mallan, tr.), "The Japanese Are Still in Peru," *Asia and the Americas* 43, No. 12 (December 1943): 675.

20. Orazio A. Ciccarelli, "The Sánchez Cerro Regimes in Peru, 1930-1933" (Ph. D. diss., University of Florida, 1969), pp. 224-28: Victor J. Guevara, *Las grandes cuestiones nacionales: El petróleo–Los ferrocarriles–La inmigración japonesa–El problema moral* (Cuzco: Talleres Tipográficos de H.G. Rozas sucesores, 1939), pp. 140, 142 and Willard Price, "The Far-Flung Japanese," *Asia* 38, No. 2 (February 1938): 131. Guevara's essay "La inmigración japonesa" (pp. 127-173) summarized this chapter in Peruvian journalism.

21. Guevara, *Las grandes cuestiones,* pp. 144-47, 153.

22. Ibid., pp. 148, 150.

23. Ibid., pp. 153-54.

24. Ibid., pp. 154-56 162.

25. Ibid., pp. 156, 158-60, 164, 166-67.

26. Gaimushō mf, roll S449, S 10.1.1.0-12, frames 724-58 contain photographic copies of these two pamphlets.

27. *Perū kiroku,* pp. 95, 107-109 and "Okinawans," pp. 609-14. See Janet Evelyn Worrall, "Italian Immigration to Peru, 1860-1914," Ph.D. diss., Indiana University, 1972), p. 138 concerning ethnic associations of the Italian colony in Peru.

28. *Perū kiroku,* pp. 95-98, 181-83, 228-29 and "Okinawans," pp. 611, 612, 616. A chronological listing of the Central Japanese Association's activities, 1917-39, is in *Perū kiroku,* pp. 252-60.

29. Ibid., p. 237.

30. Ibid., pp. 265-66.

31. Comisión Organizadora del Monumento a Manco Capac, *La independencia del Perú y la colonia japonesa* (Lima, 1926 [?]), pp. 129-33; *Perū kiroku,* pp. 102-104, 107-108, 265-66 and "Okinawans," p. 615.

32. *Perū kiroku,* pp. 278-79.

33. "Okinawans," p. 589.

34. *Memoria RREE 1922,* p. 113; Sterling to Hughes, Lima, September 19, 1922, 823.00/425, PIA (M-746), roll 4 and *Perū kiroku,* p. 37.

35. Gustav Eckstein, *Noguchi* (New York: Harper & Brothers, 1931), pp. 296-300.

36. Comisión, *La independencia,* pp. 1-6, 8, 10-18 and Kurt Severin, "The Japanese Inca of Peru," *Travel* 82, No. 4 (February 1944): 5. Carleton Beals considered this Japanese focus on the Peruvian Indians a sort of "Pan Japaneseism"; see "Japan Invades Latin America," *The American Mercury* 34, No. 133 (March, 1935): 303. See also Antonello Gerbi, "The Japanese in Peru," *Asia and the Americas* 43, No. 1 (January 1943): 43.

37. Comisión, *La independencia,* pp. 23-30; "Japanese Migration," p. 663; *Mensaje presentado al Congreso ordinario de 1926 por el Presidente de la República Sr. Dn. Augusto B. Leguía* (Lima, 1926) p. 7; Poindexter to Secretary of State, Lima, April 6, 1926, 823.00/515, PIA (M-746), roll 5 and Boal to Secretary of State, Lima, October 29, 1927, 823.00/543; ibid., roll 7.

38. Idem to idem, Lima, November 16, 1927, 823.00/544, PIA (M-746), roll 7.

39. *The Japan Advertiser* (Tokyo), August 16, 1940, p.5.

Chapter 5

1. *Peru–Yearbook of Foreign Trade–1942* (Lima, [n.d.]), pp. 81-82, 84; Compañía Peruana de Negocios Internacionales S.A., *1941 Peru – Yearbook of Foreign Trade* (Lima, [n.d.]), p. 35; *The Japan Year Book 1943-44*, pp. 463-64; *Japan Statistical Yearbook 1949*, pp. 481-82 and *Japan Statistical Yearbook 1954*, p. 260.

2. "La cuota de importación a los tejidos de algodón de orígen japonés," *Boletín de la Cámara de Comercio de Lima* 11, (December 1940); 614-15 and Manuel Prado, *Mensaje presentado al Congreso por el Señor Doctor Don Manuel Prado Presidente Constitucional de la República 1941* (Lima, 1941), p. 25.

3. John Gunther, *Inside Latin America* (New York: Harper & Brothers, 1940), p. 187 and *NYT*, December 1, 1942, p. 19.

4. J.F. Normano and Antonello Gerbi, *The Japanese in South America* (New York: The John Day Company, 1943), pp. 79-80.

5. *Perū kiroku*, p. 45.

6. Gunther, *Inside Latin America*, pp. 204-205, 214.

7. *FRUS 1941*, vol. 10, pp. 110-11; *BPAU*, vol. 76, No. 4 (April 1942): 234; *Memoria RREE 1941-1942*, p. xviii, *Perū kiroku*, p. 46 and Donald Marquand Dozer, *Latin America: An Interpretive History* (New York: McGraw-Hill, 1962), p. 534.

8. *NYT*, February 7, 1942, p. 7.

9. Ciro Alegría and Alfredo Saco, "Japanese Spearhead in the Americas," *Free World* 2, No. 1 (February 1942): 81-84 and ibid., No. 2 (March 1942): 181-84; Fernando de los Ríos, "South American Perplexities," *Foreign Affairs* 20, No. 4 (July, 1942): 654-55. The impact of the Peruvian allegations was greater because of earlier statements by foreigners, such as Carleton Beals's insistence that "Huaral, on the coast, is completely a Japanese city" in *The Coming Struggle for Latin America* (Philadelphia: J.B. Lippincott Company, 1938), p. 18.

10. Edward N. Barnhart, "Japanese Internees from Peru," *Pacific Historical Review* 31, No. 2 (May 1962): 170-72; *NYT*, March 31, 1942 p. 3, and Manuel Prado, *Mensaje presentado al Congreso por el Señor Doctor Don Manuel Prado Presidente Constitucional de la República 1942* (Lima, 1942), p. 18. The Japanese-Peruvians interned in the United States, as well as other wartime Japanese internees from Latin America, were in the custody of the Immigration and Naturalization Sevice (INS) and subject to investigation and review by the Federal Bureau of Investigation. The file on each unmarried person and every head of family gradually expanded, including "Report of Enemy Alien in Custody," "Petition for Repatriation," and the "General Information Form." The last-named item, a twenty-page form which included fifty-eight multipart questions, covered in detail the social, political, and economic background of the individual.

The Department of Justice, through the INS, has kindly permitted the writer to study scores of those files. Committed to protect the identity of the individuals concerned, the writer finds it desirable to cite the cases simply by file number.

11. *Memoria RREE 1942-1943*, pp. vii-viii.

12. U.S. Department of Justice, INS Files 146-13-2-528, 146-13-2-1319, 146-13-2-512 and 146-13-2-1326.

13. Ibid., Files 146-13-2-439 and 146-13-2-483.

14. For a general treatment of this theme, see Barnhart, "Citizenship and Political Tests in Latin American Republics in World War II," *HAHR* 42, No. 3 (August 1962): 297-332.

15. U.S. Department of Justice, INS File 146-13-2-1864.

16. Severin, "The Japanese Inca of Peru," p. 31; Seoane, "The Japanese Are Still in Peru," p. 676; and "Okinawans," p. 587.

17. *NYT*, March 31, 1942, p. 3; April 6, 1942, p. 4; Norweb to Secretary of State, Lima, September 1, 1942, 894.246/2, JIA (M-422), roll 18.

18. Barnhart, "Japanese Internees," p. 172, n13; *FRUS 1941*, vol. 6, p. 102; *FRUS 1945*, vol. 9, p. 326; *NYT*, March 7, 1942, p. 5; May 10, 1942, p. 2; December 1, 1942, p. 19; May 21, 1944, p. 12; "Okinawans," p. 588; Gardiner, "Los japoneses y Colombia," p. 228; C. Harvey Gardiner, "The Japanese and Central America," *Journal of Interamerican Studies and World Affairs* 14, No. 1 (February 1972): 22-23 and idem, "Los japoneses y el Ecuador," *Boletín de la Academia de Historia del Valle del Cauca* 41, Nos. 161-64 (December 1973): 796-97.

19. A complete telling of the internment of the Latin-American Japanese, unlike the oft-told internment of Japanese-Americans, awaits scholarly attention.

20. Prado, *Mensaje 1942*, p. 18 and *NYT*, May 10, 1942, p. 38.

21. *Perū kiroku*, p. 31 and *NYT*, June 30, 1942, p. 6; July 13, 1942, p. 13. For locations and dates of the establishment of the Japanese schools, see "Okinawans," p. 615, n63 and *Perū kiroku*, pp. 265-66.

22. "Okinawans," pp. 593, 601, 604, 607.

23. *FRUS 1943*, vol. 6, pp. 720-71, 723-24. Concerning one Japanese-related fire, see "Japanese in Peru," *The Inter-American* 2, No. 5 (May 1943):5.

24. "Okinawans," pp. 593, 624; *BPAU*, vol. 77, Nos. 9 and 11 (September and November 1943), pp. 521, 656 and vol. 78, No. 1 (January 1944), p. 37; *FRUS 1943*, vol. 6, pp. 731-33; *FRUS 1944*, vol. 7, pp. 1558-60, 1565-66 and Gaimushō mf, roll S580, S 1.7.0.0-39, frame 675.

25. John W. White, "Japan's Amazon Dream," *Asia and the Americas* 43, No. 10 (October 1943): 582.

26. *NYT*, February 13, 1945, p. 16; J. Fred Rippy, "The Japanese in Latin America," *Inter-American Economic Affairs* 3, No. 1 (Summer 1949): 64 and *FRUS 1945*, vol. 9, pp. 1330-31.

27. Ibid., pp. 298-99; Alfred Steinberg, " 'Blunder' Maroons Peruvian Japanese in the U.S.," *The Washington Post*, September 26, 1948; Barnhart, "Japanese Internees," pp. 173-77; U.S. Department of Justice, *Annual Report of Attorney General of the United States for the Fiscal Year Ended June 30, 1946*, pp. 12-13; *Annual Report . . . 1947*, p. 19; *Annual Report . . . 1949*, p. 23; United Nations, General Assembly Ad Hoc Commission on Prisoners of War, August 27, 1951; *NYT*, September 15, 1951, p. 2, and "Okinawans," pp. 587,588. Tigner insists ("Okinawans," 588) that of the approximately 1771 deportees to the United States only thirty-four were allowed to reenter Peru while 364 remained in the United States, all the others having been sent to Japan.

28. "Okinawans," pp. 617-19. Concerning the Shindō Renmei in Brazil, see James Lawrence Tigner, "Shindō Remmei: Japanese Nationalism in Brazil," *HAHR* 41, No. 4 (November 1961): 515-32.

29. "Okinawans," pp. 596, 610-11, 615-16, 625.

Chapter 6

1. United Nations, *Treaty Series*, vol. 136 (1952), pp. 46, 126-45 and *NT*, January 18, 1955, p. 3; February 18, 1956, p. 3.

2. *Memoria RREE 1954-1955*, pp. 92-94 and *NT*, October 23, 1954, p. 1; February 16, 1955, p. 1; February 23, 1955, p. 2; July 24, 1955, p. 7; July 28, 1955, p. 4; September 20 1955, p. 3; February 18 1956, p. 3.

3. *JT*, July 17, 1956, p. 3; August 21, 1956, p. 3.

4. United Nations, *Security Council Official Records, Tenth Year, 704th Meeting*, December 13, 1955, p. 14; *Security Council Official Records, Eleventh Year, 756th Meeting*, December 12, 1956, pp. 1-8 and United Nations, *Official Records of the General Assembly, Eleventh Session, Plenary Meetings*, Vol. 2 (Plenary Meeting 623, December 18, 1956), pp. 723-27.

5. *Memoria RREE 1956-1957*, pp. 110, 504-506 and *JT*, June 16, 1957, p. 2; June 27, 1957, p. 3.

6. *JT*, June 15, 1958, p. 2; June 22, 1958, p. 2; June 28, 1958, p. 2; July 2, 1958, p. 2; July 6, 1958, p. 2; August 3, 1959, p. 1; August 4, 1959, p. 1; August 5, 1959, p. 1.

7. Ibid., January 3, 1960, p. 3; August 31, 1960, p. 10; March 22, 1961, p. 4; April 1, 1961; p. 3; May 10, 1961, p. 4; May 11, 1961, p. 1; May 12, 1961, p. 1; June 8, 1961, p. 6; July 13, 1961, p. 6; December 26, 1963, p. 7; and *HAR 14*, (1961): 241.

8. *JT*, July 28, 1962, p. 5; July 28, 1965, p. 3; July 28, 1966, p. 7; July 28, 1967, p. 7.

9. Ibid., January 5, 1966, p. 2; February 8, 1966, p. 3; July 28, 1968, p. 3.

10. Ibid., April 16, 1967, p. 4; April 19, 1967, p. 4; May 12, 1967, p. 4; May 16, 1967, p. 2.

11. Biblioteca Nacional, *Anuario bibliográfico peruano de 1951-1952* (Lima, 1957), pp. 243-45; *Anuario . . . 1953-1954* (Lima, 1959), pp. 273-75; *Anuario . . . 1955-1957* (Lima, 1961), pp. 372-75; *Anuario . . . 1958-1960* (Lima, 1964), pp. 392-96; *Anuario . . . 1961-1963* (Lima, 1966), pp. 357-60; and *Anuario . . . 1964-1966* (Lima, 1969), pp. 402-404.

12. The activities of various official emigration agencies attest to this; see Kaigai Ijū Jigyōdan ("Japan Emigration Service"), *Kaigai Ijū Jigyōdan jūnenshi* [Ten year history of the Japan Emigration Service] (Tokyo: Dai Nihon Publishing Company, 1973) and Yoshinori Ohara, *Japan and Latin America* (Santa Monica: The Rand Corporation, 1967), p. 64. Tigner's study of the Okinawans in Latin America was facilitated by official American desire to promote their immigration in postwar years.

13. *Memoria RREE 1954-1955*, p. 92; *NT*, October 23, 1954, p. 1 "Migration: Immigration Policies of Countries of South America," *International Labour Review 55*, No. 5 (May 1947): 442-44 and Arturo Nieves Ayala, *El Perú y la inmigración de post-guerra* (Lima: Imp. E.R. Lulli 1946), pp. 85-86.

14. Kaigai Ijū Jigyōdan ("Japan Emigration Service"), *Kaigai ijū tōkei (Shōwa 27-45)* [Overseas emigration statistics: 1952-1970] (Tokyo, 1972), pp. 35-36; Tadashi Akasaka, "Nihon-nambei tōgan kōro: Ijūsha yusōshi [Japan-South America east coast route: emigrant transport history]," *Ijū Kenkyū* [Emigration research], No. 10 (March 1974): 64, 66; and John Sasaki, "Impressions of a Japanese Migration Director in the Two Americas," *Migration News* 5, No. 5 (September-October 1956): 12.

15. Kaigai Ijū Jigyōdan, *Kaigai Ijū Jigyōdan jūnenshi*, pp. 263-64.

16. Ibid., pp. 293-94.

17. *JT*, October 6, 1959, p. 7.

18. *NT*, February 18, 1956, p. 3.

19. "Okinawans," pp. 593, 597-99, 602, 606, 608.

20. Ibid., pp. 589, 624 and *NT*, March 31, 1956, p. 3.

21. *Perú kiroku*, pp. 286-90.

22. Ibid., pp. 290-96.

23. Ibid., 297; *JT*, January 6, 1967, p. 3; Kaigai Nikkeijin Kyōkai ("The Overseas Japanese Association"), *Dai kyūka kaigai nikkeijin taikai, Hawai 1968 (9th Convention of Japanese Abroad, Hawaii 1968)*, (Tokyo, 1968), p. 16.

24. *NT*, June 20, 1956, p. 3 and *JT*, April 15, 1959, p. 2; August 4, 1959, p. 1.

25. Ibid., April 1, 1961, p. 3, July 28, 1963, p. 3.

26. Ibid., February 9, 1966, p. 3; January 6, 1967, p. 3; April 25, 1967, p. 3; Ernst Zierer, *Introducción a la lengua japonesa hablada* (Trujillo, 1964), a second, enlarged edition was published in 1965; and *Poesía japonesa* (Lima, 1967).

27. *Perú kiroku*, pp. 211-13. For details concerning some of the earliest Japanese doctors, dentists, and pharmacists in Peru, see ibid., pp. 87-91.

28. *NT*, February 26, 1956, p. 3 and *JT*, April 29, 1957, p. 2; August 23, 1957, p. 2; June 5, 1960, p. 3; June 9, 1960, p. 3; April 9, 1966, p. 4; October 9, 1966, p. 3.

29. Ibid., January 20, 1957, p. 2; March 14, 1959, p. 3; January 21, 1960, p. 5; January 25, 1960, p. 6; November 3, 1960, p. 3; April 4, 1961, p. 3; May 1, 1961, p. 4; July 30, 1961, p. 3 and Ernesto Cáceres B., *La luz viene del oriente* (Lima: Editora Médica Peruana, 1960), pp. 1-67, 80-104.

30. *JT,* May 9, 1958, p. 3; May 5, 1961, p. 4.

31. Ohara, *Japan and Latin America,* p. 11.

Chapter 7

1. "Japan: Tariffs and Trade Controls: SCAP Trade and Financial Mission to Latin America," *Foreign Commerce Weekly,* September 19, 1949, p. 21 and *JT,* May 16, 1961, p. 6.

2. United Nations Economic Commission for Latin America, "Export Promotion in Japan and Its Application to Latin America," *Economic Bulletin for Latin America* 15 No. 1 (1970): 92.

3. Ibid., pp. 91, 95.

4. Kanoh Hironaka, "Japan's Floating Fair," *Keidanren Review,* No. 2 (1965): 45-53.

5. *NT,* October 30, 1954, p. 10 and *JT,* October 4, 1957, p. 10; November 5, 1958, p.7.

6. Ibid., December 5, 1958, p. 6; July 14, 1959, p. 6; February 15, 1961, p. 9; July 3, 1963, p. 10; September 22, 1963, p. 7; December 6, 1965, p. 10; December 11, 1965, p. 10; *JEJ,* July 9, 1963, p. 11; March 16, 1965, p. 3; October 17, 1967, p. 8; December 26, 1967, p. 6.

7. United Nations, *Treaty Series,* Vol. 451 (1963), pp. 21-45.

8. *JT,* April 3, 1965, p. 10; September 14, 1965, p. 10; June 6, 1968 p. 8; July 19, 1968, p. 8.

9. "Sengo ni okeru Nippon no Rabei shokoku to no bōeki jisseki suii [Japanese postwar trade development with various Latin American countries]," *Raten Amerika Jihō* [Latin America News], 12, No. 14 (May 11, 1969): 16-26. The term Latin America is meant to include the following twenty independent states: Argentina, Bolivia, Brazil, Chile, Colombia, Costa Rica, Cuba, the Dominican Republic, Ecuador, El Salvador, Guatemala, Haiti, Honduras, Mexico, Nicaragua, Panama, Paraguay, Peru, Uruguay, and Venezuela.

10. *NT* February 10, 1954, p. 9; June 16, 1956, p. 10 and *JT,* July 15, 1957, p. 6.

11. Ibid., October 10, 1962, p. 10; May 19, 1963, p. 7.

12. "Sengo ni okeru," *Raten Amerika Jihō,* 12, No. 14 (May 11, 1969): 16-18, 23, 25; United States Bureau of the Census, *Statistical Abstract of the United States; 1951* (Washington, 1951), p. 849; *Statistical Abstract 1956,* p. 917; *Statistical Abstract, 1960,* p. 899; *Statistical Abstract 1964,* p. 879; *Statistical Abstract 1968,* p. 816; *Statistical Abstract 1972,* p. 780.

13. Ibid.

14. Japan External Trade Organization, *Foreign Trade of Japan: 1964* (Tokyo, 1964), p. 245; *Foreign Trade 1967,* p. 159, *Foreign Trade 1969,* pp. 151-52.

15. *JEJ,* April 20, 1965 p. 4. Two general treatments of the issues of Peruvian fisheries and territorial waters, set in broader contexts than Peruvian-Japanese relations alone, are in Gerald Elliot, "The Fishing Industry of Peru," in Claudio Véliz (ed.), *Latin America and the Caribbean: A Handbook* (New York: Frederick A. Praeger, 1968), pp. 646-51 and David C. Loring, "The Fisheries Dispute," in Daniel A. Sharp (ed.), *U.S. Foreign Policy and Peru* (Austin: University of Texas Press, 1972), pp. 57-118. See also Harvey Nelson Gardiner, "Guano in American Agriculture, Politics and Diplomacy During the mid-Nineteenth Century," (M.A. thesis, Southern Illinois University, 1974), pp. 77-108.

16. *JEJ,* April 23, 1963, pp. 1-2; Christopher Eckenstein, "The Latin American Free Trade Association," in Véliz, *Latin America,* pp. 542-50 and Alberto Fuentes Mohr, "The Central American Common Market," in ibid., pp. 551-57.

17. *HAR* 9 (1956): 490; *JT,* April 16, 1957, p. 6 and United Nations Economic Commission for Latin America, "Export Promotion," *Economic Bulletin for Latin America* 15, No. 1 (1970): 97.
18. *JT,* October 4, 1958, p. 6: October 28, 1958, p. 6; November 21, 1958, p. 7; December 1, 1958, p. 14 and *HAR* 11 (1958): 686.
19. *JT,* April 20, 1958, p. 7; March 21, 1962, p. 10; August 22, 1965, p. 6.
20. United Nations Economic Commission for Latin America, *Economic Survey of Latin America 1965* (New York: United Nations, 1967), pp. 326-27; *JT,* March 17, 1964, p. 10; August 15, 1966 p. 10; *HAR* 17 (1964): 441-42 and *JEJ,* September 8, 1964, pp. 19-20; December 8, 1964, p. 10.
21. *JT,* May 28, 1965, p. 15; August 14, 1965, p. 10; July 28, 1966, p. 9; December 18 1967, p. 9; *PT,* March 6, 1970, p. 1 and *JEJ,* August 24, 1965, p. 6.
22. *Comercio Exterior* 14, No. 7 (Mexico, July 1964): 494 and *JT,* June 20, 1964, p. 10; February 3, 1966, p. 11, February 27, 1966, p. 7.; October 27, 1967, p. 9.
23. Ibid., November 4, 1964, p. 4 and *JEJ* June 4, 1963, p. 11; January 17, 1967, p. 7; September 19, 1967, p. 14.
24. Ibid., February 23, 1965, p. 6.
25. "Migration: Immigration Policies of Countries of South America," *International Labour Review* 55, No. 5 (May 1947): 437 and *JT,* August 21, 1956, p. 3; April 16, 1957, p. 6; April 20, 1958, p. 7; October 25, 1958, p. 3.
26. *Japan's Economic Co-operation with Developing Nations* (n.p., n.d.), pp. 19-21, 28-32.
27. *JT,* January 3, 1960, p. 3; August 31, 1960, p. 10; November 11, 1961, p. 10; December 22, 1961, p. 10; October 18, 1967, p. 3; *JEJ,* February 20, 1968, p. 14; and *The Christian Science Monitor,* June 27, 1962, p. 10.
28. *JT,* April 1, 1961, p. 3; July 28, 1965, p. 3; July 28, 1966, p. 7.
29. Ibid., July 28, 1967, p. 7.

Chapter 8

1. *JT,* July 28, 1972, p. 7. For early assessments of Peru in this period, see three articles by George W. Grayson, Jr., "Peru's Military Government," *Current History* 58, No. 342 (February 1970): 65-72, 114-15; "Peru's Military Populism," *Current History* 60, No. 354 (February 1971): 71-77, 116 and "Peru Under the Generals" *Current History* 62, No. 366 (February 1972): 91-97, 116-17. See also "Peru tokushū [Peru—special edition]," *Raten Amerika Jihō* [Latin America News] 12, No. 17 (June 11, 1969): 5-48.
2. *PT,* February 14, 1969, p. 12; March 14, 1969, p. 16; March 28, 1969, p. 62; May 30, 1969, p. 16; *JT,* January 15, 1969, p. 8; March 28, 1969, p. 8; March 29, 1969, p. 9, and Grayson, "Peru's Military Government."
3. Edward S. Milenky, "From Integration to Developmental Nationalism: The Andean Group 1965-1971," *Inter-American Economic Affairs* 25, No. 3 (Winter 1971): 81, 83-85.
4. "How Will Multinational Firms React to the Andean Pact's Decision 24?" *Inter-American Economic Affairs* 25, No. 2 (Autumn 1971): 55-65.
5. *PT,* January 8, 1971, pp. 3-5 and *JT,* July 22, 1971, p. 10; August 14, 1971, p. 11; October 15, 1971, p. 11.
6. Ibid., June 20, 1970, p. 4; July 3, 1970, p. 4; July 13, 1970, p. 3; July 20, 1970, p. 3; July 25, 1970, p. 3; August 30, 1970, p. 4; September 7, 1970, p. 3 and *PT* September 25, 1970, p. 17.
7. *JT,* June 24, 1970, p. 8; December 19, 1970, p. 11; and *PT,* December 25, 1970, p. 4.
8. Ibid., July 25, 1969, p. 2; October 24, 1969, p. 1 and *JT,* July 25, 1969, p. 4; July 26, 1969, pp. 3, 8; November 16, 1969, p. 10; June 24, 1970, p. 8.

9. Kaigai Ijū Jigyōdan ("Japan Emigration Service"), *Ijūchi kyōiku no genjō to mondaiten* [Present conditions and problems of education in the immigrant settlements] (Tokyo: Supido Printing, 1966), pp. 59-61.

10. Kaigai Ijū Jigyōdan ("Japan Emigration Service"), *Kaigai ijū no keizaiteki kōka* [Economic results of overseas emigration] (Tokyo: Japan Emigration Service, 1968), pp. 10, 30.

11. Ibid., pp. 20-27, wherein the statistics cover eleven other Latin American countries, the United States, and Canada as well as Peru. The values have been converted from yen to dollars at the rate of 360:1. See also Stephen I. Thompson, "Survival of Ethnicity in the Japanese Community of Lima, Peru," *Urban Anthropology* 3, No. 2 (Fall 1974): 243-261.

12. *NT,* February 18, 1956, p. 3, *JT,* April 1, 1961, p. 3; July 28, 1971, p. B1, and Kaigai Ijū Jijyōdan, *Kaigai ijū no,* p. 30.

13. Kaigai Ijū Jigyōdan, *Kaigai ijū tōkei,* p. 40.

14. *Statesman's Yearbook 1972-73* (London: Macmillan St. Martin's Press, 1972), p. 1231.

15. *PT,* September 12, 1969, p. 22; June 16, 1972, p. 15.

16. *Perū kankō* [Peru sight-seeing] (Lima, 1971) and *PT,* May 7, 1971, p. 30.

17. Ibid., January 15, 1971, p. 14; August 13, 1971, p. 15.

18. Ibid., August 20, 1971, p. 17.

19. Kaigai Nikkeijin Kyōkai, ("The Overseas Japanese Association"), *Dai jūka kaigai nikkeijin taikai, Tokyo 1969* [10th Convention of Japanese Abroad, Tokyo 1969] (Tokyo: The Overseas Japanese Association, 1969) and *JT,* April 24, 1973, p. 9.

20. Ibid., January 1, 1970, p. 7; July 28, 1970, p. 17; July 28, 1972, p. 7.

21. Ibid., December 28, 1971, p. 5, *PT,* December 31, 1971, p. 16 and *Perū Tayori* [Peru News] (Tokyo) 1, Nos. 1-6 (June-November 1972), *passim.*

22. *JT,* February 6, 1969, p. 4; July 25, 1969, p. 4; May 7, 1970, p. 4; July 11, 1970, p. 10; August 20, 1970, p. 11; August 25, 1970, p. 12; August 30, 1970, p. 4; June 5, 1971, p. 13; November 28, 1971, p. 11; April 13, 1972, p. 10; July 28, 1972, p. 7 and *PT,* July 25, 1969, p. 2; August 21, 1970, p. 1; January 15, 1971, p. 14; February 26, 1971, p. 14; April 16, 1971, p. 65; December 15, 1972, p. 15.

23. *JT,* January 15, 1969, p. 8; March 23, 1970, p. 4; May 7, 1970, p. 4; July 3, 1970, p. 4; August 25, 1970, p. 12; August, 28, 1970, pp. B1,3.

24. Ibid., October 12, 1970, p. 11; October 17, 1970, p. 9; February 26, 1972, p. 11; March 2, 1972, p. 10 and *PT* October 9, 1970, p. 16; October 16, 1970, p. 1; August 13, 1971, p. 15; February 25, 1972, p. 15; February 9, 1973, p. 15; June 29, 1973, p. 15.

25. *JT.,* July 28, 1969, p. 9; August 28, 1970, p. B3; July 28, 1972, p. 7 and *PT,* October 17, 1969, p. 18; March 6, 1970, p. 3; September 25, 1970, p. 13, June 2, 1972, p. 10.

26. Ibid., July 25, 1969, p. 2 and *JT,* February 6, 1969, p. 4; July 25, 1969, p. 4; July 26, 1969, p. 3.

27. Ibid., July 28, 1969, p. 8; September 22, 1969, p. 12; May 1, 1970, p. 5 and *PT,* May 8, 1970, p. 3.

28. Japan External Trade Organization, *Foreign Trade of Japan: 1971* (Tokyo: Japan External Trade Organization, 1971), pp. 167, 170; Japan External Trade Organization, *White Paper on International Trade Japan: 1973* (Tokyo: Japan External Trade Organization, 1973), pp. 198, 200-201; United Nations Department of Economic and Social Affairs Statistical Office, *Yearbook of International Trade Statistics 1972-1973* (New York: United Nations, 1974), p. 436.

29. JETRO, *Foreign Trade of Japan: 1971,* p. 167; JETRO, *White Paper on International Trade Japan: 1973,* p. 198 and UN, *Yearbook of International Trade Statistic 1972-1973* p. 436.

30. Ibid.

31. JETRO, *Foreign Trade of Japan: 1971,* p. 173 and JETRO, *White Paper on International Trade Japan: 1973,* p. 205.

32. Ibid., p. 206 and JETRO, *Foreign Trade of Japan: 1971*, p. 173.
33. This tabulation is derived from the following: "Sengo bōeki," *Raten Amerika Jihō* 12, No. 14 (May 11, 1969); 16-26; JETRO, *Foreign Trade of Japan: 1971*, p. 167; JETRO, *White Paper on International Trade Japan: 1973*, pp. 198, 201 and UN, *Yearbook of International Trade Statistics 1972-1973*, p. 436.
34. *JT*, March 2, 1972, p. 10.
35. Doreen Gillespie, "Japan Grows in Importance in the Peruvian Financial Scene," *PT*, September 29, 1972, pp. 11, 13, 15 and All Cullison, "Big Increase in Japanese Investing Abroad," ibid., p. 19.
36. Ibid., December 12, 1969, p. 3; October 16, 1970, p. 2; January 15, 1971, p. 4; February 26, 1971, p. 2; October 29, 1971, p. 4; January 7, 1972, p. 15; March 3, 1972, pp. 5, 83 and *JT*, August 10, 1970, p. 13; December 12, 1970, p. 10; May 12, 1971, p. 13; November 15, 1971 p. 3.
37. Ibid., December 1, 1970, p. 9; March 31, 1972, p. 11; April 30, 1972, p. 10; June 29, 1972, p. 11 and *PT*, July 9, 1971, p. 16; July 7, 1972, p. 4; September 29, 1972, p. 11.
38. Ibid., January 15, 1971, p. 4; February 26, 1971, p. 2; December 31, 1971, p. 4; February 18, 1972, p. 6; September 29, 1972, p. 11 and *JT*, December 29, 1971, p. 10; February 8, 1973, p. 12; December 4, 1973, p. 8.
39. Charles T. Goodsell, "Diplomatic Protection of U.S. Business in Peru," in Sharp (ed.), *U.S. and Peru*, pp. 246-52; Bruce A. Blomstrom and W. Bowman Cutter, "The Foreign Private Sector in Peru," in *ibid.*, p. 260 and *JT*, October 9, 1969, p. 10.
40. *PT*, March 6, 1970, p. 1; June 25, 1971, p. 3.
41. *JEJ*, January 19, 1971, p. 6; *JT*, May 12, 1971, p. 13; February 28, 1972, p. 12; May 8, 1972, p. 10; May 9, 1972, p. 11 and *PT*, December 17, 1971, p. 4; April 20, 1973, p. 1; March 1, 1974, p. 5.
42. *JEJ*, August 22, 1972, p. 7; September 5, 1972, p. 7; September 19, 1972, p. 6 and *JT*, September 2, 1972, p. 10; May 27, 1973, p. 4.
43. Ibid., October 27, 1972, p. 10; *JEJ*, November 14, 1972, p. 6 and *PT*, October 27, 1972, p. 6.
44. *JT*, November 4, 1970, p. 11; November 9, 1970, p. 10; December 12, 1970, p. 10; *JEJ*, September 14, 1971, p. 3 and *PT*, September 17, 1971, p. 4; January 28, 1972, p. 4; September 29, 1972, p. 17.
45. *JT*, May 4, 1969, p. 13; August 20, 1970, p. 11; *Mainichi Daily News* (Tokyo), May 5, 1969, p. 4 and *PT*, February 27, 1970, p. 1; August 21, 1970, p. 1.
46. Ibid., March 7, 1969, pp. 2, 15; May 16, 1969, p. 3; September 5, 1969, p. 3; May 1, 1970, p. 12; September 29, 1972, p. 13.
47. Ibid., August 15, 1969, p. 1; January 16, 1970, p. 13; September 4, 1970, p. 3; October 20, 1972, p. 6; January 19, 1973, p. 2; Gillespie, "Japan Grows in Importance" p. 13 and *JEJ*, April 7, 1970, p. 16. Nippon Steel cancelled this order on the grounds that the high sulfur content produced unacceptable levels of air pollution; see *PT*, March 26, 1971, p. 1.
48. Ibid., October 16, 1970, p. 2; May 21, 1971, p. 3; September 17, 1971, p. 5; January 7, 1972, p. 15; March 3, 1972, p. 5; October 20, 1972, p. 6; February 2, 1973, p. 1; Gillespie, "Japan Grows in Importance," p. 13 and *JT*, September 26, 1972, p. 10; October 2, 1972, p. 11, November 1, 1972, p. 11.
49. *PT*, September 12, 1969, p. 3; October 29, 1971, p. 4.
50. *JT*, April 10, 1970, p. 11; March 5, 1971, p. 12; June 19, 1972, p. 10; November 9, 1972, p. 11; April 26, 1973, p. 11; May 22, 1973, p. 12; December 7, 1973, p. 2 and *PT*, January 22, 1971, p. 5; May 7, 1971, p. 4; May 28, 1971, p. 1; August 18, 1972, p. 15; September 29, 1972, pp. 13, 154 November 2, 1973, p. 15; December 7, 1973, p. 9.
51. Ibid., January 25, 1974, pp. 3-4.
52. *JEJ*, October 8, 1968, p. 13; November 5, 1968, p. 18 and *PT*, March 28, 1969, p. 21.

53. Ibid., March 3, 1972, pp. 60-62, 68; July 27, 1973, p. 2 and Michael Roemer, *Fishing for Growth: Export-led Development in Peru, 1950-1967* (Cambridge: Harvard University Press, 1970), pp. 117, 124.

54. *PT*, March 28, 1969, p. 35 and *JT*, May 12, 1969, p. 9.

55. *PT*, February 19, 1971, p. 15; February 26, 1971, p. 14; March 5, 1971, p. 17; April 16, 1971, p. 65; April 16, 1971, p. 3; November 5, 1971, p. 4; December 3, 1971, p. 16 and *JT*, June 5, 1971, p. 13; January 22, 1973, p. 10; May 18, 1973, p. 11.

56. Ibid., February 24, 1970, p. 10; July 24, 1970, pp. 26-27; September 14, 1970, p. 12; November 23, 1972, p. 10 and *PT*, September 3, 1971, p. 15; September 29, 1972, p. 15.

57. Ibid., April 25, 1969, p. 1; October 9, 1970, p. 10; March 26, 1971, p. 17 and *JT*, September 1, 1970, p. 12.

58. Ibid., August 7, 1969, p. 9; August 11, 1969, p. 9; February 25, 1970, p. 9 and *PT*, April 24, 1970, p. 1; August 21, 1970, p. 1.

59. United States Bureau of the Census, *Statistical Abstract of the United States: 1973* (Washington: Government Printing Office, 1973), p. 776.

60. U.S., *Statistical Abstract 1960*, p. 869; United States Bureau of the Census, *Statistical Abstract of the United States: 1971* (Washington: Government Printing Office, 1971) p. 755; *Statistical Abstract . . . 1972*, p. 767 and *Statistical Abstract . . . 1973*, p. 769.

61. *JT*, July 20, 1972, p. 2; July 28, 1972, p. 7; March 1, 1973, p. 2; May 18, 1973, p. 11; July 28, 1973, pp. B1, 3; August 22, 1973, p. 2; August 25, 1973, p. 2 and *PT*, June 29, 1973, p. 15; August 24, 1973, p. 52.

Bibliography

Bibliographical Aids

Andrade, Gustavo. "Latin American Studies in Japan." *Latin American Research Review* 8, No. 1 (Spring 1973): 147-56.

Borton, Hugh; Elisséeff, Serge; Lockwood, William W.; and Pelzel, John C. *A Selected List of Books and Articles on Japan in English, French and German.* Revised edition. Cambridge: Harvard University Press, 1954.

Bureau for Economic Research in Latin America, Harvard University. *The Economic Literature of Latin America: a Tentative Bibliography.* 2 vols. Cambridge: Harvard University Press, 1935-36.

Jones, Tom B.; Warburton, E.A.; and Kingsley, A. *A Bibliography on South American Economic Affairs: Articles in Nineteenth-Century Periodicals.* Minneapolis: University of Minnesota Press, 1955.

Kaigai Ijū Jigyōdan ("Japan Emigration Service"). *Kaigai Ijū Jigyōdan jūnenshi* [*Ten year history of the Japan emigration service*]. Tokyo: Dai Nihon Publishing Company, 1973, pp. 265-85.

Kosaka, Masao. *Latin American Studies and Library Materials in Japan, 1969 - A Preliminary Report.* Washington: Pan American Union, 1970.

"Migration Bibliography: Japanese Colonization in Latin America," *Migration News* 18, No. 5 (September-October, 1969): 27.

Mitani, Hiroshi. "Latin American Studies in Japan." In *Handbook of Latin American Studies No. 27.* Gainesville: University of Florida Press, 1965, pp. 457-63.

Sable, Martin H. *Latin-American Studies in the Non-Western World and Eastern Europe.* Metuchen, N.J.: Scarecrow Press, 1970.

Uyehara, Cecil H. *Checklist of Archives in the Japanese Ministry of Foreign Affairs, Tokyo, Japan, 1868-1945 Microfilmed for the Library of Congress 1949-1951.* Washington: Library of Congress, 1954.

Wionczek, Miguel S. "Literatura reciente sobre la economía del Japón." *Comercio Exterior* 21, No. 2 (Mexico) (February 1971): 159-60.

Manuscripts

Ciccarelli, Orazio A. "The Sánchez Cerro Regimes in Peru, 1930-1933." Ph.D. dissertation, University of Florida, 1969.

Clark, Thomas Dean. "A Survey of Japanese Foreign Trade 1952-1957." Master's thesis, University of Illinois, 1959.

Gardiner, Harvey Nelson. "Guano in American Agriculture, Politics and Diplomacy during the mid-Nineteenth Century." Master's thesis, Southern Illinois University, 1974.

Karno, Howard Laurence. "Augusto B. Leguía: the Oligarchy and the Modernization of Peru, 1870-1930." Ph.D. dissertation, University of California at Los Angeles, 1970.

Nihon ("Japan"), Gaimushō ("Foreign Office"). Chū-. nam-, hokubei engan gyogyō kankei: Perū [Documents relating to fishing along North, Central, and South America: Peru]. Microfilm rolls S291-292, S 5.4.9.0-2.

———. Gaikoku ni okeru hai-Nichi kankei zakken: Perū no bu [Miscellaneous documents relating to anti-Japanese movements in foreign countries: Peru]. Microfilm roll S449, S 10.1.1.0-12.

———. Gaikoku ni okeru hai-Nichi kankei zakken: Perū hai-Nichi bōdō jiken [Miscellaneous documents relating to anti-Japanese movements in foreign countries: anti-Japanese riots in Peru}. Microfilm roll S450, S 10.1.1.0-13.

———. Ippan oyobi shō-mondai: Zaitekkoku hompō-jin kyūjutsu mondai [General and specific problems: problems of the relief of Japanese nationals residing in enemy countries]. Microfilm roll S580, S 1.7.0.0-39.

———. Kaigai kakuchi zairyū hompō-jin shokugyō-betsu jinkō-hyō [Tables on the population of Japanese residing abroad classified by occupation]. Microfilm roll SP 44, SP 125.

———. Kakkoku taigai seisaku kankei zassan: Hikoku no bu [Miscellaneous documents relating to the foreign policies of various countries: Peru]. Microfilm roll 46, MT 1.2.2.1.

———. Nihongo gakkō chōsa ikken [Documents relating to investigations of Japanese-language schools [in foreign countries]]. Microfilm roll S309, S 9.1.5.0-10.

———. Perū imin kankei zakken [Miscellaneous documents relating to [Japanese] immigration to Peru]. Microfilm rolls 734-35, MT 3.8.2.205.

———. Teikoku shō-gaikoko gaikō kankei zassan: Nippi kan [Miscellaneous documents relating to diplomatic relations: Japanese-Peruvian relations]. Microfilm roll 28, MT 1.1.3.3.

———. Chū-nambei ni gaikōkan kara gaimudaijin e denshin [Telegrams from diplomatic officials in Central and South American countries to the Minister of Foreign Affairs: Peru]. Microfilm roll WT 37, IMT 259, IPS Doc. No. 1333.

———. Zaigai hōjin shōyō - shōgyō - kaigi-sho kankei zakken: Perū Shōkō Kyōkai [Miscellaneous documents relating to Japanese chambers of commerce and chambers of commerce and industry in foreign countries: the chamber of commerce and industry in Peru]. Microfilm roll S275, S 5.2.6.0-19.

Sinclair, Joseph T. "Lima, Peru: a Study in Urban Geography." Ph.D. dissertation, University of Michigan, 1959.

Tigner, James Lawrence. "The Okinawans in Latin America." Ph.D. dissertation, Stanford University, 1956.

U.S. Department of Justice, Immigration and Naturalization Service. Files of Japanese-Peruvian wartime internees. Washington, D.C.

———. National Archives, Department of State. Consular Despatches: Hakodate, T-113 (2 rolls).

———. Decimal File, 1910-1929: Japan: Internal Affairs, M-422 (43 rolls).

———. Decimal File, 1910-1929: Peru: Internal Affairs, M-746 (30 rolls).

———. Diplomatic Dispatches: Japan, M-133 (82 rolls).

———. Diplomatic Instructions, M-77 (175 rolls).

———. Notes from Foreign Legations, T-802 (6 rolls).

Werlich, David Patrick. "The Conquest and Settlement of the Peruvian Montaña." Ph.D. dissertation, University of Minnesota, 1968.

Worrall, Janet Evelyn. "Italian Immigration to Peru, 1860-1914." Ph.D. dissertation, Indiana University, 1972.

Printed Documents

Asociación Cultural Peruano-Japonesa. *Estatutos*. Lima: Imprenta Minerva, 1954.

Cavalcanti, T.B., ed. *Las constituciones de los Estados Unidos del Brasil*. Madrid: Instituto de Estudios Políticos, 1958.

Great Britain, Foreign Office. *British and Foreign State Papers 1927 Part I*. London: His Majesty's Stationery Office, 1932.

Japan, Bureau of Statistics, Office of the Prime Minister. *Japan Statistical Yearbook* [for the years 1949, 1954]. Tokyo: Nihon Statistical Association, [1950, 1955].

Japan External Trade Organization (JETRO). *Foreign Trade of Japan* [for the years 1964-1971]. Tokyo: Japan External Trade Organization, 1964-71.

———. *White Paper on International Trade Japan: 1973*. Tokyo: Japan External Trade Organization, 1973.

Japan. Ministry of Foreign Affairs. *Case of the Peruvian Barque Maria Luz*. Yokohama, 1872.

Japan. Foreign Office. *Treaties and Conventions between the Empire of Japan and Other Powers . . . since March, 1854*. Revised edition. Tokio, 1884.

Japan. Foreign Office. *Treaties and Conventions between the Empire of Japan and Other Powers*. Tokio, 1899.

Japon, Cabinet Impérial, Bureau Général de Statistique. *Résumé Statistique de l'Empire du Japon*. 54 vols. Tokio, 1887-1940.

Japan's Economic Co-operation with Developing Nations. [n.p.], 1968.

League of Nations. *Treaty Series*. Vol. 102. Geneva: League of Nations, 1930.

Martens, G. Fr. de, *et al. Nouveau recueil général de traités*. 3rd series. Leipzig; Libraire Dieterich, 1909.

México, Secretaría de Relaciones Exteriores. *Memoria de labores de la Secretaría de Relaciones Exteriores de Agosto de 1926 a Julio de 1927 presentada al H. Congreso de la Unión*. México: Imprenta de la Secretaría de Relaciones Exteriores, 1927.

Nihon (Japan), Gaimushō (Foreign Office). *Dai Nihon gaikō bunsho* [Japanese diplomatic correspondence]. 10 vols. Tokyo: Dai Nihon Publishing Company, 1936-40.

———. *Waga gaikō no kinkyō* [The present state of our diplomacy]. Vols. 1-12. Tokyo: Japan Foreign Office, 1957-68.

Paz-Soldan, José Pareja, ed. *Las constituciones del Perú*. Madrid: Ediciones Cultura Hispánica, 1954.

Perú, Biblioteca Nacional. *Anuario bibliográfico peruano* [for the years 1951-66]. Lima, 1957-69.

Perú. Ministerio de Fomento. *Memoria de la Dirección de Fomento al Sr. Ministro del Ramo 1899*. Lima, 1899.

Perú. Ministerio de Hacienda y Comercio, Dirección Nacional de Estadística y Censos. *Anuario Estadística del Perú 1966*. Lima: Imprenta del Ministerio de Hacienda y Comercio, [1969].

———. *Censo nacional de población y ocupación 1940*. 9 vols. Lima: Imprenta Tórres Aguirre, S.A., 1944-49.

Perú. Ministerio de Relaciones Exteriores. *Boletín del Ministerio de Relaciones Exteriores*. 52 vols. Lima, 1904-14.

———. (Ricardo Aranda, ed.) *Colección de los tratados, convenciones, capitulaciones, armisticios y otros actos diplomáticos y políticos . . .* 14 vols. Lima: Imprenta del Estado, 1890-1911.

———. *Memoria . . . de Relaciones Exteriores . . .* [for the years 1874, 1885, 1887, 1890-94, 1896-1903, 1909, 1912, 1914-18, 1920-29, 1934-43, 1953-57, 1962-63]. Lima, 1874-[1963].

Perú. Presidencia. *Mensaje presentado al Congreso . . . por . . . Augusto B. Leguía*. Lima: Imp. "Garcilaso", 1926.

———. *Mensaje presentado al Congreso por . . . Manuel Prado . . .* [for the years 1941 and 1942]. Lima, 1941-42.

Perú. Senado. *Diario de los debates del Senado legislatura ordinaria de 1940*. Lima: Imprenta Torres Aguirre, S.A. 1940.

United Nations, Economic Commission for Latin America *Economic Survey of Latin America 1965*. New York: United Nations, 1967.

United Nations. General Assembly. *Ad Hoc Commission on Prisoners of War*. New York: United Nations, [1951].

———. *Official Records of the General Assembly, Eleventh Session, Plenary Meetings* II. New York: United Nations, [1957].
United Nations. Security Council. *Security Council Official Records, Tenth Year, 704th Meeting*. New York: United Nations [1956].
———. *Security Council Official Records, Eleventh Year, 756th Meeting*. New York: United Nations, [1957].
United Nations. *Treaty Series*. Vols. 136 (1952) and 451 (1963).
———. Department of Economic Affairs, Statistical Office. *Yearbook of International Trade Statistics* [for the years 1951-73]. New York: United Nations, 1952-74.
U.S. Bureau of the Census. *Statistical Abstract of the United States* [for the years 1951-73]. Washington: Government Printing Office, 1951-73.
U.S. Congress. *Statutes at Large,* XII. Boston, 1865.
———. 82nd Congress, 2nd session, House of Representatives, Committee on the Judiciary. *Hearings before the President's Commission on Immigration and Naturalization*. Washington: Government Printing Office, 1952.
U.S. Department of Justice. *Annual Report of the Attorney General of the United States for the Fiscal . . .* [years 1946, 1947, and 1949]. [Washington, n.d.].
U.S. Department of State. *Papers Relating to the Foreign Relations of the United States*. (volumes 1873 I, 1941 X, 1943 VI, 1944 VII and 1945 IX). Washington: Government Printing Office, 1874-1969.
———. "Removal of Alien Enemies" *The Department of State Bulletin* 13, No. 317 (July 22, 1945): 107-108.
———. "Removal of Alien Enemies" *The Department of State Bulletin* 13, No. 324 (September 9, 1945): 361.
———. Supreme Court (Richard Peters, ed.). *Reports of Cases Argued and Adjudged in the Supreme Court of the United States*. Vol. 15. Philadelphia, 1845.

Books

Arispe A., Alfredo. *!Peligro! !America!–Japón, amenaza para el Perú y para el continente*. Lima: Editorial Minerva, 1939.
Asahi, Isoshi. *El por qué del éxito comercial del Japón*. La Habana: Editorial Hercules 1939.
Basadre, Jorge. *Historia de la República del Perú*. 5th ed. rev. 8 vols. Lima: Ediciones "Historia", 1961-63.
Beals, Carleton. *The Coming Struggle for Latin America*. Philadelphia: J.B. Lippincott Company, 1938.
Borton, Hugh. *Japan's Modern Century*. New York; Ronald Press Company, 1955.
Bradley, Anita. *Trans-Pacific Relations of Latin America*. New York: Institute of Pacific Relations, 1942.
Cáceres B., Ernesto. *La luz viene del oriente*. Lima: Editoria Médica Peruana, 1960.
Chaplin, David. *The Peruvian Industrial Labor Force*. Princeton: Princeton University Press, 1967.
Cintra, José Thiago. *La migración japonesa en Brasil (1908-1958)*. México: El Colegio de México, 1971.
Comisión Organizadora del Monumento a Manco Capac. *La independencia del Perú y la colonia Japonesa*. Lima, [1926].
Compañía Peruana de Negocios Internacionales S.A. *1941 Peru–Yearbook of Foreign Trade*. Lima: Compañía de negocios internacionales, S.A., [n.d.].
Dew, Edward. *Politics in the Altiplano; the Dynamics of Change in Rural Peru*. Austin: University of Texas Press, 1969.

Dozer, Donald Marquand. *Latin America: an Interpretive History*. New York: McGraw-Hill, 1962.
Eckstein, Gustav. *Noguchi*. New York: Harper & Brothers, 1931.
Fujii, Yukio and Smith, T. Lynn. *The Acculturation of Japanese Immigrants in Brazil*. University of Florida Monograph No. 5 Gainesville: University of Florida Press, 1959.
García Calderón, Francisco. *Latin America: Its Rise and Progress*. London: T.F. Unwin, 1911.
Guevara, Victor J. *Las grandes cuestiones nacionales: el petróleo–los ferrocarriles–la inmigración japonesa–el problema moral*. Cuzco: Talleres Tipográficos de H.G. Rozas sucesores, 1939.
Gunther, John. *Inside Latin America*. New York: Harper & Brothers, 1940.
Inahara, K., ed. *The Japan Yearbook 1934*. Tokyo: The Foreign Affairs Association of Japan, [n.d.].
———. *The Japan Year Book 1936*. Tokyo: The Foreign Affairs Association of Japan, [n.d.].
Izumi, Seiichi and Sono, Toshihiko. *Andes 2: Excavations at Kotosh, Peru, 1960*. Tokyo: Kadokawa Publishing Company, 1963.
Japan Biographical Encyclopedia & Who's Who. Tokyo: The Rengo Press. Ltd., [1958].
The Japan Year Book 1939-40. Tokyo: The Foreign Affairs Association of Japan, [n.d.].
The Japan Year Book 1943-44. Tokyo: The Foreign Affairs Association of Japan, [n.d.].
Jones, Clarence F. *Commerce of South America*. Boston: Ginn and Company, 1928.
Kaigai Ijū Jigyōdan ("Japan Emigration Service") *Ijūchi kyōiku no genjō to mondaiten* [Present condition and problems of education in the immigrant settlements]. Tokyo: Supīdo Printing, 1966.
———. *Kaigai Ijū Jigyōdan jūnenshi* (Ten year history of the Japan Emigration Service). Dai Nihon Publishing Company, 1973.
———. *Kaigai ijū nó keizaiteki kōka* (Economic results of overseas emigration). Tokyo: Japan Emigration Service, 1968.
———. *Kaigai ijū tōkei (shōwa 27-45)* (Overseas emigration statistics: 1952-1970). Tokyo: Japan Emigration Service, 1972.
Kaigai Nikkeijin Kyōkai ("The Overseas Japanese Association"). *Dai jūka kaigai nikkeijin taikai, Tokyo 1969* [10th convention of Japanese abroad, Tokyo 1969]. Tokyo: The Overseas Japanese Association, 1969.
———. *Dai kyūka kaigai nikkeijin taikai, Hawai 1968* [9th convention of Japanese abroad, Hawaii 1968]. Tokyo: The Overseas Japanese Association, 1968.
Kerr, George H. *Okinawa: the History of an Island People*. Tokyo: Charles E. Tuttle Company, 1959.
Li, Kisang. *Introducción a la escritura de la lengua japonesa*. Trujillo: Universidad Nacional de Trujillo, 1965.
Mizukami, Tatsuzo, et al. *1965 Nambei keizai shisetsudan hōkokusho* [Report of the 1965 economic mission to South America]. [Tokyo: Marui Kōbunsha, 1965].
Moore, John Bassett. *History and Digest of the International Arbitrations to Which the United States Has Been a Party*. (53d Cong. 2nd session H.R. Misc. Doc. 212). 6 vols. Washington, 1898.
Nieves Ayala, Arturo. *El Perú y la inmigración de post-guerra*. Lima: Imp. E.R. Lulli, 1946.
Nihon Bōeki Kenkyūkai ("Foreign Trade Research Association of Japan"). *Sengo Nihon no bōeki nijūnenshi* (History of twenty years of Japanese postwar trade). Tokyo. Commerce Industry Investigation Company, 1967.
Normano, J.F. and Gerbi, Antonello. *The Japanese in South America*. New York: The John Day Company, 1943.
Ohara, Yoshinori. *Japan and Latin America*. Santa Monica, Calif.: The Rand Corporation, 1967.
Perū kankō (Peru sight-seeing). Lima: Peru Shimpō [1971].
Peru–Yearbook of Foreign Trade–1942. Lima: Sanmarti y Cía., S.A., [n.d.].

Pike, Frederick B. *The Modern History of Peru*. New York: Frederick A. Praeger, 1967.
Poesía japonesa. Lima, 1967.
Poppino, Rollie E. *Brazil: the Land and People*. New York: Oxford University Press, 1968.
Raten Ámerika Kyōkai ("Latin America Society"). *Nihonjin Perū ijū no kiroku* [Record of Japanese emigration to Peru]. Tokyo: Shinkyōsha Publishing Company, 1969.

―――. *Nihon no Raten Amerika chōsa kenkyūsho gaisetsu* [Introduction to Latin American investigations and research in Japan]. Tokyo, 1965.

―――. *Raten Amerika Jiten 1964 nenban* [Latin America handbook 1964 edition]. Tokyo: Tōkō Seihan Publishing Company, 1964.

―――. *Raten Amerika Jiten 1968 nenban* [Latin America handbook 1968 edition]. Tokyo: Tōkō Seihan Publishing Company, 1968.

―――. *Raten Amerika shokoku e no nihonjin ijūshi* [History of Japanese emigration to various countries of Latin America]. Tokyo: Shūeisha Publishing Company, 1965.

Río, Mario E. del. *La inmigración y su desarrollo en el Perú*. Lima: Sanmartí y Cía., 1929.
Roemer, Michael. *Fishing for Growth: Export-led Development in Peru, 1950-1967*. Cambridge: Harvard University Press, 1970.
Saito, Hiroshi. *O Japonês no Brasil; Estudo de Mobilidade e Fixação*. São Paulo: Editora "Sociologia e Política", 1961.
Sharp, Daniel A., ed. *U.S. Foreign Policy and Peru*. Austin: University of Texas Press, 1972.
Smith, T. Lynn. *Brazil: People and Institutions*. Revised edition. Baton Rouge: Louisiana State University press, 1954.
The Statesman's Yearbook 1972-73. London: Macmillan St. Martin's Press, 1972.
Stewart, Watt. *Chinese Bondage in Peru: a History of the Chinese Coolie in Peru, 1849-1874*. Durham: Duke University Press, 1951.
Takenobu, Y., ed. *The Japan Year Book* [for the years 1920-21, 1921-22 and 1929]. Tokyo: The Japan Year Book Office, [n.d.].
Treat, Payson J. *Diplomatic Relations between the United States and Japan 1853-1895*. Reprinting. 3 vols. Gloucester: P. Smith, 1963.
Ugarte, Manuel (introduction by Jorge Abelardo Ramos). *El porvenir de América Latina*. Buenos Aires: Editorial Indoamérica, 1953.
Ulloa [y Sotomayor], Alberto. *Perú y Japón*. Lima: Impr. Torres Aguirre, 1943.
Uribe Gaviria, Carlos. *La verdad sobre la guerra*, 2 vols. Bogotá: Editorial Cromos, 1936.
Uyehara, S. *The Industry and Trade of Japan*. Rev. ed. London: P.S. King & Son, Ltd., 1936.
Véliz, Claudio, ed. *Latin America and the Caribbean: a Handbook*. New York: Frederick A. Praeger, 1968.
Vivero, León de. *Avance del imperialismo fascista en el Perú*. Mexico: Editorial Manuel Arévalo, 1938.
Wagner de Reyna, Alberto. *Historia diplomática del Perú (1900-1945)*. 2 vols. Lima: Ediciones Peruanas, 1964.
Willoughby, Westel W. *The Sino-Japanese Controversy and the League of Nations*. Baltimore: The Johns Hopkins University Press, 1935.
Zierer, Ernst. *Introducción a la lengua japonesa hablada*. Trujillo: Universidad Nacional de Trujillo, 1964.

―――. *Introducción a la lengua japonesa hablada*. 2nd edition. Trujillo: Universidad Nacional de Trujillo, 1965.

Articles

Akasaka, Tadashi, "Nihon-Nambei togan kōro; Ijūsha yusōshi [Japan-South America east coast route: emigrant transport history]." *Ijū Kenkyū* [Emigration Research], No. 10 (March 1974): 55-84.

Alegría, Ciro and Saco, Alfredo. "Japanese Spearhead in the Americas." *Free World* 2, No. 1 (February 1942): 81-84; and No. 2 (March 1942): 181-84.
Arbaiza, Genaro. "Acute Japanese Problem in South America," *Current History* 21, No. 5 (February 1925): 735-40.
Barnhart, Edward N. "Citizenship and Political Tests in Latin American Republics in World War II." *The Hispanic American Historical Review* 42, No. 3 (August 1962): 297-332.
———. "Japanese Internees from Peru." *Pacific Historical Review* 31, No. 2 (May 1962): 169-78.
Beals, Carleton. "Japan Invades Latin America." *The American Mercury* 34, No. 133 (March 1935): 299-306.
———. "Totalitarian Inroads in Latin America." *Foreign Affairs* 17, No. 1 (October 1938): 78-89.
Bloch, Kurt. "Poor Prospects for Japan in Latin America." *Asia* 40, No. 7 (July 1940): 362-63.
Blomstrom, Bruce A. and Cutter, W. Bowman. "The Foreign Private Sector in Peru." in Sharp *U.S. Foreign Policy and Peru*, pp. 258-88.
Cullison, All. "Big Increase in Japanese Investing Abroad." *Peruvian Times,* September 29, 1972, p. 19.
"La cuota de importación a los tejidos de algodón de orígen japonés." *Boletín de la Cámara de Comercio de Lima* 11, (December 1940): 614-15.
Eckenstein, Christopher. "The Latin American Free Trade Association." in Véliz *Latin America,* pp. 542-50.
Elliot, Gerald. "The Fishing Industry of Peru." in Véliz, *Latin America,* pp. 646-51.
"Foreign Trade Gains Marked in Central and South America." *Trans-Pacific* 22, No. 23 (June 7, 1934): 3.
Fuentes Mohr, Alberto. "The Central American Common Market," in Véliz, *Latin America,* pp. 551-57.
Fung Pineda, Rosa. "El Museo Amano," *Fanal* 23, No. 85 (1968): 13-22.
Gardiner, C. Harvey. "A Coolie Contribution to Diplomacy," *Peruvian Times,* April 27, 1973 pp. 13-14.
———. "El desarrollo del sentimiento antijaponés en el Perú, 1899-1941." *Boletín de la Academia de Historia del Valle del Cauca* 41, Nos. 161-64 (December 1973): 811-23.
———. "The Japanese and Central America." *Journal of Interamerican Studies and World Affairs* 14, No. 1 (February 1972): 15-47.
———. "Los japoneses y Colombia," *Boletín de la Academia de Historia del Valle del Cauca,* 40, Nos. 158-60 (August 1972): 219-40.
———. "Los japoneses y el Ecuador." *Boletín de la Academia de Historia del Valle del Cauca* 41, Nos. 161-64 (December 1973): 788-810.
Gerbi, Antonello. "The Japanese in Peru." *Asia and the Americas* 43, No. 1 (January 1943): 43-46.
Gillespie, Doreen. "Japan Grows in Importance in the Peruvian Financial Scene." *Peruvian Times,* September 29, 1972, pp. 11, 13, 15.
Goodsell, Charles T. "Diplomatic Protection of U.S. Businessman in Peru." in Sharp, *U.S. Foreign Policy and Peru,* pp. 237-57.
Gordon, Ronald M.J. "A Japanese Colony in Peru." *Peruvian Times,* January 5, 1973, pp. 6-8.
"Government Plans Big Trade Company." *Trans-Pacific* 21, No. 43 (October 26, 1933): 21.
Grayson, George W. Jr. "Peru's Military Government." *Current History* 58, No. 342 (February 1970): 65-72, 114-15.
———. "Peru's Military Populism." *Current History* 60, No. 354 (February 1971): 71-77, 116.
———. "Peru Under the Generals." *Current History,* 62, No. 366 (February 1972): 91-97, 116-17.

———. "Peru's Revolutionary Government." *Current History* 64, No. 378 (February 1973): 61-65, 87.
Hironaka, Kanoh. "Japan's Floating Fair," *Keindaren Review*, No. 2 (1965), 45-53.
Hodges, G. Charles. "Japanese Ambitions and Latin America." *Sunset* 36, No. 4 (October 1916): 16-17, 82-85.
"How Will Multinational Firms React to the Andean Pact's Decision 24?" *Inter-American Economic Affairs* 25, No. 2 (1971): 55-65.
Idei, Seishi. "Japan's Migration Problem." *International Labour Review* 22, No. 6 (December 1930): 773-89.
Irie, Toraji (William Himel, tr.). "History of the Japanese Migration to Peru." *The Hispanic American Historical Review* 31, No. 3 (August 1951): 437-52; 31, No. 4 (November 1951): 648-64; and 32, No. 1 (February 1952): 73-82.
"Japan: Tariffs and Trade Controls: SCAP Trade and Financial Mission to Latin America." *Foreign Commerce Weekly* 36 No. 12 (September 19, 1949): 20-21.
"Japan Trade Shifts to Central and South America." *Trans-Pacific* 21, No. 44 (November 2, 1933): 20.
"Japanese Emigration Machinery." *Migration News* 7, No. 1 (January-February 1958): 17.
"Japanese Expansion in Latin America." *The American Review of Reviews*, 42, No. 3 (September 1910): 363.
"Japanese in Peru." *The Inter-American* 2, No. 5 (May 1943): 5-8.
"Japanese Prosper Along West Coast." *The Americas* 7, No. 3 (December 1920): 18.
"Kaigai ijū hyakunen nenpyō [One hundred year chronology of overseas emigration]." *Ijū Kenkyū* [Emigration Research], No. 3 (November 1968); unnumbered folding chart, following p. 50.
Kamizono, Yoshifusa. "Seinen ijū kobōsha no keikō—Aichi-ken ni okeru tōkei wo chūshin ni shite [The inclinations of youthful emigration applicants—based on statistics in Aichi Prefecture. *Ijū Kenkyū* [*Emigration Research,*], No. 6 (March 1970): 33-48.
Kearns, Kevin C. "The Andean Common Market." *Journal of Interamerican Studies and World Affairs* 14, No. 2 (May 1972): 225-51.
Kinney, Henry Walsworth. "Japan's Problems in South American Trade." *Trans-Pacific* 3, No. 6 (December 1920): 69-77.
Kurusu, Saburō. "El Japón mira hacia la América Latina." *Trans-Pacific* 21, No. 44 (November 2, 1933): 3-4.
Loring, David C. "The Fisheries Dispute." in Sharp, *U.S. Foreign Policy and Peru,* pp. 57-118.
Macedo, J.M. "Los japoneses como cultivadores de arroz en el Estado de Texas." *Boletín del Ministerio de Fomento* (Peru) 4, No. 1 (January 1906): 80-81.
Machida, Chūji. "Machida desea promoción del comercio libre para el bienestar del mundo." *Trans-Pacific* 22, No. 36 (September 6, 1934): 3, 9, 11.
"Memorandum on Japanese Migration Policies." *Far Eastern Survey* 1, No. 15 (August 17, 1932): 1-4.
"Migration: Immigration Policies of Countries of South America." *International Labour Review* 55, No. 5 (May 1947): 436-44.
Milenky, Edward S. "From Integration to Developmental Nationalism: The Andean Group 1965-1971." *Inter-American Economic Affairs* 25, No. 3 (1971): 77-91.
"More Trade Sought with Latin America." *Trans-Pacific* 21, No. 40 (October 5, 1933): 21.
Ogishima, Tōru. "Japanese Emigration." *International Labour Review* 34, No. 5 (November 1936): 618-51.
Ohara, Yoshinori. "Conditions of Economic Development in Latin America—with Special Reference to Capital Formation." *The Developing Economies* 2, No. 2 (June 1964): 171-89.

Okuchi, Nobuo. "A Hundred Years of Japanese Migration." *Migration News* 14, No. 4 (July-August 1965): 1-4.
Oshimoto, Naomasa. "Kaigai ijū hyakuneshi nenpyō ni soete" [A commentary on the chronology of one hundred years history of emigration]. *Ijū Kenkyū* [Emigration Research], No. 3 (November 1968): 45-49.
———. "Tōkei kara mita sen-eki kaigai ijū no keikō" [Statistical tendency of postwar emigration]. *Ijū Kenkyū* [Emigration Research], No. 1 (October 1967): 9-17.
Paulet, Pedro E. "Peru Has Many Riches." *Trans-Pacific* 21, No. 44 (November 2, 1933): 7.
"Peru Limits Japanese." *Trans-Pacific* 22, No. 32 (August 9, 1934): 9.
"Perū tokushū" [Peru - Special Edition]," *Raten Amerika Jihō* [Latin America News] 12, No. 17 (June 11, 1969): 5-48.
[Porter, Catherine]. "Japanese in Peru Seek Cotton Market in Japan." *Far Eastern Survey* 7, No. 18 (September 7, 1938): 212-13.
[———.] "South American Wool Gaining in Japan." *Far Eastern Survey* 6, No. 14 (July 7, 1937): 163-64.
"Post-War Migration Problems in Japan." *International Labour Review* 75, No. 1 (January 1957): 53-67.
Price, Willard. "The Far-Flung Japanese." *Asia* 38, No. 2 (February 1938): 129-32.
"Comercio de la colonia japonesa." *Boletín mensual de la Cámara de Comercia de Lima'* 11, (May 1940): 227.
Ríos, Fernando de los. "South American Perplexities." *Foreign Affairs* 20, No. 4 (July 1942): 650-62.
Rippy, J. Fred. "The Japanese in Latin America." *Inter-American Economic Affairs* 3, No. 1 (1949): 50-65.
Sakisaka, Masao. "Desarrollo de la economía japonesa en el período posterior a la segunda guerra mundial." *Revista de Economía Latinoamericana* (Caracas) 2, No. 7 (July-September 1962): 109-41.
Sasaki, John. "Impressions of a Japanese Migration Director in the Two Americas." *Migration News* 5 No. 5 (September-October 1956): 8-12.
———. "Japanese Migration and Its Future." *Migration News* 18 No. 5 (September-October 1969): 3-6.
"Sengo ni okeru Nippon no Rabei shokoku to no bōeki jisseki suii" [Japanese postwar trade development with various Latin American countries]. *Raten Amerika Jihō* [Latin American News] 12, No. 14 (May 11, 1969): 16-26.
Seoane, Manuel (Lloyd Mallan, tr.). "The Japanese Are Still in Peru." *Asia and the Americas* 43, No. 12 (December 1943): 674-76.
Severin, Kurt. "The Japanese Inca of Peru." *Travel* 82, No. 4 (February 1944): 4-9, 31.
"South America and Asiatic Labor." *The American Review of Reviews* 36, No. 5 (November 1907): 622-23.
Steinberg, Alfred. "'Blunder' Maroons Peruvian Japanese in the U.S." *The Washington Post*, September 26, 1948.
Switzer, Kenneth A. "The Andean Group: a Reappraisal." *Inter-American Economic Affairs* 26, No. 4 (1972): 69-81.
Thompson, Stephen I. "Survival of Ethnicity in the Japanese Community of Lima, Peru." *Urban Anthropology* 3, No. 2 (1974): 243-61.
Tigner, James Lawrence. "Shindō Remmei: Japanese Nationalism in Brazil." *The Hispanic American Historical Review* 41, No. 4 (November 1961): 515-32.
Titiev, Mischa. "The Japanese Colony in Peru." *Far Eastern Quarterly* 10, No. 3 (May 1951): 227-47.
"Trade Chance Seen in South America." *Trans-Pacific* 16, No: 34 (September 1, 1928): 20.

United Nations, Economic Commission for Latin America. "Export Promotion in Japan and Its Application to Latin America." *Economic Bulletin for Latin America* 15, No. 1 (1970): 52-107.
"Want More Sales in Latin America." *Trans-Pacific* 21, No. 41 (October 12, 1933): 18.
"Want Trade Pacts in South America." *Trans-Pacific* 21, No. 29 (July 20, 1933): 17.
Weil, Elsie F. "Training Japanese for Emigration." *Asia* 17, No. 11 (November 1917): 722-28.
White, John W. "Japan's Amazon Dream." *Asia and the Americas* 43, No. 10 (October 1943): 580-83.
Wood, Robert. "Kotosh." *Americas* 20, No. 10 (October 1968): 36-41.
Yonekura, Isamu. "The Last Outpost of Resistance: Enomoto Takeaki and the Republic of Hokkaido." *The East* 8, No. 2 (February 1972): 48-56.

Files of Journals and Newspapers

Andean Air Mail & Peruvian Times (Lima). 1963-73.
Andean Quarterly (Chile). 1942-47.
Asia. 1917-32.
Asia and the Americas. 1942-46.
Asian Studies. 1963-1970.
Asian Survey. 1961-71.
Boletín de la Cámara de Comercio de Lima. 1940.
Boletín del Ministerio de Fomento (Peru). 1906.
Boletín del Ministerio de Relaciones Exteriores (Peru). 1904-14.
The China Weekly Review. 1938-40.
The Christian Science Monitor. 1922, 1960-62.
El Comercio (Lima). 1940.
Comercio Exterior (México). 1961-71.
Contemporary Japan. 1964-70.
Current History. 1925-73.
The Developing Economies (Tokyo). 1962-70.
Economic Bulletin for Latin America. 1965-73.
The Far Eastern Quarterly. 1941-56.
Far Eastern Survey. 1932-49.
Foreign Commerce Weekly. 1949.
The Hispanic American Historical Review. 1918-73.
Hispanic American Report. 1948-64.
Ijū Kenkyū [Emigration research] (Tokyo). 1967-73.
The Inter-American. 1942-46.
Inter-American Economic Affairs. 1948-73.
International Labour Review. 1928-70.
The Japan Advertiser (Tokyo). 1940.
The Japan Economic Journal (Nihon Keizai Shimbun) (Tokyo). 1963-73.
Japan Quarterly (Tokyo). 1954-71.
Japan Report. 1955-73.
The Japan Times (Tokyo). 1956-73.
The Journal of Asian Studies. 1956-72.
Keidanren Review (Tokyo). 1965-68.
Kobe Economic & Business Review. 1953-69.
Kyoto University Economic Review. 1926-58.
Mainichi Daily News (Tokyo). 1969.

Migration News. 1956, 1964-71.
The New York Times. 1895-1973.
Nippon Times (Tokyo). 1955-56.
Pacific Affairs. 1959-69.
Perū Tayori [Peru News] (Tokyo). 1972.
Raten Amerika Jihō [Latin America News] (Tokyo). 1967-69.
The Trans-Pacific. 1928-34.
The Wall Street Journal. 1959-70.
The Washington Post. 1948.

Index

Abraham Lincoln School, 106
ACM. *See* Andean Common Market
Aeroperu, 158
Agencies, of Peruvian government, 158
Agreement, regarding commerce, 160, 161
Aiba, Kōji, 62, 159
Aid: from United States, 153; statistics, 153
Ajinomoto, 133
Akihito, Crown Prince, visit by, 98, 137, 161
Akiyama, Masatoshi, Minister to Panama, 82
Alcoser, Remigio, "anti-yellow" proposal of, 67
Alegría, Ciro: anti-Japanese sentiments of, 84; novel by, 84
Alianza Popular Revolucionaria Americana, 94
Allende, Dr. Salvador, 129
Amari, Zōji: in Peru, 24; communication from, 67
Amazon basin, 28, 30
American Smelting and Refining Company, failure of, 147-48
Amistad case, cited, 5
Ancón, Peru, immigrants in, 24
Andean Common Market, 142; decisions of, 129; launching of, 128-29; mission visits Japan, 129, 161; plans of, 152; Toyota's response to, 149
Andean Development Corporation Treaty, 128
Andean Institute of University of Tokyo, 134
Andes Petroleum Company, 145
Andes Times. See Andesu Jihō
Andesu Jihō, 75, 159
Anti-Asiatic Patriotic League, 66
Aoyagi, Ikutarō, 18, 42
APRA. *See* Alianza Popular Revolucionaria Americana
Arai, Kinta, propagandist, 47
Arequipa, Peru, 63; Department of, 120; honorary consulate in, 160; Japanese association in, 74; Japanese school in, 76; university in, 106
Argentina, 87, 128, 135; claim of, 118; diplomat in, 82; embassy in, 96; Japanese in, 101, 133; population comparison, 115;

trade, 60, 81, 140, 141; trade statistics, 116, 117; treaty with, 101
Arroyo del Río, Carlos (report by Ecuadorian president), 88
Asama, calls at Callao, 45
Associations, of Japanese, 73
Ate Valley, Japanese school in, 76
Athletics, 109
Atico, Peru, fishing operation out of, 150
Atlas Maru, calls at Callao, 112, 160

Balta, José, President, 6
Ban, Tetsuo, Ambassador to Peru, 135
Bank of Tokyo, 133
Barbers, Japanese, in Peru, 52, 63
Barber shops, Japanese, in Peru, 64, 66
Bayovar, Peru, 123
Bazaars, Japanese, 65
Belaúnde, Victor A., at United Nations, 96
Belaúnde Terry, Fernando, 116, 127; activity of president, 123; ouster of, 130; policies of, 97
Benavides, José, Minister of Agriculture, 151
Benavides, Oscar, President, 49
Benson, E.S., 8
Bokuyō Maru, immigrants aboard, 66
Boletín Informativo, 98, 136
Bolivia, 25, 71, 103, 124, 128, 135, 149; deportees from, 86, 87, 88; Japanese in, 101, 133; treaty with, 101
Brazil, 1, 18, 23, 57, 87, 124, 128, 135; claim of, 118; constitution of, 37; cultural agreement with, 110; diplomat in, 82; embassy in, 96; immigrant quota, 37; Japanese in, 37, 101, 133; population comparison, 115; proposal regarding, 15; trade, 60, 81, 140, 141; trade statistics, 116, 117; training center in, 125; treaty with, 101
The British Sugar Company, Ltd., 31
Business associations, Japanese, 64
Bustamante, José Luis, 94

Cáceres, Andrés, President, 19, 20
Cáceres B., Ernesto, 110
CACM. *See* Central American Common Market

193

Cajamarca, Peru, 147
Callao, Peru, 4, 86, 122, 123, 155; deportees from, 86; development of harbor of, 126; fishing plans for, 150; immigrants in, 24, 25, 35, 62, 66, 89; Japanese association in, 73; Japanese naval units at, 45, 78, 98, 161; Japanese schools in, 104, 105; Okinawans in, 103; Shindō Renmei in, 92
"Calling": described, 36; by Okinawans, 93; postwar, 103; by societies, 74
Canada, Japanese in, 101, 133
Cañete, Peru: deportees from, 86; Japanese school in, 75, 76
Canneries, proposals regarding, 123
Cárdenas, Lázaro, 71-72
Catholicism, conversion of Japanese to, 73, 90, 103
Cayaltí, 3, 4, 5, 7, 42; described, 1; deteriorating, 5; mutiny aboard, 4; sale threatened, 7; voyage of, 2, 159
Census: of 1940, 39-41, 102; of 1961, 102; of 1972, 102, 132
Centeno Bravo, Juan, 68
Central American Common Market, 124; founding of, 119; purpose of, 119
Central Japanese Association of Peru. *See* Perū Chūō Nihonjinkai
Cerro Azul, Peru: immigrants in, 25
Chala, Peru, 120
Challwa del Perú, S.A., 151
Chancay, Peru: Japanese association in, 73; Japanese in, 24; Japanese school in, 76
Chancay Valley, Peru, 89; "Japanized," 70
Chanchamayo Valley, Peru, Japanese in, 49
Chapi copper mine, 123
Chiclayo, Peru: Japanese association in, 74; Japanese school in, 76
Chile, 22, 45, 87, 128; claim of, 118; diplomat in, 82; embassy in, 96; Japanese in, 133; population comparison, 115; research project in, 125; trade, 57, 60, 81, 140, 141; trade statistics, 116, 117
Chimbote, Peru: deportees from, 86; fertilizer plant at, 121; fisheries experts at, 125; fishing plans for, 150; Japanese association in, 73; Japanese school in, 76; power line for, 143
Chincha, Peru, Japanese school in, 76
Chinese, 8; aboard *Cayaltí,* 1; aboard *María Luz,* 7; ashore in Japan, 9; in Peru, 62, 72; need for, 6; release of, 12; testimony of, 9; mentioned, 8
Chrysler, production in Peru by, 149
Claims, regarding maritime zone, 118
Coffee, 57
Colombia, 59, 88, 128; deportees from, 86, 87; diplomat in, 82; embassy in, 96; Japanese in, 133; Patia River project in, 125; trade, 141
El Comercio (Lima), president of, 109
Compañía Ballenera del Kinkai, S.A., activity of, 150-51
Compañía Peruana de Vapores: activity of, 115; plans of, 151-52
Consulate, requested in Kobe-Osaka area, 115
Consuls, opinions held by, 10
Contracts, immigrant: termination of, 46; terms of, 24, 27, 31
Contracts, oil: for "La Pampilla" oil refinery, 122; with Petroperu, 145
Copper, 6, 121, 123, 146, 147
Costa Rica: deportees from, 87; plant in, 124
Cotton, 57, 63, 81, 98
Cotton goods: decree concerning, 50
Cruz Montero, Alejandro: article by, 68-69; quoted, 69
Cuba, 130; embassy in, 96; trade, 141
Cudina, Juan, 5
Cultural activities, 108-109
Cultural agreement: with Brazil, 110; with Mexico, 110
Cuzco, Peru, 121

Dai Nambei, 75
Davidson, John N., attorney, 11
Davis, Edward Clarence, consul in Yokohama, 31, 159
Debts, refinancing of, 136
Decrees: Peruvian, 45, 51, 63, 103-104, 118, 122, 161; Portuguese, 17
DeLong, C.E., 5, 9, 12, 15; absence of minister, 7; action by, 13, 15; claims *Cayaltí,* 7; communications from, 9, 10, 11, 14; communications to, 12, 13; correspondence problem of, 166; instructions for, 6-7, 159; offer of, 7; opinion by, 9; sells *María Luz,* 15
Deportees, specific cases, 86
Devéscovi, Ernesto, 66
Dickens, Frederick V., 11
Dickover, E.R., U.S. consul in Kobe, 46
Diez Canseco, 55
Diplomatic relations, severance of, 160
Diseases, Japanese afflicted by, 25
Dominican Republic: deportees from, 87; embassy in, 96; Japanese in, 101
Dōshikai, 74
Dunn, A.C., 5, 7
Dysentery, 25

Earthquake, Japanese response, 130, 161
Ecuador, 128; boundary disputed, 28, 82; claim of, 82, 118; deportees from, 86, 87, 88; trade, 141

Index   195

Electric Power Development Company, study by, 144
Electroperu, 158
Elguera, César A., 44
Elías Bonnemaison, Manuel, Minister to Japan, 160
Emigrants' Protection Law, violation of, 29
Emigration: statistics concerning Japanese in Peru, 29, 33-34, 36, 100, 156; summary of activity by companies, 33
English, Earl, 3, 4
Entelperu, 143, 158
EPCHAP, 158
Escuela Japonesa de Lima, 76, 131
Escuela Victoria, 105
Espantoso, Guillermo, honorary consul in Lima, 25, 43, 159
Eten, Peru, 24, 30
Ethnicity, Japanese, 156
Etolin, deportees aboard, 87
European Economic Community, 119
EXPO '70: aids Peruvians, 130; Peruvian participation in, 128, 137, 161
Export-Import Bank of Japan, 112
Extraterritoriality, 11, 18, 19, 20

Feasibility studies, 136-37, 142, 145, 148
Federation of Economic Organizations. *See* Keidanren
Federal Bureau of Investigation, 85, 91
Fencing. *See* kendō
Fernández Dávila, Julio: activity of minister, 113; Ambassador to Japan, 96, 160; Minister to Japan, 95, 160
Fernández Maldonado, Jorge, 136, 146, 147, 152, 161
Ferreyros, José Carlos, 98, 126, 135
Fertilizer, 121, 146
Fertiperu, 158
Figueroa y Parra, Eusebio, 30
Fish, Hamilton, 6-7, 9, 12, 13, 14, 15, 159
Fisheries Agency, 138, 150
Fishing, 136, 150
Fishing agreement, signatories of, 119
Fishing fleets, proposals regarding, 123
Fish meal, 150; basis of, 146; importance of industry, 119; Japanese purchases of, 98, 150
"Floating fair": objectives of, 112; of 1959, 112; of 1969, 128
Flor Valle, Miguel Angel de la, 155
Flower-arranging. *See* ikebana
Ford Motor Company, 148
Foreign Office, Japanese, 24; activity of, 42, 142; communications to, 8, 10, 15; communications from 7, 10-11, 12, 30; demand by, 53; its estimate of Latin America, 82; mission of, 1; petition to, 45; pressure on, 45; prominent Peruvians invited by, 109; protest by, 38; report to, 32
Formosa, sugar of, 57
France, 60; activity of, 120; as creditor, 130; offer from, 152
Freyre, Manuel, Peruvian Minister to the U.S., 12
Fuji, publication of, 99
Fujimura, Nobuo, 51
Fukuda, Takeo, 130
Furuya affair, 52, 54
Furuya, Tokijiro, barber, 52

García Calderón, Francisco, quoted, 65
García y García, Aurelio, 154, 159; captain appointed Minister to Japan, 13; instructions for, 13-14; presents case, 14; pressures Japanese, 15; trade effort by, 17; treaty talks by, 15
García y García, José Antonio, 6
General Motors, 148, 149
General Randall, deportees aboard, 91
"Gentlemen's Agreement," sought by Peru, 50
Germany, 60
Gómez de la Torre, Francisco, honorary consul in Arequipa, 160
Gonzáles M., Pedro, anti-Japanese stance of, 70
González Tello, Manuel, anti-Japanese stance of, 71
Goods, Japanese, opinion about, 112
Goyburu Elias, José B., Peruvian consul in Kobe, 46
Grau, Miguel, Chargé, 95
Great Britain, 60; activity of, 120; regarding guano, 117
Greater South America. See Dai Nambei
Gripsholm, in repatriation service, 88
Guano, 6, 17, 22, 48, 57, 117, 121, 146
Guano Development Public Corporation, proposal by, 121
Guatemala, deportees from, 87
Guidebook, for Japanese, 134

Habeas corpus, action by internees, 91
Hacienda San Nicolás, 78
Haiti, deportees from, 87
Hakodate, Japan, U.S. consul at, 2, 3, 4, 5, 7
Hakuryū Maru, detention of, 138
Hara, Kichihei, president of JETRO visits Peru, 161

Harris, Townsend, Consul General in Japan, 4
Hawaii, Japanese in, 23
Haya de la Torre, Víctor Raúl: of APRA, 94; pro-Japanese sentiment of, 97, 107, 126
Hayakawa, Takashi, 161
Hayasaka, H., counselor departs, 52; pamphlet by, 72
Heeren, Oscar, 16, 18
Herrera, Ricardo: action by captain, 11; appeal by, 7; ashore, 9; complaint of, 8; counsel for, 11; pronounced guilty, 9; request of, 10; ruling against, 159; quoted, 8-9, 10
Herrera Larco, Rafael, visits Japan, 160
Hioki, Eki, Minister to Peru, 43, 74, 159
Honduras, 88; claim of, 118; deportees from, 87
Hong Kong, 6, 12, 13
Hooper López, René, Ambassador to Japan, 135, 138
Hoshi, Tōru, 20
Hoshi, Yoshino, 105
Hoshi Pharmaceutical Company, 93
Hoshi School, 105
Houghton, Edward L., 31
Huacho, Peru: deportees from 86; playground in, 78; Japanese school in, 76
Huancayo, Peru: Japanese association in, 74; Japanese school in, 76
Huancayo Observatory, coronograph at, 109
Huánuco, Peru, 44, 63, 93; monument in, 134, 161
Huánuco Department: Japanese in, 71
Huaral Valley: excavation in, 109
Humboldt Current, 118

Ica, Peru: Japanese school in, 76
Igei, Gino, 104
Ikebana, courses in, 77
Ilo, Peru, 147
Immigrants, Japanese: activities of, 41; age groups of, 41; arrivals of, 24, 26, 27, 159; generations of, 103; marital status of, 41; sex of, 40; survey of, 37; totals, 29
Immigration: Peruvian attitude regarding, 124; Peruvian law, 51; Peruvian policy, 22
Immigration and Naturalization Service, wartime role of, 88
Inca Rubber Company: contract with, 29; workers for, 28
Income: comparisons, 139; of Peruvians, 139
Independencia, calls at Japanese ports, 98, 154, 161
Induperu, 158
Industrias Marítimas de Supe, S.A., 123, 150

Insurance, cancellation of, 89
Intermarriages, number of, 103
International Petroleum Company, 144; nationalization of, 127
Internees, records concerning, 173
Investment, 153; advantages of, 121; by Japanese, 120; from United States, 154; in mining, 123; in oil, 122; Japanese role in, 142; mission, 137; statistics, 154
IPC. *See* International Petroleum Company
Iquique, Peru: nitrate of, 57
Iquitos, Peru, 59
Irigoyen, José María, 19, 20
Irigoyen, Manuel, 19
Iron, 121
Iron Duke, 8
Iron ore, Japanese purchase of, 98
Ishii, Itarō, Ambassador to Brazil, 82
Ishikawajima-Harima Heavy Industries, 151
Isomura, Ryōsuke, emigration agent, 26
Isuzu Motors Ltd., 122
Italy: as creditor, 130; Italians in Peru, 62, 72: offer from, 152
Itō, Keiichi, consul in Peru, 30
C. Itoh and Company, 148
Iwate: calls at Callao, 45
Izumi, Seiichi, 109, 134, 161

Japan: merchant marine of, 17; position regarding territorial waters, 118-19
The Japan Advertiser (Tokyo), 54
Japan Chamber of Commerce and Industry, 125, 113
Japan Consulting Institute, in Peru, 152
Japan Emigration Service. *See* Kaigai Ijū Jigyōdan
Japan External Trade Organization, 119, 155; meeting of, 128; purpose of, 112; sponsors exhibition, 113, 160
Japan Gasoline Company, 122, 142, 143-45
Japan Mail Line. *See* Nippon Yūsen Kaisha
Japan Mining Industry Association, 124
Japan-Peru Cultural Association, 51, 52, 160
Japan-Peru News. See Nippi Shimpō
Japan-Peru Society, 107
Japan Petroleum Development Corporation, 145
Japan Plant Association, 121, 124
Japan Porcelain and Ceramic Ware Export Association, 122
Japanese Association. *See* Nihonjin Kyōkai
Japanese Brotherhood Association. *See* Nihonjin Dōshikai
Japanese Chamber of Commerce, in Peru, 133
Japanese Credit Society, 69

Japanese Foreign Office. *See* Foreign Office, Japanese
Japanese Overseas Electrical Industry Survey Institute, 126
Japanese Red Cross, 90
Japón al día, 98
Jauja, Peru: Japanese association in, 74; Japanese school in, 76
JETRO. *See* Japan External Trade Organization
Jiménez de Lucio, Alberto, Minister of Industry and Commerce, 136, 161
Jiritsu, 74
Joint ventures: examples of, 145, 151; nature of, 152; regarding automobiles, 122
José de Gálvez School, in Callao, 104, 105
Jus sanguinis, principle of, 87

Kaigai Ijū Jigyōdan: operations of, 101; survey by, 133
Kaigai Nikkeijin Kyōkai: meetings of, 135
Kairin School, in Callao, 104
Kaiyō Maru: research ship, 150
Kanagawa Prefecture: authorities of, 8; decision by authorities, 9; reply of authorities, 10
Kasuga, Yoshio: Ambassador to Peru, 133, 135
Katori: calls at Callao, 155
Kawasaki Dockyard Company, 148
Kawasaki Kisen Kabushiki Kaisha: activity of, 115, 152
Kawasaki Steamship Company. *See* Kawasaki Kisen Kabushiki Kaisha
Keidanren, 119
Kendō, 77
Kikuzuki: calls at Callao, 155
Kina, Kame, 34, 89
Kinjyō Travel Service, in Lima, 134
Kishi, Nobusuke, 97, 107, 160
Kitada, Masamoto, 51-52, 53
Kitsutani, S.G., 67, 79
K.K.K.K. *See* Kawasaki Kisen Kabushiki Kaisha
Kobe, Japan, 46
Kokumin (Tokyo), 54
Korea, 34
Kotosh, Peru: ruins of, 134
Kubo, Hidemasa, 146
Kurile Islands, 2
Kurimoto, Shinzō, barber, 52
Kurino, Schinichirō, 19
Kurotibi, T., pamphlet by, 72
Kurusu, Saburō, 160; activity of, 48; background of, 48; colonization plan of, 49; departure of, 49; vigilantes organized by, 49;

LAFTA. *See* Latin American Free Trade Association
Lansa Air Line, 126
Lansing, Robert, 43, 44
Larco Herrera, Carlos: honorary consul at Trujillo, 160; honored, 107; renamed honorary consul at Trujillo, 160; visits Japan, 95
Latin America: Japanese communities in, 133; perspectives on, vii
Latin American Free Trade Association: access to, 124; founding of, 119; frustration within, 128
LaValle, José A. de, 17
Lead, 121, 123, 146, 147
The League of the New Way. *See* Shindō Renmei
Leguía, Augusto B., 24, 25, 26, 31, 36, 45, 46, 47, 79; action by President, 45; interests of, 23; revolt against, 160; toppled, 48
Leticia, Colombia, 59
Libao, César F.F.: in Japan, 125
Libertad Department: astronomers in, 51
Lima, Peru: deportees from, 86; Japanese in, 30, 62, 64, 89; Japanese associations in, 73; Japanese schools in, 76; lure of, 35; Okinawans in, 103; power line for, 143; project in, 78; rioting in, 39, 52, 160; Shindō Renmei in, 92; trade fairs in, 113
Lima Daily News. See Rima Nippō
Loan, terms of, 143, 144, 146, 147
Loayza, Francisco A., 79
Lodge, Henry Cabot, 96
Lorca, Miguel, employees of, 63
Lurín, valley of, 89

Macao: Peruvian consul at, 4; Portuguese in, 6
McColley, J.H., 4, 5
Macera, César Francisco, anti-Asian stance of, 67-68
McMillin, Benton: U.S. Minister to Peru, 43
Madre de Dios, Peru, region of, 145
Malaria, 25, 27
Maldonado, Peru, Japanese school in, 76
Manco Capac, statue of, 78-79, 159
Manganese, 147
Marañón River, Peru, project on, 142
María Luz, 8, 11, 13, 14, 42; abandoned by captain, 12; arbitral award regarding, 16-17, 159; case of, 159; in Japanese waters, 7, 8; sale of, 15; survey of, 9
Mariátegui, José Carlos: Ambassador to Japan, 127, 137, 135; lists Japanese contributions, 136
Marquina, María de, proposal by, 68

Marubeni-Iida Company: activity of, 143-45; agreement by, 130; contract of, 122
Masamari River, Peru, region of, 35
Matsonia, deportees aboard, 91
Meiji Colonization Company: activity of, 28, 29, 33; collapse of, 29
Mercado Jarrín, Edgardo, 135
Metal Empresa S.A., 151
Mexico, 19, 24, 43, 44, 87, 128; comparison of Peru with, 48; cultural agreement with Japan, 110; Japanese diplomat in, 82; Japanese embassy established in, 96; example of, 71; Japanese in, 33, 133; offer from, 152; population comparison, 115; precedent from, 11; trade, 60, 81, 140, 141; trade statistics, 116, 117
Michiko, Princess, visit by, 98, 161
Michiquillay, Peru, copper deposit at, 143
Mikasa, Prince: exhibit opened by, 110; visits Peru, 96, 137, 160
Minato School, in Callao, 104
Minerals: joint venture production of, 136
Mineroperu, 158; negotiation by, 147; request of, 143
Mining, activity regarding, 146; investment in, 123; laws regarding, 147; mission regarding, 123
Ministry of Agriculture and Forestry, Japanese, research facility of, 150
Ministry of International Trade and Industry, Japanese, 119; activity of, 112
Miró Quesada, Aurelio, 109, 160
MITI. *See* Ministry of International Trade and Industry
Mitsubishi Heavy Industries, 122
Mitsubishi Mining Company, 120
Mitsubishi Shōji: agreement by, 130; capital provided by, 120
Mitsubishi Trading Company. *See* Mitsubishi Shōji
Mitsui Bussan Kaisha, 115
Mitsui Consultants Company Ltd., 126
Mitsui and Company, Ltd., 123, 151, 130
Mitsui Mining & Smelting Company, 123
Mitsui Products Company. *See* Mitsui Bussan Kaisha
Miura, Yoshiaki, Minister to Mexico, 82
Miyahara School, in Callao, 104
Mizutani, Ryōichi, 81
Mollendo, Peru, 123
Momoi Fishing Net Manufacturing Company, 150
Montagne Sánchez, Ernesto, 161
Montaña, 30, 35; proposal regarding, 72; quota concerning, 71; slogan for, 49
Monterey, deportees aboard, 87

Morales Bermúdez, President, death of, 20
Morales Bermúdez, Francisco, Minister of Economy and Finance, 152; discusses debts, 130; visits Japan, 136, 161
Morioka Emigration Company, 33, 34; activity of, 23, 24, 26, 27; competition for, 28; rumor about, 25
Morishita, Kunio, Vice Minister for Foreign Affairs, report by, 124; visits Peru, 95
Muelle, Eduardo: consul in Yokohama, 159; optimism of, 57; quoted, 56, 57; survey by, 56
Mundo Gráfico, publication suspended, 55
Murakami, Yoshiatsu: Minister to Peru, 50
Murota, Yoshibumi: communication to Minister, 25; Minister to Peru, 24, 43, 159
Mutsu, Munemitsu, activity of Japanese Minister to the U.S., 19

Nacional, El (Lima), anti-Asian stance of, 68
Nagasaki, Hiroshi, Ambassador to Peru, 135
Nakao, Kenkichi, 30
National Council for Immigration and Alien Affairs, Peruvian, report of, 100
Nicaragua: claim of, 118; deportees from, 87, 88
Nichi Nichi (Tokyo), 54
Nicolini, Manuel de, Captain, 2
Nihonjin Dōshikai, founding of 73, 74
Nihonjin Kyōkai, activity of, 74; founding of, 74, 159
Nihon Kinkai Hogei Company, 151
Nikai, Shigeto: Ambassador to Peru, 135; activity of, 155
Nikkō, 98, 104
Niño Current, importance of, 150
Nippi Shimpō, founding of, 75
Nippon Densō, in Peru, 149
Nippon Electric Company: activity of, 143; agreement by, 130
Nippon Green Coffee Association, 143
Nippon Mining Company, 146
Nippon Steel Corporation, 147, 179
Nippon Yūsen Kaisha, 24
Nisei: number of, 103; Peruvianization of, 102
Nissan Motor, 133; in Peru, 148; plans of, 122; production in Peru by, 149
Nitrates, 6, 17, 57
Noda, Ryōji, 26
Noguchi, Dr. Hideyo, 78, 159, 78
Norweb, R. Henry, U.S. Ambassador to Peru, 83, 87;
Noticias sobre Japón, publication of, 98-99

Occupations: of deportees, 86: statistics concerning, 108; survey of, 108
Odría, Manuel, President, 94; decree by, 103-04
Okazaki, Katsuo, Foreign Minister: his views regarding emigration, 100; visits Peru, 95, 160
Okinawa Association, 93
Okinawans, 36; activity of, 73, 134; described, 32; experiences of, 34; in Shindō Renmei, 93; occupations of, 102-103; survey of, 102
Onaga, Ryōshin, 36, 89
Orbegoso Alvarado, Jaime Luis de, honorary consul in Trujillo, 160
Orient Steamship Company. See Tōyō Kisen Kaisha
Oroya, Peru, Japanese association in, 74
Oroya fever, 78
Ortíz de Zevallos, Ricardo, Foreign Minister, 20
Osaka Steamship Company, vessel of, 112
Overseas Development Company, 33
Overseas Japanese Association. See Kaigai Nikkeijin Kyōkai
Overseas Mineral Resources Development Association, in Peru, 121
Overseas Technical Cooperation Agency, 125
Oye, Taku, 12, 13
Ozawa, Takeo, 95, 160

Pacasmayo, Peru, 2; immigrants in, 24; Japanese association in, 73
Pachacamac, Peru: ruins of, 98; valley of, 89
Paita, Peru, 123
Pakistan, 125
Palpa, Peru, deportees from, 86
La Pampilla: oil refinery of, 122; expansion of refinery, 143-45
Panama, 1; claim of, 118; deportees from, 87, 88; diplomat in, 82; trade, 141
Paraguay, 135; Japanese in, 101, 133; treaty with, 101
Pardo, José, 28, 30
Pardo, Manuel, 13
Paz Soldán, Dr. Carlos Enrique, 71
Pérez de Cuéllar, Javier, Deputy Foreign Minister, 138; visits Japan, 136, 161
Peru: action by congress of, 44; activity of senate of, 55; belligerency of, 91; census of 1940, 39-41, 102; census of 1961, 102; census of 1972, 102, 132; communication from Foreign Office, 12, 53; communication to Foreign Office, 9, 11, 12, 44, 66; conditions in, 3; decrees of, 39, 50, 63, 118, 122, 160; Departments of, 32; deportees from, 86, 87; Director of Immigration quoted, 36; immigration law of, 38, 51; Japanese in, 40, 132, 133; laws concerning Axis subjects, 90, 160; merchant marine of, 17; modification of constitution of, 49; neutrality of, 28; peace treaty ratified by, 95; peace treaty signed by, 95; population comparison, 139; Proclaimed List applied to, 91; regarding economic prospects of, 6; regarding return of deportees, 92; request of Foreign Office, 6; ruling by, 31; severs diplomatic relations with Axis, 83; trade, 140, 141; treaty denounced by, 46, 50
Perū Chūō Nihonjinkai, 50; activity of, 76, 78, 134; founding of, 74, 159; role in "calling," 36
Peru-Japan Cultural Association, statutes of, 107
Peru-Japan Cultural Center: activity of, 134; in Lima, 107, 155
Perū kankō, 134
Peru News. See Perū Tayori
The Peru News. See Perū Shimpō
Perū Shimpō, 93, 134
Peru Sight-seeing. See Perū kankō
Perū Takushoku Kumiai, 49, 70, 160
Perū Tayori, 136, 161
Peruvian Colonization Association. See Perū Takushoku Kumiai
Pescaperu, 158
Petroperu, 144-45, 146, 158
Piérola, Nicolás de, President, 20
Piscina Nippon, gift of Japanese colony, 160
Pisco, Peru: fishing plans for, 150; Japanese association in, 73
Polar Ugarteche, Mario, Vice President, visits Japan, 98, 161
Polo, Solón, Foreign Minister, 50
Ponce, Aníbal, Ambassador to Japan, 97-98, 107
Pongo de Manseriche, proposed project at, 142
Prado, Manuel, President, 97, 107; honorary degree for, 97; plan of, 126; quoted, 88; visits Japan, 95, 113, 161
Prefectures, associations related to, 73
Prensa, La (Lima), anti-Japanese stance of, 67-68, 69-70
Proclaimed List, applied to Peru, 91
Protocol: in *María Luz* case, 159; terms of, 15; quoted, 114
Publications, nature of, 133-34
Puebla, deportees aboard, 87
Puno Department, project in, 125

Quillabamba Valley, proposal regarding, 121

Ramírez y González, José Manuel, anti-Japanese stance of, 70, 71
Remittances: by Japanese, 131; comparison of, 132; statistics, 132
Rice, 17
Rice, E.E., 3, 4, 5; U.S. Consul at Hakodate, 2; informs Japanese authorities, 4; informs U.S. minister, 3; instructed by minister, 3
Rima Nippō, founding of, 75
Rimac River, valley of, 89
Ríos, Fernando de los, anti-Japanese sentiments of, 84
Rioting: claims, 83; commission concerning, 54; coverage of, 170; effects of, 77; in 1940, 52, 160; Peruvian activity concerning, 55; reported in Japan, 54
Riva Agüero, Enrique de la, Foreign Minister, 44; communication from, 13
Rivera Pando, T.A.: proposal by, 68
Romero la Puente, Manuel, anti-Japanese stance of, 69
Roosevelt School, sansei attending, 106
Rowan, J.C., Rear Admiral commanding U.S. Asiatic Squadron, 3, 4, 5
Rumania, 152
Russia, arbitration by czar of, 15
Russo-Japanese War, 28

Sakamoto, Ryūki, Minister to Peru, 82, 83
Sakura, publication of, 98
Sakura Maru (1899), immigrants aboard, 24
Sakura Maru (postwar), calls at Callao, 128, 161
Salaverry, Peru, immigrants in, 24
Salina Cruz, Mexico, port of, 33
Salinas Cossio, Dr. G., anti-Japanese stance of, 69, 70
Salvador, El: claim of, 118; deportees from, 87, 88
Sánchez Cerro, Luis Miguel, President, 69; revolution led by, 48, 160
San Juan Vanguard, launching of, 148
San Marcos University, 105
Sansei: number of, 103: Peruvianization of, 102; schooling of, 106
Santa Barbara School, 75
Sanjō Electric Company, 123
Sarmiento, General, comment by, 59
Satō, Chargé, 53
Satō, Eisaku, Prime Minister, 107, 128
Satō, Ichirō: Director General of Japanese Economic Planning Agency, visits Peru, 161
Schools, Japanese-language, 75, 76, 77

Seishō Maru No. 5, detention of, 138
Self Support. See Jiritsu
Senjō Maru, immigrants aboard, 35
Seoane, Manuel, 87
Seoane Corrales, Edgardo, Vice President, visits Japan, 161
Seve, Eduard, communication from, 13
Severin, Kurt, 87
Seward, William H., Secretary of State, 4, 5
Shawnee, deportees aboard, 87
Shepard, C.O., Chargé, 7, 9
Shillacoto, Peru ruins of, 134
Shimazaki School, in Callao, 104
Shimizu, Seizaburō: Chile visited by Minister, 47; Minister to Peru, 45, 159; sentiments of, 79
Shindō, Michitarō, emigration agent, 29
Shindō Renmei, movement in Peru, 92
Shipbuilding, terms of contract, 115
Shipping, role of Ishikawajima-Harima Heavy Industries in, 151
Siderperu, 158
Silk, 17
Sima, Peru, drydock at, 152
Sino-Japanese War, 23
Sociedad Internacional de Comerciantes de Lima, anti-Asian stance of, 67
Solf y Muro, Alfredo, Foreign Minister, 83
Sotil, D., proposal of Deputy, 69
Soyeshima, Foreign Minister, 13; communication to, 8; query by, 14; quoted, 10, 11, 12
Spain, announcement by embassy of, 86; wartime role of, 84
Steel, cargoes for Japanese producers, 148
Sugimura, Toraichi, Minister to Peru, 28
Sumac, Yma, vocalist, 109
Supe, Peru: immigrants in, 24; Japanese school in, 76
Supreme Commander for the Allied Powers, mission from, 111
Survey: by Japan Emigration Service, 133; mineral, 121; occupations, 108; of Japanese, 62
Switzerland, wartime role of, 84
Syrians, in Peru, 62

Tacna, Peru, Department of, 30, 121; Japanese association in, 74
Taiyō Fishery Company, 150
Takada, Minoru, consul in Lima, 160
Takahashi, Korekiyo, 18, 42
Talara, Peru, 146; fertilizer plant at, 143
Tambopata River, Peru, region of, 29
Tanaka, Teikichi, activity of emigration agent, 23, 26; quoted, 25
Tantaleán Vanini, Javier, Minister of Fisheries visits Japan, 136, 151, 161

Tarea, operation of, 28
Tarma, Peru, Japanese association in, 74
Tatsuke, Shichita, communication from Minister, 44
Tea, 17
Technical assistance: by Japanese 125; nature of, 124; obstacles to, 125; offers of, 152; programs of, 151
Technical mission, 146
Technical trainee, in Japan, 125
Technical training center, program of, 125
Teijin Limited, activity of, 150
Terada, Kazuo, in Peru, 137
Teraoka, Kōhei, Ambassador to Peru, 96, 160: Minister to Peru, 95, 160
Testimony, of Chinese, 4
Thompson, Wallace, interview by, 47
Thompson and Bewick, trading firm of, 2
Tiempo, El (Lima): anti-Japanese crusade of, 66, 67; anti-Japanese sentiment in, 47
Tokyo, Japan: Andean Institute, 134; Peruvian exhibits in, 110; treaty signed in, 159; University of, 109
Tokyo Shibaura Electric, 121
Tomii, Shū, Ambassador to Argentina, 82
Torre Bueno, Felipe de la, Peruvian consul in Macao, 4
Toshiba. *See* Tokyo Shibaura Electric
Tōyō Emigration Company, 33
Tōyō Engineering Company, 146
Tōyō Kisen Kaisha, sailings of, 57
Toyota Motor, 133; in Peru, 148-49; plans of, 122
Trade, Japanese: agreement, 111; Argentina, 140, 141; Brazil, 140, 141; categories, 117, 118, 140; Chile, 140, 141; Colombia, 141; comparisons, 60, 139; Cuba, 141; developments in, 81; increase of, 70; Mexico, 140, 141; missions regarding, 113, 114; Panama, 141; Peru, 56, 59, 114, 116, 117, 118, 139, 140; pickled radish, 131-32; promotion of, 136; restrictions on, 114-15; role of, 157; statistics, 56, 58, 59, 114, 116, 117, 118, 139, 140; terms agreed upon, 113; unfavorable balance, 139; Venezuela, 141
Trask, Benjamin C., 13
Treaties: concerning Japanese immigration, 101; denounced, 46, 50, 160; signed, 20, 95, 156, 159, 160; terms of, 16, 20, 46; quoted, 4; with Mexico, 19; with U.S., 4; of Shimonoseki, 21
Trueblood, Chargé quoted, 91
Trujillo, Peru, 34; deportees from, 86; Japanese association in, 73; Japanese school in, 76; Japanese consulate in, 160; publications in, 107; university in, 106
Tulumayo area: Japanese holding in, 93
Typhoid fever, 25

Uchima, Yasuhiro, 104
Ueda, J., astronomer, 109
Uesugi, Masami, rumor regarding, 87
Ulloa, Alberto, Foreign Minister, 18, 38
Umitaku Maru, 125
Unión Regional Tacna, Arica y Tarapacá, anti-Asian stance of, 66
Union Stadium, gift of, 107, 135
United Nations, Japan seeks admission to, 96
United States, 11, 60; activity of, 120; aid from, 153, 159; announcement by, 91; as creditor, 130; as "whipping boy," 127; challenge by, 118; concern of, 43; detention facilities of, 92; Gentlemen's Agreement of, 31; interest of, 44, 66-67; investment from, 154; Japanese in, 101, 133; market in, 121; population comparison, 115; regarding guano, 117; report for, 35, 37, 45; report quoted, 45; response of, 6; trade, 140; trade statistics, 116, 117
Uruguay, claim of, 118
U.S.S. Iroquois, calls at Hakodate, 3

Van Valkenburgh, R.B., 3, 4, 5; Minister informed by consul, 3; instructs consul, 3; seeks instructions, 5
Vehicles: action regarding industry, 148; statistics, 149
Velasco Alvarado, Juan: General assumes presidency, 127; changes by, 129-30; opposition to, 158
Venezuela, 96, 141
Verruga peruana, 78
Victoria Japanese Educatiom Association, of Lima, 105
Vidarte, Carlos, anti-Japanese stance of, 67
Vigil, Enrique A., honorary consul in Tokyo, 159
Visas, bilateral elimination of, 161
Volkswagen, production in Peru by, 149
Volvo, production in Peru by, 149

War: declared by Latin American countries, 83-84; declared by Peru, 160
War of the Pacific, 18, 22
Washington, D.C., diplomatic activity in, 19, 20, 42, 159
Watson, Robert G., British consul, 8
West Germany, 120, 130
White, John W., 90
Wiese, Fernando, 54
Woodworkers' Union of Callao, anti-Japanese stance of, 67

Yamagata, Kiyoshi, Minister to Chile, 82
Yamazaki, Keiichi, Minister to Peru, 47-48
Yamekawa, Sobuku, 34, 89
Yanai, Tsuneo: Minister to Colombia, 82

Yavari, voyage of, 115
Yellow fever, 25
Yodogawa, Masaki, Consul, 49, 82, 84
Yokohama, Japan, consulate in, 35

Zappe, E., Acting Consul General of Germany, 10

Zegarra, Félix C.C., Peruvian Minister to U.S., 19
Zenkō Maru No. 30, detention of, 138
Zinc, 98, 121, 123, 146, 147
Zorritos, Peru, ship detained at, 138